Praise for *Apparently There Were Complaints*

An Amazon Best Book of the Month
An Apple Books Must-Listen Audiobook of the Month
An AudioFile Earphones Award Winner

"A good Hollywood memoir is a little bit dishy, a little bit honest, and a lot like sitting down for a candid conversation with an old friend, and [Sharon] Gless shares all the dirty details of her unlikely journey to stardom with a wry chuckle. . . . Celebrity memoir fans will find lots to enjoy here, as well as anyone with fond memories of *Cagney & Lacey* or *Queer as Folk*. Discussions of mental health, alcoholism, and relationships, and a connected Hollywood family, bring strong comparisons to Carrie Fisher's *Wishful Drinking* (2008). A perfect book to get lost in this winter."
—*Booklist* (starred review)

"Her memoir is as unfiltered, self-deprecating, and funny as you would expect, with great stories from each period of her career covering the stars she rubbed shoulders with (Steven Spielberg, James Garner, Robert Wagner, and more), an insider's look at an eternally fascinating industry, the alcoholism that crept up on her, and the people who looked out for her and helped shape a remarkable career."
—Vannessa Cronin, Amazon Books editor

"Emmy Award–winning actor Gless debuts with a no-holds-barred look at her long and storied career. . . . Written by a masterful storyteller, this smart account boldly reveals both the grit and the glamour of Gless's life, candidly contending with her substance abuse, various affairs, and the fact that writing her memoir took almost seven years. Fans will be delighted."
—*Publishers Weekly*

"Once I started, I couldn't stop. . . . Being in Gless's company is often as riveting as spending time with Billy Porter. That's part of the fun of a celebrity memoir—when it just *goes there* with no filter and pretension. And Gless is a brassy dame. . . . I especially dug the story about a fake fight she staged at one of her own parties with the late Lynn Redgrave to amuse her guests. That doesn't happen enough at Hollywood get-togethers these days."

—Marshall Heyman, *Vulture*

"Actor Sharon Gless's animated yet intimate tone, gentle pacing, and husky timbre will keep listeners glued to her fascinating memoir. Gless holds little back as she exposes her flaws and vulnerabilities. . . . Listeners will enjoy spending time with the fiercely independent, frank, and appealing Gless."

—Michelle J. Ritholz, *AudioFile*

"A refreshing, witty memoir."

—Lorrie Lynch, *AARP The Magazine*

"It's such a good book. Really a fun read."

—Jane Lynch

"It's a brilliant book. The stories come to life. I was literally on the edge of my seat, laughing and crying. It's everything you want a great book to be. I could not stop reading it, start to finish."

—Nina Tassler, former chairman of entertainment at CBS

"It's simply amazing. Heartfelt and funny."

—Rosie O'Donnell

Apparently There Were Complaints

≡ A MEMOIR ≡

Sharon Gless

SIMON & SCHUSTER PAPERBACKS

New York   London   Toronto   Sydney   New Delhi

Simon & Schuster Paperbacks
An Imprint of Simon & Schuster, Inc.
1230 Avenue of the Americas
New York, NY 10020

First Simon & Schuster trade paperback edition December 2022

SIMON & SCHUSTER PAPERBACKS and colophon are registered trademarks of Simon & Schuster, Inc.

For information about special discounts for bulk purchases, please contact Simon & Schuster Special Sales at 1-866-506-1949 or business@simonandschuster.com.

The Simon & Schuster Speakers Bureau can bring authors to your live event. For more information or to book an event, contact the Simon & Schuster Speakers Bureau at 1-866-248-3049 or visit our website at www.simonspeakers.com.

Interior design by Carly Loman

Photographs courtesy of the author.

Manufactured in the United States of America

10   9   8   7   6   5   4   3   2   1

Library of Congress Cataloging-in-Publication Data
Names: Gless, Sharon, author.
Title: Apparently there were complaints : a memoir / Sharon Gless
Description: New York : Simon & Schuster, [2021]
Identifiers: LCCN 2021013758 (print) | LCCN 2021013759 (ebook) |
ISBN 9781501125959 (hardcover) | ISBN 9781501125973 (ebook)
Subjects: LCSH: Gless, Sharon. | Television actors and actresses—United States—Biography.
Classification: LCC PN2287.G55354 A3 2021 (print) | LCC PN2287.G55354 (ebook) |
DDC 791.4502/8092 [B]—dc23
LC record available at https://lccn.loc.gov/2021013758
LC ebook record available at https://lccn.loc.gov/2021013759

ISBN 978-1-5011-2595-9
ISBN 978-1-5011-2596-6 (pbk)
ISBN 978-1-5011-2597-3 (ebook)

For the men in my life—

my husband, Barney Rosenzweig

and my brothers, Michael Gless and Aric Gless

*I could always knock Michael over
with a feather.*

Introduction

Eight years old at Beverly Jacks and Jills summertime day camp in the San Fernando Valley of Los Angeles.

This is my favorite photo of me as a child, taken at summer day camp in the San Fernando Valley of Los Angeles. I am eight years old.

I wasn't sent to camp looking like this, my French braids askew and coming loose, my shorts twisted to the side, sloppy. My legs are scuffed with dirt. There is a long chocolate ice cream stain running down the front of my white Bluebird blouse, which is only half tucked in. It matches the chocolate moustache above my lip, topping my ear-to-ear grin. Every time I look at this photo, I think, "That is the happiest kid in the world."

Being happy has always been my goal. I've been defined with many labels over the years, some great, others not. I've been called the poor relative, a rich kid, a spinster, impudent, naïve, funny, darling, boring, fat, perfect, unusual, forgettable, and unforgettable. I've heard too sexy, too unsuitable, too angry, too dykey, and the blonde, the bitch, worst ever, best ever, Emmy loser, and Emmy winner. In the press, I've been called a gay icon, a political liberal, a home-wrecker, a sack of potatoes, and a drunk.

A more tough-skinned person would have ignored all these labels. I'm many things, but tough-skinned isn't one of them. I was a sensitive little girl who became a perceptive and vulnerable big girl. I wouldn't change that.

It's good to remember myself as happy, the way I am in this camp photo. Left to my own devices, I was usually a happy child.

Yet rarely is anything left to its own devices, not even cherished photographs. A couple of years ago, I took my small camp photo to be enlarged and framed. It now hangs in the entryway of my Studio City home. The photo editor, trying to correct what was wrong with me, airbrushed out all the chocolate stains on my blouse and on my face.

Apparently, there are still many things about me that others think need fixing.

I am seventy-eight years old now. Fuck 'em.

= One =

Bubbles

"If you ever have another drink again, don't call me. I don't do suicides."

Jesus.

The hotshot Miami doctor's tone was dismissive. He closed my file. He had better things to do.

I was seventy years old and had come to see this big-deal gastroenterologist for my debilitating stomach pain. After spending the previous week in the hospital, I had been advised to stay completely away from alcohol. I did. For about thirty-six hours.

I blamed a bag of crispy chocolate chip cookies for the first bout of major stomach pain that sent me to the emergency room. I had been watching late-night TV and eating cookies in bed, chewing quietly so as not to wake my husband. Barney can't bear crumbs in the sheets. An hour later, my stomach began to hurt.

I waited for the pain to go away. It didn't. I considered my options. Going to the emergency room would involve me getting up and putting on clothing. That seemed like way too much effort for 1:30 a.m. I decided to ignore the sharp stabbing in my stomach. My attempt only lasted the length of a MyPillow commercial. The pain was undeniably getting much worse. I hid the empty cookie bag and woke up Barney. He drove me to the emergency room.

The pain spread rapidly to my back. After multiple tests, the ER doctors were still stumped about the cause. My regular internist was called in. He couldn't figure it out either.

I begged him, "Please! Just give me morphine. Anything to stop this pain!"

My internist thought I might need surgery for gallstones. Pain drugs were out of the question until they knew the exact cause.

After five hours of MRIs, scopes, and blood tests, they had a diagnosis. Acute pancreatitis. They had figured out the culprit. It was martinis.

Martinis?!? Well, that had to be wrong!

I did look forward to a Hendrick's martini or two. Sometimes three. Every night. Starting at 5 p.m., the respectable happy hour. They made me feel happy.

I thought, "Why couldn't the pain have been caused by something that I would never miss, like exercise? Couldn't it have been a bad reaction to the lap pool? Perhaps it's a transdermal overdose of chlorine."

The only treatment for pancreatitis was to stay in the hospital, be medicated, and wait it out. I spent the next five days there on really good pain meds. I don't remember a thing about those days.

I was released, feeling fine, free to go home with my printed-out instructions on how to prevent another attack. At the top of the list was "No alcoholic beverages."

Right.

I'm not great with instructions. I don't have the patience for them. If the remote doesn't make my TV turn on when I press the green button, I call someone to come over to fix it.

The next evening, while at a restaurant with a friend, I decided to test the waters and ordered one of those pink, fizzy cocktails that comes with a paper parasol.

I never go for those sissy drinks, but I thought it seemed safe enough. It wasn't a martini, after all. An hour later, I was doubled over in pain. Pastel-colored fruity libations are not to be trusted.

Dr. Gastroenterologist concluded I must have a death wish. He had nothing else to say to me. My bottom lip started quivering. My eyes filled with tears.

He barked, "You're not gonna get all weepy on me now, are ya? I thought you were the tough one."

He was referring to my portrayal of police detective Christine Cagney in my TV show from the 1980s, *Cagney & Lacey*.

How dare he speak to me that way! I defended myself. "They *paid* me to be tough. You're not paying me."

The doctor stood over me. He was physically imposing, a retired general in the army. I wasn't sure if I was angry or developing a bit of a crush.

Either way, I followed his orders. I haven't had a drink since May 8, 2015. And I miss my Hendrick's dry martini, stirred not shaken. Every single night. Still.

— • —

I spent the first six weeks of my life in a hospital. I was born premature.

On May 28, my mother went into labor. I was supposed to be an end-of-June baby. After my mother had been in labor for seventy-four hours, the doctor said, "This baby wants to be born today." It was May 31, 1943.

They wheeled my mother into surgery, knocked her out, and performed a C-section. She was sent to recovery, and I was rushed into an incubator in the nursery, weighing less than three pounds.

After spending a week in a different ward of the hospital, unable to see or hold me, my mother scored a wheelchair from the hallway and managed to roll through the corridors to the nursery. She was certain she would be told that I had died.

But when she made her way over to the incubator, she saw I was alive. Though, according to her, I looked like a pound of butter, like she could hold me in the palm of her hand.

The nurse unwrapped the blanket to show her my tiny body, which my mother also described as "just perfect."

The next day, my mother was sent home from the hospital for a month of bed rest. She had no choice but to leave me behind, unnamed.

One of the nurses began to call me Bubbles.

My father would stop in to see me on his way home from work. He placed a tiny bottle of holy water, blessed by the pope, in the corner of the incubator.

My mother did not return. She was physically fragile and probably petrified of the possibility of losing another daughter.

Four years earlier, the year before my older brother, Michael, was born, my mother gave birth to a girl she named for her mother, Marguerite. The nuns at the hospital baptized the curly-haired baby when, after twenty-four hours, it became obvious she wasn't going to make it. Little Marguerite was laid to rest in an infant-size coffin before my mother was even released from the hospital.

No doctor ever gave my mother a reason for Marguerite's death. In the 1930s and '40s, the medical community never connected the ways smoking and drinking could affect a fetus. My mother started smoking cigarettes at age sixteen and enjoyed daily libations once she was an adult. Pregnancy pamphlets from that era encouraged women to not give up smoking or social drinking, as it kept "the expectant mother's nerves calm."

After a normal pregnancy and delivery of Michael, my mother felt a renewed sense of optimism while expecting me.

There was one other aspect that made this pregnancy different. A tea-leaf reader named me.

In the 1940s, my mother did a lot of volunteer work with the Assistance League of Los Angeles, a charitable organization of "society" women. After their events, the women would go to the adjoining Attic Tea Room, where a tea-leaf reader was often on hand to read fortunes as entertainment for the diners.

The fortune-teller looked into the bottom of my mother's cup and said, "Your life is going to change."

"Well, I am pregnant," my mother admitted.

After studying the pattern of the tea leaves once more, the fortune-teller said, "It will be a very special child." (I love that part of the story!) "May I name this baby?"

My mother was caught off guard by the request, but, as conservative as she was, she took the fortune-teller's phone number and agreed to call her after I was born.

In my baby book is an envelope that my mother had used to write down the fortune-teller's suggestions. Karen, Hillary, and Sharon were the three choices. Sharon had been circled in pencil. And so, five weeks after I was born, I became Sharon Marguerite Gless.

Good thing. I don't think "Bubbles Gless" would have worked in the *Cagney & Lacey* credits.

Two

Miss Gless Is About to Perform

I did not linger long in the three-pound-premature-infant category. I'm sure those first six weeks of my life were the one and only time anyone ever suggested that I gain weight.

I looked like Winston Churchill in my first baby photo. I had a fat face, a double chin, and wisps of white-blonde hair on my mostly bald head. It almost looks like I led the Allied coalition to victory in 1943.

As a little girl growing up in Southern California, I played softball, tetherball, danced, wrestled my brother Michael, and swam all day long. There was no opportunity for a fat cell to stick to me. That changed between fifth and sixth grade, when I went into puberty. I rapidly became rounder. All over. My mother never made mention of it.

I could sense the first complaint about my weight coming my way one summer morning, at Union Station in downtown LA, with every step my grandmother took along the train platform toward me.

My mother and I watched as weary passengers in wrinkled clothes stumbled out of various railcars until we finally spotted Grimmy (the grandchildren's name for Grandmother McCarthy). Even after a three-day train trip, she had emerged from the parlor car at the very end of the train looking fresh and dignified in her tailored light blue suit, using her thinly wrapped umbrella as a walking stick. I watched her with rapt attention as she approached, thrusting the umbrella before every determined stride. She had such power. She was extraordinary. It seemed like other passengers stepped out of her pathway. No one dared cross her.

Grimmy eyed me from head to toe, turned to my mother, and said, "She's getting fat, Marjorie."

She made this proclamation as if I weren't standing right there. My mother didn't offer up a word in my defense. She was afraid of her own mother, which was understandable. Grimmy scared the shit out of me, too.

Grimmy would extend her cheek toward me to be kissed whenever she visited. There was never a kiss offered in return. She *did*, however, offer plenty of emphatic opinions about how I should live my life and conduct myself.

She was regal and stern, with a no-nonsense tone. She always had the answers about the correct way to do everything, and she never held back her thoughts when it came to me, her first blonde look-alike granddaughter. She had a plan in place for me: a direction and a map for how I was to advance through life. It included attending grade school and Bluebirds in the upscale Hancock Park area of Los Angeles, being trained in social decorum and ballroom dancing at cotillion, attending the elite all-girl Marlborough School, as my mother and her sisters had, and then making my debut to society at the Las Madrinas Ball at age eighteen. By age twenty-two, I would hopefully have attracted and married an ambitious young attorney, set up a home in Los Angeles, be doing charity work with the ladies of the Junior League and playing bridge, golf, or tennis, and be on my way to having fabulous children who would also grow up to be attorneys or the wife of one. Being fat had no place in the plan. On that train platform, I got my first verbal warning.

Grimmy held the family purse strings, so she was the boss. Every opportunity I was afforded, from ballet lessons to boarding school, happened because she financed it. Her approval was everything to me. And it was scarce.

Grimmy was from the era where children were to be "seen and not heard." She had raised her three daughters and one son with that philosophy.

My mother and her siblings had grown up in a large home on Muirfield Road in Hancock Park. The showcase house was designed by and furnished with my grandmother's impeccable taste and built from the earnings of her husband, my grandfather, Neil S. McCarthy.

Grandpa was the most famous and powerful entertainment attorney in Los Angeles during the Golden Age of Hollywood. He represented Howard Hughes, Cecil B. DeMille, Mary Pickford, and Katharine Hepburn, along with other stars and major motion picture interests. He would often meet with his celebrity clients at the famous Beverly Hills Hotel in the Polo Lounge, where he went for lunch every weekday. A waiter would remove the white netting that kept a reserved table on the patio clean and ready for Grandpa and his guests. The most popular item on the menu was, and still is today, the famous McCarthy chopped salad, named for my grandfather. His caricature was on the wall of the famous Brown Derby restaurant on Vine Street in Hollywood.

Louis B. Mayer, Ava Gardner, and Lana Turner were also on Grandpa's extensive client list. Howard Hughes was a neighbor on Muirfield Road and would often show up, unannounced, at Grandpa's front door, for both financial and personal advice.

The McCarthys' lifestyle appeared to be charmed and impressive, but it didn't spare their marriage. After my mother and her three siblings had grown, married, and had homes of their own, my grandfather, who had fallen in love with another woman, requested a divorce.

At that time, a wife could still contest a divorce and Grimmy did just that. She had faithfully supported my grandfather's goals through his college years, his early career, and the raising of their children. She had helped him go from being the poor son of an alcoholic stagecoach driver to a powerful and wealthy lawyer.

"I'm much better off being the present Mrs. McCarthy," was her response to his divorce request.

"Who told you that?" Grandpa asked.

"The finest attorney I know," she replied.

"And, that would be?"

"You."

Grimmy's wise strategy was based on stories Grandpa had brought home over the decades. He would tell his female clients to never accept divorce, warning them that it would play out in the man's favor, and they could end up with nothing. Grimmy always remembered that. She was not about to give up being Mrs. McCarthy, especially since she was still in love with Mr. McCarthy.

He moved out nonetheless, though he remained legally married to my grandmother for the rest of her life. Grimmy moved away to Hillsboro, New Hampshire. She renovated an old 1700s structure that had once been a stagecoach post into a wonderful home. She then devoted her time to writing cookbooks, one of which became a national bestseller. Everything Grimmy put her hand to became a success, except the one thing that mattered most: her marriage. Now, on her own, she was determined to not lose her influence over other areas of her life. I was at the top of her list.

Since Grimmy no longer lived in Los Angeles full-time, she invited my mother and father to move from their tiny home in LA's Carthay Circle to the huge Muirfield house. There were specific instructions attached to the invitation. We were to occupy "the children's quarters." My mother and father used what was once my mother's childhood bedroom as the master bedroom. Michael was given my uncle's childhood bedroom and, at age three, I was in the nursery. We all shared one bathroom, though the house had at least eight more. Happily, the swimming pool and badminton court were not off-limits.

My father readily acclimated to the upgrade. He would host impressive cocktail parties and backyard barbecues.

Grimmy kept her own private wing of the Muirfield house,

which was beyond a closed door, past the children's quarters. My brothers and I were not allowed to go in. Around age six, I began to defy that order, but only if Grimmy wasn't visiting Los Angeles. Her quarters had the prettiest dressing room and bathroom, both wallpapered in light gray felt, and a built-in, wall-to-wall mirrored table, with her lotions, perfumes, and powders on top. I made sure I didn't leave my fingerprints behind as evidence. There was a fireplace in her bedroom with a chaise longue upholstered in pale pink brocade, with a cashmere throw perfectly folded at the bottom.

Grimmy's bed had pink satin sheets which tempted me most of all. On one of my trespassing adventures, I stripped off all my clothes and jumped between the sheets completely naked to see what satin felt like against my bare skin.

=·=

Unlike Grimmy, my mother was very shy and gentle with her opinions. She always made sure her children were well mannered and compassionate. I had the compassion part down early but struggled with her definition of well mannered. In a household where public displays of emotion were discouraged, I was often quietly reprimanded: "Sharon Marguerite, will you please modulate your voice."

My mother would kindly call me "a case of arrested development." I perplexed her. I stayed young, very young, for a long time.

In my heart, I still feel like a six-year-old. At my last birthday party, my best friend, Dawn Lafreeda, asked if I was now going to turn seven.

"Not a chance," I said. "According to the Catholic Church, seven is the age of reason. I have no intention of accepting that responsibility."

I've been rambunctious and expressive my whole life. The condition of my sterling silver baby cup is evidence. The bottom of the cup is loaded with deep dents from my hitting it on my high chair.

According to my mother, I spent my toddler years vacillating between being the sweetest child and then suddenly, without provocation, having a meltdown and "becoming airborne, flying into the walls." Worried, my mother confided to one of her friends about the flip in my personality.

"What's her birth date?" her friend asked.

"May 31. Why?"

"Well, that explains it. Your daughter is a Gemini. The sign of the twins. Two personalities."

I find that laughable. I have many more than two personalities.

The nursery was the only place where I could drop my guard and let loose. A full-length mirror on the nursery door became my first acting coach. Whenever I had been punished, I would sit in front of the mirror and watch myself cry. It wasn't easy to keep the tears flowing and observe myself at the same time at age four, but I managed. When the tears ran out, I would put a children's album on my little record player and perform it for myself in the mirror.

Moderation never came easily to me as a child. It still doesn't. I associate it with all the other *m*-words that seem so *m*undane: *modified, mediocre, modest, middle-of-the-road*, and *marginal*. Even maturity seems a dull goal. What's after that? Mortem?

If Grimmy wasn't around, I never thought about the consequences of indulging. I liked treats. I would take the quarter I had earned for doing chores and buy five candy bars with it and eat them all.

Whenever my parents would host their friends at the house, the children would often be sent to play miniature golf on Olympic Boulevard. I was pretty good at it, but the game wasn't the reason I wanted to go. The highlight was the snack stand at the end.

At age fourteen, in boarding school, I was in an ice cream sandwich–eating contest. One day my total was seventeen ice cream sandwiches. I was the champ. There was no prize. I walked away only with 3,200 extra calories.

By ninth grade, it was no longer a question of *if* I was getting fat. I *was* fat. During my Christmas break from school, I couldn't fit into any of my regular clothing. I had to wear my school uniform at home. Grimmy was in Los Angeles for the holidays. She took one look at me and her eyes filled with tears. They were not tears of happiness.

"She looks just like her grandmother Gless," she said to my mother, and walked out of the living room, crying. This was not a compliment. Grandma Gless was short and portly, about as wide as she was tall.

My mother stayed silent, staring at the floor.

I went upstairs to my room and closed the door.

= • =

My other grandmother, Nellie Gless, maiden name Duggan, had been an orphan from New Orleans. Her oldest brother, a Jesuit priest in Los Angeles, brought twelve-year-old Nellie to the West Coast to live in a convent school.

At age sixteen, Nellie had fallen madly in love with my grand-father Constánt Simón Gless, the oldest son of wealthy sheepherders, descendants from the Basque country bordering both Spain and France.

On the Gless side of the family, I'm a fifth-generation Angeleno. There aren't many people in Los Angeles who can make that claim. The Gless family owned about 44,000 acres of land, now known as Encino, California. They also owned most of Gardena, Los Feliz, and Boyle Heights, thousands of acres covered with sheep. There are still five streets named after my family in Los Angeles. That and a dime will get you nothing.

Grandma told me that the first time Constánt kissed her, she fainted dead away. They married not long after. No one was ever rude enough to comment, but my father, Dennis Gless, was born rather early, a nine-pound "preemie."

A few years later, Nellie gave my father a new baby sister, Juanita, my "Aunt Hoonie."

After decades of trying to make ends meet with her "silver

spoon" husband who wasn't interested in keeping a real job for long, Nellie sought a divorce. That's what she got. Divorce papers. No money. No child support. Constánt's mother had squandered the family fortune on ridiculous indulgences, including her very own train car so she wouldn't have to sit with other passengers. They had to sell off most of the land. Any inherited money was gone, and so was Constánt from Nellie's life. Nellie was left to find a job and support her two children. Ironically, she spoiled my father, giving him her full attention and even writing his valedictorian speech for his Hollywood High School graduation. Her daughter, Juanita, on the other hand, was taught to work hard, sacrifice for her brother, and help out. There was no question which child was Nellie's favorite.

If Grandma Gless was heavyhearted or work-weary from her hard life, she never showed it when I was around. Once a month, my mother would pick me up from grammar school on a Friday afternoon and take me to Grandma's to spend the night. She did this reluctantly.

"Your grandmother Gless sleeps in the nude. It's not healthy," my mother told me.

How could she know that? I had never noticed Grandma being naked when I stayed overnight at her studio apartment, and I shared her Murphy bed with her. Her entire place was probably no more than three hundred square feet in total, but for me it was a haven of acceptance, where I was encouraged to tell stories, sing, and perform to my heart's content. All of my emotions were welcome, as was my big appetite. The one place in my childhood where there was never any reprimanding or complaints was at my grandma Gless's apartment.

Grandma's apartment building was near the famous Ambassador Hotel in Los Angeles and was very old. The elevator was the type with a heavy iron door on every floor, each painted with a floor number that was chipped and faded. Once you were inside the elevator, a metal accordion gate had to be drawn across the entrance before it would go up or down. I found it fascinating, watching the floors come into view from above and then drop below me, until we arrived at the iron door with the painted 6. I could sense the disapproval from my mother, who would stand in uncomfortable silence as the outdated elevator rose, clanging loudly. When it finally jerked to a stop, she would pull the gate open, push the iron door, and there would be Grandma, waiting for me in the hallway. I would feel so excited to have her see me! A moment later she would have me in her arms.

Grandma loved me so much that she would cover my face with kisses as soon as she could get her hands on me. It was the only unappealing part of the visit. Her fondness for good whiskey caused her nose to run, and with each kiss she planted on my cheeks, she would leave dampness behind. I waited for her to look away before wiping off my face—clearly an example of my newly learned compassion.

I would "help" Grandma make a delicious homemade dinner; then we would wash and dry the dishes while she taught me a new song to sing. When it was dark outside, Grandma would run my bath. Her small bathroom always smelled of her perfumes and face cream. She had beautiful skin. Even today, if I catch the scent of original Nivea lotion, it will instantly take me back to those Friday nights.

After I was bathed and in my nightie and robe, it was showtime! I would go to my dressing room, which was the tiny passageway between the living room area and the bathroom. Grandma's clothing hung in a shallow closet on one side of the passageway, but the other side had a small dressing table with a mirror. There was a settee that tucked under the table. A suspension rod in the doorway held up a curtain of tropical-print fabric on wooden rings that allowed it to slide open and closed. When I was completely ready, I would signal Grandma from behind the closed curtain and wait for her announcement.

The preshow routine was always the same. I would stand by

"backstage" while Grandma subdued the "crowds," using impresario-like tones of authority.

"May I have your attention please? Please. Quiet everyone! No more talking! Quiet in the peanut gallery. Please take your seats. The show is about to begin!"

From behind the curtain, the imaginary crowd's energy left me trembling with excitement and nerves. She made it seem like hundreds of people were waiting for me. I could hear the pounding of my heartbeat. I knew once Grandma announced me, I had to go on. Finally, when I thought my chest would explode, Grandma would softly say: "Miss Gless is about to perform."

I'm sure I had a full lineup of songs, but I only remember the one Grandma taught me, "Christopher Robin Is Saying His Prayers." It was always my big opener.

I threw the curtain aside and made my grand entrance.

The applause was thunderous every time.

And so it began.

Miss Gless is about to perform.

Three

So Everyone Can See You

On the wall in my Los Angeles home office is a photo of my mother with her six bridesmaids. Each of my mother's attendants carried a lavish bouquet of cascading sweet pea flowers that matched the color of her individual bridesmaid dress.

My mother's parents gave her the wedding of her dreams: an elaborate, no-expense-spared Catholic ceremony with hundreds of LA's high-society names on the guest list, including Bank of America founder A. P. Giannini, and movie moguls Louis B. Mayer and Cecil B. DeMille.

My father, Dennis Gless, had abundant charm and matching good looks. My mother fell madly and deeply in love with him. I like to imagine that, at least early on, he felt the same way about her. However, my brothers and I never once saw our parents kiss or even share a moment of true physical affection.

Later in her life, my mother divulged to me why she was never fond of Grandma Gless. She was convinced that Grandma had pressured her only son to marry for the wealth and social status of the McCarthys. However, my mother had no money of her own. After the elaborate wedding reception and the gift of a new car, my grandparents expected my father to fully support their daughter. And he did.

I'm sure it was huge pressure for my father to try to emulate the success of his legendary father-in-law. Grandpa took him in like a son, even using his influence as a board member and attorney to get my father a job with an impressive title: head of public relations at Desmond's, which was a famous clothing chain store in LA.

My dark-haired dad had thick wavy locks and piercing blue eyes, and was a jock at heart, just like my grandfather. He would go along to any sporting event Grandpa wanted to attend. Grandpa always had the most expensive ringside seats to the biggest boxing matches that came through Los Angeles. The two of them would triumphantly return home with the fighters' blood spattered on their shirts.

My father's biggest sports obsession was the University of Southern California's Trojans football team. He had seats on the fifty-yard line. He had attended USC for one year out of high school before the money ran out. Even though he wasn't technically an alumnus, he focused on being a "hero" to the Trojans organization by entertaining team members at the Muirfield house, and also providing gifts to the players and organization that were beyond his means. It became his life. No sacrifice seemed too great to keep Trojans management thinking he was "the guy," even when what he sacrificed should have supported our family.

My father's USC Trojans obsession became a deep source of embarrassment for my conservative mother, who was naturally very shy and who would never make a show of money or gifts in hopes of impressing anyone. She referred to my father as "the perennial sophomore."

My father knew the power of his God-given natural assets of charm and good looks, and he knew how to work them to his benefit. The Trojans football association wasn't alone in thinking my father was swell. Ladies loved Dennis Gless. And he loved them in return.

As a child, I was completely smitten with my father. I used to imagine that I was the most loved of all the women in his life. It quickly became pretty clear to me that my mother didn't hold that place.

A couple of times a year, my father would take me to the Pike amusement park in Long Beach. It was always my favorite father-daughter day. On one of our outings, he had to first make an appearance at a fashion show for his job at Desmond's. My father was the host and announced the style and designers worn by the runway models. I was spellbound watching him hold the attention of everyone in the room. The women in the audience were falling all over themselves to see him. During his opening remarks he said, "I have my daughter with me today."

Many of the people attending turned to look for me at a table off to the side.

"Darling, stand up on the chair so everyone can see you," my father coaxed me.

I slowly stood up on the chair and smiled at the crowd. There was applause. Quite a bit. I liked the attention, but I knew my mother would have been horrified by this public display.

While my mother allowed Michael and me to wrestle and yell at each other in the house, rude or showy behavior was never tolerated if we were in public or with other people. Using the wrong tone of voice around my mother could get me grounded for a month.

I never heard my mother raise her voice, and swearing was out of the question. Only one time did I hear her say "damn." But not really. She spelled it out loud, "D-A-M-N." I'm sure she confessed that travesty to a priest.

One Sunday morning, we were having breakfast together in the kitchen. This was rare, as my father ate very few meals at home. My mother never sat at the table with us. She always stood at the sink.

Suddenly, I heard my mother tell my father, with great urgency, "Dennis, not in front of the children!!"

I had no idea what he had done, and, apparently, neither did he. We all stopped eating and my father, bewildered, said, "What? What did I do?"

She replied, "You are dunking your toast in your yolk!"

In his defense, my father said, "Marjorie, we are here, in our kitchen."

"I don't care," she insisted. "The children are going to watch you do that, and then they will dunk their toast in their yolk in public."

My father turned to Michael and me and said, "Children, are you going to dunk your toast in your yolk when you are out in public?"

"No, Daddy," Michael and I answered in unison.

"You see, Marjorie. They are not going to dunk their toast in their yolk when they are in public," my father repeated for emphasis.

He then returned to dunking his toast.

My mother resented my father's nonchalance about what she thought of as crucial life lessons. She'd tell both Michael and me: "I'm the one who loves you enough to take the time to train you, to teach you manners. Then your father sweeps in and takes you out to show you off."

It was true. Daddy didn't monitor our behavior. He taught Michael to extend his hand when meeting someone and me to curtsy. The hard day-to-day detail work was left to my mother.

"Someday you will thank me," she used to tell us.

The truth is, I do. Every day, I do.

⇒ • ⇐

My father was a great entertainer. He would make us laugh by doing spot-on imitations of my mother's friends. When he played the piano in the family room, his hands would move across the keys with a dramatic flair and his upper body would sway. He would sometimes teach me songs and we would sing them together, side by side on the piano bench.

Grandpa McCarthy was known across Beverly Hills for his spectacular Christmas trees, and my father adopted Grandpa's hobby as a way to connect with him. The two of them would go to the train yards in downtown Los Angeles to pick out the largest and freshest Christmas trees coming in from the Northwest. Boxes and boxes of oversize ornaments were brought in from storage, and my father would place each ornament, one at a time, on the branches himself, stepping back to get the overall effect.

The very first color photo on the cover of the *Los Angeles Times* was of my father's beautiful Christmas tree.

As if to counter my father's grand version of the holiday, my mother would get small Christmas trees—about three feet tall—and set them up in each of our bedrooms, a child-size tree with our personal small ornaments and strings of mini lights. Every night she would sit on the edge of my bed while she gave me a back rub or ran her fingers through my hair. She would listen to my prayers and then leave the little tree lights plugged in until after I had fallen asleep. My father's trees may have been stunning and memorable, but my mother's little bedroom trees were simply magical. She created a tradition that meant the most to me. Her trees were my favorite part of the Christmas season.

Daddy's gift to my mother every Christmas Eve was a rolling garment rack full of beautiful, tailored clothes. Shopping for herself was never a priority for my mom. A brand name meant little to her. She never appeared to be impressed or happy about her whole new wardrobe. Years later, I finally understood the reason. One of my father's not-so-secret lovers was his secretary, Yvonne. She shared the same body type as my mother, long and lean. My dad would have Yvonne try on the clothing he had picked out for Mom. Whatever looked good on his mistress, he would buy for his wife.

I was oblivious to the affair and was a big fan of Yvonne's. She would let me sit at her desk, punch the keys on her typewriter, and play with the intercom system. My father would be very professional around Yvonne when I visited his office. He thought my mother had no idea what was going on, and she kept up the ruse.

I often heard my mother's anguish, through the locked bathroom door, as she cried alone. I was too young to understand the cause of her tears. I would cry as well, standing on my side of the closed door. By the time she emerged from the bathroom, she would be poised and gently dismissive of my concerned face, as if I were being "silly."

When I was nine, I heard my parents arguing in the middle of the night, their voices traveling through the hallways of our "children's quarters."

The next day, I was sitting with my mother in the station wagon in the driveway when I began to cry.

"Are you and Daddy getting a divorce?"

My mother turned toward me.

"No, darling. Why would you think that?"

"I heard you and Daddy arguing last night and he said, 'So, do you want a divorce?'"

"Oh, darling. Daddy and I never argue. We were merely having a discussion. You must have been having a nightmare."

I really wanted to accept my mother's explanation.

I said, "Do you promise me that you'll never get a divorce?"

"I promise."

I relied on her promise. And for the longest time I think my father counted on it, too. It would take a lot for my mother, a devout Catholic and daily communicant, to divorce my father. Plus, my father would always manage to find a way to get sympathy and concern from my mother.

I was still awake one night, months later, when he came home very late. From my bed, I could see his profile in the hallway, carrying a large kitchen knife. He went into the nursery across the hall, headed straight to the window, and cut the cord off of the venetian blinds. I heard my mother make a phone call to my father's sister, my aunt Hoonie, and ask her to please come over right away.

I was terrified. I got up and ran down the hallway and sat on the end of my parents' bed.

About thirty minutes later, Aunt Hoonie came to find me. She waved her hand through the air, dismissing any notion that something serious had happened.

"Darling. Everything is going to be fine," she said, ushering me back to my room and into my bed.

Years later, Aunt Hoonie told me the truth about that night. It seems my father was very drunk and threatening suicide. Hoonie had found him downstairs, passed out on the couch in the library, with the venetian blind cord loosely strung around his neck and the knife on the coffee table. She knew her brother never really wanted to do any self-harm. He only wanted to frighten my mother into not ending their marriage.

Aunt Hoonie could always call his bluff. She told me that she shook him awake saying, "Dennis, if you're going to do the job, use the knife to slit your throat. But do it outside on the badminton court so you don't make a mess in the house."

A few years later, I gave my father a case of the mumps. Mumps are usually relatively harmless for children but can cause large swelling in the testicles of adult men. For days, he stayed in the guest room with two heat lamps over his sore and swollen parts. Once he recovered, he never returned to sharing the master bedroom with my mother. Ultimately, they both seemed happier with the new arrangement.

The stress of their marriage caused my mother health complications, yet she never complained. She suffered through cases of pneumonia once or twice a year, and severe nosebleeds, probably induced by the stress of being married to an errant husband. I would be sent to stay with Aunt Hoonie and her husband, my uncle Jack, for a week or two while she "recovered."

When my father was home, which wasn't often, he never failed to capture my full attention. I, in turn, wanted his. I wanted to be the center of his world.

On the days my father would take me, by myself, to the Pike, he would buy a string of tickets and then stand nearby and wait for me as I went on the Tilt-a-Whirl or the Hurricane. As the ride picked up speed, I would catch a glimpse of my father, handsome in his seersucker suit and straw boater hat, standing out from the crowd, as always. It was only a fleeting moment before the ride spun me around, and he was gone once more.

Four

If It Walks Like a Duck

"Where is it?" I bellowed from my mother's bedroom doorway. "Is it here?"

I tried to catch my breath after running up the staircase.

My mother said, "Darling, it's a he. Don't call him 'it.'"

"Okay. But, where is it?"

It seemed too real to call my new little brother, Aric, a "him." I was trying to figure out if this brand-new person was really ours to keep.

He was with a private nurse in the guest room. I was allowed to hold him, but only if I wore a mask. The fear of germs around a newborn was of great concern in the 1950s. Ironically, cigarette smoke seemed to be inconsequential.

With Aric's arrival, I was moved out of the nursery. Michael's large bedroom was renovated into two smaller ones, each with a set of bunk beds.

I was seven and a half when Aric was born; Michael was ten. Although I didn't realize it until much later, my mother had miscarried a number of times between my birth and Aric's.

I'd like to say that there was never a more cherished infant than our new little brother, but, in our enthusiasm, I think Michael and I gave Aric a case of full-blown PTSD by the time he was six months old.

In the first month of Aric's life, I decided that I wanted to show him off to one of our visitors. My mother had made me promise to never remove Aric from his bassinet, but, luckily for me, she wasn't home. Oops! Promise broken.

I tiptoed into the nursery and lifted Aric out of his bassinet and headed toward the flight of twenty stairs. Then, five steps from the bottom, I slipped. I was airborne, headfirst, but I held on tight to Aric. When my chest hit the bottom step the wind was knocked out of me. The baby rolled out of my arms and onto the floor. He was silent. I couldn't breathe and I thought I had killed my baby brother. After a few gasping moments, my breath returned and Aric started crying. I picked him up and he stopped. No one ever knew what I had done. Sorry, Aric.

Often Michael and I would boisterously flail about the nursery as my mother sat in a chair feeding Aric or as she changed him. His little eyes would blink rapidly and his head would swivel around, trying to keep up with the action.

"Children, you must stop tantalizing your brother!" my mother would say in frustration when Aric would spit up his entire bottle from sensory overstimulation.

Michael and I didn't purposely intend to upset Aric. We loved him, but he was often an easy target for our childish pranks.

My mother was always of the opinion that a child should not be raised alone without a sibling. From a very young age, her only ambition was to fall in love, get married, and have many children. The love and marriage didn't live up to her dreams, but she was determined to have the children.

She got pregnant again before Aric was one. She wanted him to have a playmate near his age. It wasn't to be.

One night we woke up to a commotion. Michael and I met up in the hallway. We watched through the slats of the upstairs banister as my mother, six months pregnant, was carried on a gurney down the stairs by two EMTs. She was crying.

I was terrified. I asked my brother what was happening.

"She's crying because she might lose the baby," Michael told me.

The ambulance pulled out of the driveway with sirens blaring. Michael and I sat on the floor in the hallway. The middle-of-the-night silence seemed overwhelming. I didn't know what to do. The neighbor, our "aunt Tommy," came over to stay with us.

Most often, the only time Michael and I would have physical contact with each other was to wrestle or occasionally punch each other. We were both too cool to show physical affection.

"Want to sleep in my room on the bottom bunk with me?" Michael asked.

"Yes, please," I said. I crawled under the covers and faced the wall so he wouldn't regret his offer. Michael put his arm over my shoulder for a while. I fell asleep.

The next morning, my father sat on the edge of the bed and stood me in front of him. He looked exhausted.

"Mommy had a baby boy last night. He was born too early and he died this morning."

My mother had named the baby Donal, which is Gaelic for Neil, my grandfather's name.

That afternoon, I was sent to stay with Aunt Hoonie, Uncle Jack, and my little cousin Lizzie for a few weeks.

When I came back home, it was as if my mother had never been pregnant. Donal was never discussed. There would be no other chances for Aric to have a sibling near his age.

≡ • ≡

One Saturday morning, I woke up to the sound of continuous banging coming from outside. I decided to investigate. I followed the noise into the backyard and up the brick steps to the swimming pool, where I saw my grandfather's head, barely showing from the deep end of the empty pool, which had been drained for the winter. The only time he came to the Muirfield house was if he knew Grimmy was on the East Coast.

Grandpa was sitting on a wooden sawhorse, placed on the floor of the deep end, that replicated the height of a polo pony, four legs and a body. He held a polo mallet and was repeatedly slamming a wooden ball into the shallow end of the pool. It would ricochet with loud cracking sounds off the walls and eventually roll back down to the deep end, where my grandfather would smack it again. He was there to practice for an upcoming polo match at Will Rogers Park. I stood on the edge of the pool, thrilled to watch him practice.

When he finished, he wiped his brow and turned to look at me. With seventeen grandchildren, he didn't even try to guess.

"Which one are you?"

"I'm Sharon, Grandpa."

That was enough for him.

"Well, of course you are. That's fine. Yes. That's fine."

As I was walking with him to put his mallet and wooden horse away in the garage, he stopped and made me walk ahead of him.

"You walk like a duck," he said.

I felt both embarrassed and excited that he noticed the way I walked, that he noticed me at all!

He led me by the shoulders to the long, narrow crack dividing the driveway. He told me to walk the straight line with my feet only on the crack. I fought tipping over with each step, but I practiced over and over until I could walk the line smoothly.

Grandpa's attention made me feel like he cared about me. He was probably thinking, "A McCarthy granddaughter can't walk around like a duck." Whatever. It still made me feel special. After ten minutes, Grandpa brushed his hands together, satisfied that he had discovered the cure to my problem, got in his car, and left. I had been given my instructions.

I spent so much of my life trying to walk that line. As a child, I never spent individual time with Grandpa, only seeing him for special occasions.

On one such occasion, Cecil B. DeMille invited Grandpa and our family to his home on a Sunday afternoon for dinner. We sat at round tables covered with white tablecloths and formal settings in the large front room in Mr. DeMille's home, which was in a gated enclave in the Los Feliz district of Los Angeles. I did my best to keep my Mary Janes pointing straight forward when I walked in. I hoped Grandpa would notice. He didn't.

Following dinner, a very large movie screen was lowered on the wall and a film projector was set up. I was so excited to be part of an actual screening of a Hollywood movie. The rest of the evening was spent seeing a brand-new film starring Charlton Heston and Yul Brynner. We were the very first private group of people to see Mr. DeMille's then recently completed *The Ten Commandments*, before it was released to the theaters. Prior to that evening, I had no idea what Mr. DeMille did. I only knew that he was a friend of my grandfather's, and that he loved racehorses. So did Grandpa. I thought that's what they had in common.

When I was a young girl, Grandpa told me that the movie industry is "a filthy business" and that I should stay out of it.

I didn't believe him. Why would *he* be in it, if it were so awful? To me, show business seemed like a beautiful way to make a living. From my earliest days, I loved the energy of Hollywood, the way it seemed to permeate everything. There was an excitement about the moviemaking business. You could buy maps to the movie stars' homes, where they actually lived. You could cross paths with a celebrity having a hot fudge sundae at C. C. Brown's on Hollywood Boulevard. The stories on the screen that were being shown all around the world were created mere miles from our front door. At night, I would walk onto our sleeping porch, hoping to see the huge Hollywood Boulevard klieg lights sweep the sky in their crossing pattern announcing the premiere of a new film.

I dreamed about being a part of it. I wasn't sure what my job in Hollywood would be, but whatever it was, it would be important.

Five

Inevitable

I could have become a famous virtuoso pianist. It could have happened. I had enthusiasm, passion, and a true love of music.

When I was in the first grade at Cathedral Chapel School, my teacher asked if anyone wanted to participate in beginner piano lessons. I raised my hand. So did about six other kids. We followed the nun who would be teaching us to the empty kindergarten classroom. We sat on the floor behind a row of varnished wooden planks that had been painted to resemble piano keyboards. In my excitement, I whispered to the little girl sitting next to me.

"These don't make any sound. That's later."

The nun abruptly stopped her lesson.

"Sharon, if that is all the respect you have for the piano, then I want you to please leave now! And do not come back."

This happened five minutes into the class. Five minutes. I returned to my regular classroom, red-faced and ashamed. No apology to the angered nun sufficed. My brilliant piano career, shattered.

≡ • ≡

The next year, when I was seven, my mother enrolled me in ballet lessons because, as she told me later, "You were leaping all over the house."

As a girl, my mother had taken ballet classes from the famous Russian-born ballet star and movie actor Theodore Kosloff. In his late sixties, he had opened a successful ballet school on Hollywood Boulevard, where my mother took me for classes. Mr. Kosloff was impressed with my muscular calves and the arch of my feet. He said I had great potential.

One of Mr. Kosloff's requirements was that every student had to own a pair of pointe ballet slippers. Grandma Gless took me to the Capezio store on Vine Street, where all the professional dancers shopped. I felt so important as my foot was measured from all angles and the beautiful pale pink slippers with the wooden toe boxes were fitted.

The ballet slippers cost fifty dollars, an outrageous sum for the 1950s, but Grandma Gless paid for them "on time," sending in checks every month. I'm not sure they were even paid off when my father's fifty-pound iron dumbbell rolled off the chaise lounge in my parents' bedroom and onto my bare foot, crushing my big toe.

A week later, after I could limp in to class, Mr. Kosloff took one look at my misshapen toe and declared, "This girl will never dance ballet." And that was that.

My brilliant ballet career. Gone forever.

I never held a grudge against my dad for the rolling dumbbell. Even without the broken toe, my ballet slippers would have most likely been retired by the time I was fifteen. It's tough to leap and float through the air like a leaf when gravity is pulling on one hundred and seventy pounds and D-cup-size breasts.

Those satin ballet slippers now hang in a shadow box in my bedroom in LA.

≡ • ≡

I had political aspirations. I was elected seventh-grade class representative at Marlborough School. My victory over Kay Sutton was by one vote. My own. For myself. I represented the seventh grade at all council meetings.

I only served for four months, until I got a C in citizenship for talking in class. You don't get to be the class representative if you have a C in citizenship. I was thrown off the council. Impeached! Kay Sutton took over. My groundbreaking political career, ruined.

≡ • ≡

After four years of boarding at Santa Catalina School, an all-girl high school run by Dominican nuns, I had no idea what to do after graduation. Whenever my classmates talked about college applications and higher education, I'd leave to find an ice cream sandwich.

Occasionally the sisters would gently suggest that we consider the vocation of becoming a nun. By April of my senior year, I thought, "I could do that. I could sit around and pray for people."

I was afraid to go out into the world. I didn't want any responsibility. I also thought that if I were a nun no one would care that I was fat. It would all be hidden under my long, black habit. It seemed like a really good plan. I knew my mother would think it was a lovely calling. Grimmy, a non-Catholic, would probably shit herself when she heard.

One spring evening, I asked Sister Kieran, the principal, if I could speak to her after dinner. She had never liked me, but I thought my new ambition to join the convent would win her over.

I perched, as delicately as possible, across from her in the corner of the dining hall's window seat.

"Yes, Sharon," she said with barely restrained impatience. "What is it?"

In my mind's eye, I was already envisioning a halo around my head. With all the piety I could muster, I said: "Sister Kieran, I'd like to enter the order."

I put my hands in the prayer position and lowered my head.

I waited for the enthusiastic response. Nothing. I waited another thirty seconds, figuring it had not quite sunk in for her. Silence.

I finally looked up.

After a moment, she said, "Sharon, it's a wonderful calling. But in your particular case, I think you should go away to college for one year. Then, if you still want to join the order, come back and we'll talk."

I was humiliated. I had no response, but it didn't matter. She had already moved on.

I realized later that I'd been spared. The Dominican nuns were a teaching order. Jesus. What was I thinking? The world of academia held no interest for me.

My luminous career as a bride of Christ ended before it began.

⇒ • ⇐

I wasn't too heartbroken that none of those jobs worked out for me, because, in the back of my mind, I never forgot my dream to work in movies. I'd always loved the movies.

My mother loved movies, too, but only in the privacy of our living room, where she could have a cocktail, smoke cigarettes, and escape into the fantasy romance that her life lacked. She would rent the large reels that came in two or three metal cans. We had a portable screen on a stand and a Bell & Howell projector. By age five, I could easily thread the projector from the full reel to the empty one.

Some days, I would come home from school and notice the screen had been set up. I knew my mother had watched the movie again, by herself.

The only person to take me to an actual movie theater was Grandma Gless. She would ride the city bus to Hancock Park, where my mother would wait with me at the bus stop and deliver me into Grandma's arms. It was during one of our movie outings that my eyes were opened to exactly who could become an actor. Me!

Grandma took me to see *The Kid from Left Field*. To my jaw-dropping surprise the young actor that played the "kid" was Billy Chapin. Billy was in my class at Cathedral Chapel School! Billy seemed to be just a regular little boy who was now on the huge screen in front of me! And he was the star!

I began plotting out my future that afternoon. "If Billy Chapin can do that, so can I."

I knew I had a resource. "Uncle Jack" was Jack Baur, the head of casting at 20th Century Fox. My uncle Jack worked with countless stars!

In fact, one of my favorite holiday traditions was going over to Uncle Jack and Aunt Hoonie's house and looking at all the greeting cards Jack received from various stars. I'd run my fingers over the signatures of Elizabeth Taylor, Kirk Douglas, Eva Marie Saint, Lana Turner, Susan Hayward, Cary Grant, and so many more.

Soon after seeing Billy's film debut, I asked my mother if she'd talk to Uncle Jack about my becoming an actress.

I don't think my mother saw that request coming. "Darling, I think you're very young. And there is school."

I usually wouldn't have dared to argue, but I really wanted it badly.

"I can do both! Billy Chapin does!"

My mother smiled.

"Let me talk to Uncle Jack about it," she said, capping off the subject.

Time went by and she never brought me an answer. She may have forgotten all about it, but I didn't. I had the daily reminder of seeing Billy Chapin on the playground. If he could act, I could act.

A couple of months later, I brought it up again.

My mother said, "Uncle Jack and I discussed it, and we both agree that it would be best if you finish school. You're very young. Then, later, we can talk about it again."

I may have "acted" disappointed by her answer, but part of me had been terrified that Uncle Jack would suggest, "Let's put her in front of a camera and see what she can do." Then what? I had a feeling that my nightie-clad rendition of "Christopher Robin Is Saying His Prayers" that brought down the house in Grandma's tiny apartment wouldn't quite rival Natalie Wood's star turn in *Miracle on 34th Street*.

Six

Broken Promise

I wasn't shipped off to boarding school against my wishes. I had asked to go. In the eighth grade, I had a huge girl crush on my English teacher, Miss Moore. Miss Moore told me that she had attended a boarding school on the East Coast for her high school years. One day, my mother found me in tears, sitting on the floor of my bedroom.

"Darling, why are you crying?"

"I want to go away to boarding school like Miss Moore."

I expected one of the responses my mother often used when the answer was no.

"Well, darling, there are many things in life one may want but cannot have," or, "We'll see."

This time she said, "Let me talk to your grandmother."

I couldn't believe my ears. It was almost as good as a yes.

Months later, I was leaving behind my bedroom at Muirfield Road, my brothers, and my pals at Marlborough School, where I had attended seventh and eighth grade, to live in an all-girl boarding school in Monterey, California.

I wasn't given a choice of boarding schools. Grimmy had already decided upon Santa Catalina. It was close to where she lived, by this time in a new house she'd designed and built in a wooded area of Carmel, California.

At first, everything at Santa Catalina was a new adventure. I had never shared a room before. I had never been away from home for so long.

I soon regretted asking to attend boarding school. I was more homesick with each passing day, and I'd eat more and more food to try to fill the empty feeling. I didn't limit myself in any way. There was always room for another bite. My uniforms got increasingly tighter as the weeks went by. I didn't want to go to classes anymore or live in a dorm. I had to figure out how to escape the routine of Santa Catalina without breaking the rules.

One day, I spotted a box of Ivory Flakes detergent in a cupboard. I poured some of the small flakes into the palm of my hand and sniffed them up my nose. My eyes started running and my nose clogged up from the burning. I was so pleased with the results. I sounded and looked very sick.

I went to one of the nuns and said, "Sister, I have a cold."

She took one look at me and said, "Oh, boy, you sure do. Let me send you to Miss Frank."

Miss Frank was the school nurse. She decided to keep me in the infirmary and put me to bed. Somehow, even though it began as a fake cold, the irritation to my nasal passages turned into an actual infection. She would take my temperature every morning and insist I stay in bed for another day. That was exactly what I wanted. Eventually, I was diagnosed with pneumonia and pleurisy. I wasn't "hospital" sick, but I wasn't well either. I was content to stay in the infirmary, and one week turned into many.

My classmates came one evening to serenade me from below my window. They sang a few songs. For the first time at Santa Catalina, I felt loved.

I could see the local drive-in movie from a window in the infirmary sitting room. Though I couldn't hear the sound, I still watched. The days blurred together.

After I had been in bed for six weeks, Miss Frank figured out why I was not getting well.

"This child is homesick," she said. "Send her home."

Grimmy agreed to buy a ticket for me to fly back to Los Angeles. It was my first time on an airplane. My mother picked me up at the airport.

I was so relieved to be back in LA, I put my head on her lap in the car and started crying.

"Oh, Mommy. I'm so happy to see you."

"Sharon, sit up! I have to talk to you."

My mother had never spoken to me in such a sharp tone before. I didn't know what was wrong. She was usually so loving. I sat up.

"Your father and I have separated," she told me matter-of-factly.

She had promised me that they would never divorce, and now that promise was broken. Tears streamed down my face.

Her tone did not soften. "Sharon, stop crying. It's time for you to grow up."

I was shocked into silence. My mother felt so distant to me.

I was soon to find out that my father had already moved out of our house, months before, on the exact same day I left for boarding school. It had all been planned.

My brother Michael had helped Daddy pack and dropped him off at the Los Angeles Athletic Club, where he took a room, while my mother rode the train north with me to help me get settled into the dorm. It suddenly became clear to me why my mother and Grimmy had thought boarding school was such a good idea for me.

There would be no comforting driveway chat this time. I sat in silence.

Once inside, my mother told me that Grimmy had decided I should be allowed to stay in her quarters while I was home. This was a very big deal. I was actually invited to sleep in those pink satin sheets! I guess this was to be my incentive to "grow up" more quickly. I got the message. I was now a young lady and needed to act like one. No crying about the divorce. I was fourteen years old.

As I carried my suitcase to Grimmy's quarters, I walked into the guest room that my father had occupied for the last four years. Now he was gone, and there was a fine layer of dust on the furniture. His closet was empty, and I could no longer smell his cologne in the bathroom. The newspapers he would read and then leave scattered about on the floor were missing. My heart was broken. I felt that I had lost my father, and it seemed like I was losing my mother, too.

The next day, Michael, Aric, and I were sent to Aunt Hoonie and Uncle Jack's house. The visit had been arranged so Daddy could see the three of us for the first time in months. I was standing in the dining room talking to Grandma Gless. I didn't notice that my father had arrived until I heard my aunt say, "Dennis, it will be all right. Come over here with me."

I turned to see my father crying in Aunt Hoonie's arms. I had never seen my father weep. Seeing him so broken made me feel like my world was coming apart. I went over to hug him. I had no idea what to say.

After a few days home, I returned to school. I rode the train back to Monterey, feeling worse than before. Grimmy was mad at me for being fat, my parents were divorcing, and now I had to move back into the dorm and attend classes. There would be no more comforting infirmary or drive-in movies.

When I came home for Christmas break, I weighed more than I ever had and I cried almost every day.

Grimmy, even more displeased by my extra pounds, confided her concerns to Grandpa at some point. When I saw him during the holidays, he had a proposition for me.

He said: "I'll tell you what. You lose twenty-five pounds, and I will take you to lunch with Cary Grant. Is that a deal?"

As much as I adored Cary Grant, the thought of my grandfather telling him that I was losing weight so that I could have lunch with him embarrassed me way too much. It wasn't the motivating factor Grandpa expected it to be. I didn't drop a pound.

My mother and I didn't get along at all during that break. I alternated between being argumentative and teary. I probably should have been going to see a child psychiatrist for my severe adolescent depression. In the late 1950s, no one thought kids needed a mental health checkup. At least no one I knew.

My mother didn't know what to do with me, so she allowed me to do the one thing I loved most: go to the movies.

I self-medicated with Rosalind Russell in the movie *Auntie Mame*. I was besotted with that character. I wanted to become her. My mother would drop me off at the famous Grauman's Chinese Theatre on Hollywood Boulevard so I could be alone with my broken heart. I would go to the 11 a.m. show and stay for the afternoon show, never leaving the theater. I would buy a large bucket of buttered popcorn and sit in the first row of the balcony with my feet up on the railing. I would let Rosalind Russell make me forget about everything. She was my respite. I saw that movie every day, usually twice, for two weeks in a row. I memorized every line.

One afternoon in the early spring of my freshman year, the principal of Santa Catalina, Sister Kieran, came in to the study hall to make an announcement to the entire student body. A new flu strain was spreading across the United States. It was dangerous enough to cause death. There would be new rules.

"We must all be very careful about our health. Starting today we will have rest times for one hour every afternoon," Sister Kieran said. "You will lie on your bed and rest. No one may talk, read, or write letters. Is this clear to everyone?"

All one hundred girls said, "Yes, Sister."

We all went back to our rooms for our mandatory rest time. I was feeling devastated by my circumstances. I took out my stationery and wrote to my mother, pouring my heart out to her on paper. One of the nuns came into my room and caught me. She took my stationery and pen and informed me that there would be consequences for being so defiant.

I sat on the edge of my bed, crying with so much force that I thought my heart would literally break. I had no place to go and no one to go to. Then, something slowly came over me, and I could sense a shift in myself—I was going from feeling absolute despair to feeling . . . nothing at all. My tears dried, and I no longer felt any pain. I was dead inside.

I had a new way to exist, to live through my sadness, an internal place where I went "to die."

I remember going to the dining hall that night and thinking, "Nobody knows where I am. None of you can hurt me. I'm dead. And no one can even tell."

Even the next day, when Sister Kieran handed out the deportment cards, I stayed in my "dead" place. Deportment cards were marks on each girl's conduct, both good and bad, plus and minus. Sister Kieran called me out before the whole student body about how I had defied orders. I was given a minus two on my deportment card, one point away from expulsion. I took the card from her hand and returned to my seat with all of my classmates' eyes on me. Still, I felt absolutely nothing.

I was the only one who knew I was in a dead place. I could be the Sharon who was acceptable. I could talk to people, laugh, tell stories, and go to my classes. I could perform for whatever the occasion might be. But I was dead. It was the best trick in the world. It was a great success for me.

I didn't know if it was from God or some guardian angel. But some mystical being, in some other existence, had given me this new ability, a place to go "to die." It was painless. It held peace. I would go there in my head to stay alive.

And I can still do it.

⇒ Seven ⇐

Misplaced Praise

"You're getting a tone that I don't like from that fancy school of yours," Grimmy announced midway through my second year at Santa Catalina School.

She described it as a talking-through-your-teeth habit that she found unbecoming. She was the one who'd chosen the school and written the check for me to attend, so I found it ironic since Grimmy was a bit of a snob herself.

During Christmas break, when many of my classmates headed off on ski vacations, I arrived back in Los Angeles to find that I had a job. I would be a page at Bullocks Wilshire, the famous Art Deco high-end department store. I was fifteen years old—not even of legal age to be employed. I had no social security number. That didn't stop Grimmy.

Grimmy convinced my grandfather to use his connections to get me hired. Christmas Eve was my first day on the job.

I had to wear a tailored straight black skirt, a white blouse, black pumps, and stockings held up by a garter belt. No one had thought to invent pantyhose yet. Grimmy had selected and purchased it all for me.

At 8 a.m., my mother dropped me off at the back door of Bullocks Wilshire. My job was in the ultra-expensive perfume department on the main floor in the center aisle. The entire floor was marble. I stood in the middle of the traffic of harried shoppers, waiting for my cue.

The saleswomen would snap their fingers at me and call out, "Page! Oh, page!"

I then took the newly purchased items from the saleswoman and quickly walked to the gift-wrapping department, way in the back of the store, out of sight of the customers. I would wait for the purchase to be wrapped and rush it back to the impatient saleswoman. As soon as I got one package delivered, the next saleswoman would call out, "Page! Oh, page!"

Off I would run to have the next package wrapped. I did that for eight hours. The tops of my thighs hung over my stockings, and the skin rubbed together when I walked. At the end of the day, my legs were chafed and burning and my thighs were bleeding. I was coming down with a cold and felt awful. I no longer cared that it was Christmas Eve. I went to the back door to wait for my mother to pick me up that evening. The last person I expected to see was my grandmother. But there she was, sitting in the back of her chauffeur-driven town car. I was shocked she had come to take me home. I climbed in, laid my head down on the seat, exhausted, and started crying.

I heard Grimmy softly say, "I thought it was time you learned how the other half lived."

I went back to work the day after Christmas. The days were long and opened my eyes. I learned how fortunate I was. The "tone of voice from that fancy school of mine" was never heard again.

About a week after my return to boarding school, my mother called to tell me that Grimmy had decided to sell the Muirfield Road house. It was too expensive to maintain, and too enormous for only my mother and my little brother, Aric. Michael had moved into his fraternity house at USC. My father was gone, too. The place where I had spent my entire life would no longer be my home. No one else seemed to care.

My grandmother didn't demand it, but she expected gratitude

for the lifestyle she afforded my brothers, my mother, and me. Especially me. When I would go to visit her for a weekend from boarding school, she would open her mail in front of me. If she got a dividend check from one of her investments, she would set it to the side and say, "This will pay for your school next year."

I always felt indebted to Grimmy. I had been given great opportunities because of her, but what I really wanted was for her to recognize that I was a depressed, overweight teenager. I missed my father, and now the home where I'd grown up would soon be sold.

Grimmy moved my mother and Aric to Park La Brea, a multiunit complex of many identical thirteen-story apartment towers near the Farmers Market and CBS studios. They were considered very modern at the time. I found them impersonal, cold, and sterile.

Michael was never around anymore. I shared my mother's bedroom with her during my school breaks, and Aric had the other bedroom. My mother and I did not enjoy one another's company at all.

I had been arguing with her one afternoon and was in tears when the phone rang. It was my father.

He asked me, "Are you crying?"

"Yes, Daddy."

He said, "You're arguing over me, aren't you?"

"Yes, Daddy."

He told me that he loved me, but he wouldn't stay on the phone after that.

I was standing at an open apartment window, staring blankly at another look-alike tower across the courtyard from ours. I shifted my focus down to the ground from four floors up. I thought to myself, "If I just leaned out a little farther, it would all be over."

In Catholic grammar school I had been taught that those who committed suicide burned in hell forever. Even though my current life felt like hell, an eternity of burning was still worse. I slowly pulled back from the window.

That autumn I returned to Santa Catalina. I was housed in what was known as "the cottage." It was a very small old house on the school property. It had two regular bedrooms and then two very tiny rooms that were open to each other. I was given one of the little rooms and another classmate was given the other. Her name was Gibbie.

We were nothing alike. She was San Francisco and I was LA. She was dark-haired and had an angular face, defined by a Roman nose. She was very bright. She graduated summa cum laude. She excelled at classical piano. I was fair and blonde and was considered well-rounded. I excelled at nothing.

One night I asked Gibbie why she thought the nuns had paired the two of us as roommates.

She assumed that it was because both of our parents were going through divorces.

Divorce was very rare then, especially among Catholic families. Since I was so traumatized by my parents' divorce, the nuns may have thought being near Gibbie would bring me comfort.

We were in *Peter Pan* together. Gibbie was Captain Hook, and I played Hook's flunky, Smee. In addition to piano, she could sing, dance, and triumphed in sports. Though she was the heiress to a massive coffee fortune, she never mentioned it. We were just kids with similar pain.

Gibbie was always kind to everyone. It was later reported that she even looked up from the book she was reading and smiled and said hello to the young stranger who paused by her bedroom door at Sharon Tate's home in 1969, where Gibbie was a guest.

My high school roommate, Abigail "Gibbie" Folger, ran the farthest away, almost making it to the edge of the yard before falling victim to the Charles Manson murderers. I'm still not over it.

⇒ • ⇐

Near the end of my junior year, Grimmy decided that she wanted my mother to live closer to her. A famous architect named Hugh Comstock had designed and built seven tiny cottages in Carmel.

Grimmy bought one that had sat empty for quite a while. It was in total disrepair. Ivy had grown down the witch's-hat chimney and into the living room. A new challenge always invigorated her. My grandmother, with her impeccable taste, had it redone for my mom and Aric. Today the Comstock cottages are famous worldwide for their architectural quaintness.

Another chapter in my life was ending. I no longer had a home in Los Angeles. I no longer lived in the same city as Michael, my father, and Aunt Hoonie and Uncle Jack. I couldn't talk about Daddy to Grimmy or my mother, and now it would be even harder to see him.

I remained in boarding school, and that spring my father was finally permitted to attend the father-daughter weekend.

"Let Sharon see for herself," Grimmy told my mother. "He won't last the whole weekend. He'll leave."

The fathers of the girls who were from Los Angeles would always perform for the students on Saturday night at the closing event. They had rehearsed the song "Thanks for the Memories," with dance steps choreographed by the fabulous Ruby Keeler, a famous actress and dancer from Hollywood's golden era. She was the mother of one of my classmates, Terry Lowe.

When it was time for their big number, my father was not on-stage with the other Los Angeles dads. I left the school theater and searched all over the campus for him, even looking in the men's bathrooms. Daddy had vanished without saying goodbye. Grimmy had been right. He didn't stay for the weekend. I returned to the theater crying and sat in the back row.

All of a sudden the appearance of Zorro was announced from the stage and in swept my father, dressed all in black, with a wide-brimmed hat, eye mask, and full cape! The audience, even the nuns, oohed and aahed. He was impressive. He used his distinctive voice and limited Spanish to impressive effect.

Before the weekend was over, Sister Kieran ended up believing my father was a superhero, an avenger of family values. He had played the role of family patriarch to the hilt for all the nuns. He knew Sister Kieran, in particular, was easy prey, and she instantly succumbed to his spell.

Once the fathers had departed, she wasted no time finding me.

"Your father is so attractive and so very charming," she told me, as if she were the first woman to discover it.

I almost laughed out loud, thinking, "Oh my God, he got you, too. Get in line, Sister. Get way in the back of the line."

I could ignore her nearsighted admiration until she said, "Your mother is crazy. He is delightful. I don't know what's wrong with her."

Those were her exact words.

Now she was getting my Irish up.

As much as I loved having my father there for the weekend, I knew it was a forty-eight-hour show. My mother was the one who had shouldered the burden of raising my brothers and me. Sister Kieran was totally clueless.

I had to walk away before I blurted out, "The only thing wrong with my mother is that man, you ridiculous horny old fool!"

My father was not invited to attend my graduation from Santa Catalina. A gift arrived at school for me. It was from him, a beautiful watch with the words *Love, Daddy* engraved on the back. I was thrilled he remembered. I didn't show it to my mother or to Grimmy.

When I visited Aunt Hoonie later that summer in LA, I showed her the watch Daddy had given me for graduation. Aunt Hoonie had been drinking most of the evening. She was already angry with her wayward brother that day, and my graduation gift put her in the mood to stir the pot.

"Go get on the upstairs phone, darling," she said. "Let's have some fun. We'll call Yvonne. You can listen in."

I had figured out, around age thirteen, that Daddy and Yvonne were far more than boss and secretary.

Aunt Hoonie asked Yvonne, "Have you seen Dennis lately?"

Yvonne launched into a three-minute rant about what a schmuck my father was, ending by saying, "That man has the guts of Dick Tracy."

"So, Yvonne," my aunt said, "that was so wonderful, what you did for Sharon."

Yvonne responded, "Well, that son of a bitch wouldn't have gotten her anything."

Yvonne had bought me the watch and had it engraved and sent to my school. Chances are that my father didn't even know about it. I gently put the phone back in its cradle. I went downstairs. Aunt Hoonie was waiting for me with a look on her face that read, "There you have it!"

"That was so funny," I said, forcing a smile. It was one of my best acting performances to date. It was convincing enough to fool Aunt Hoonie. Inside, my heart was broken.

A few days later, on a trip to the beach with my cousin Lizzie, I accidentally wore the watch into the ocean. The salt water dissolved the face of the watch and destroyed it. It didn't matter; it was already ruined anyway.

≡ • ≡

Eighteen years old—but emotionally still very young—and weighing 170 pounds, I arrived at Grimmy's door in Carmel to learn of my postgraduation fate.

I was walking around in a fog about my future. I thought somehow I would magically attend the University of Southern California like Michael had, though the thought of filling out an application had never occurred to me and no one in my family had discussed college with me. I was soon to find out why. Grimmy had the next plan in place.

We were sitting in Grimmy's living room when she declared to my mother, as if I weren't in the room, "I'll be damned if she's going to walk down that aisle looking like Moby-Dick."

My mother and I were both speechless.

I could see Grimmy turning the calendar pages in her mind to the Las Madrinas Debutante Ball. How much time did she have to fix me so I wouldn't embarrass the whole family? A fat debutante would be a disgrace. What young man would want that? My prospects for marriage would be dismal.

With only six months to go before my debut, my grandmother made a decision that would set my course for the immediate future. As per usual, my input was not needed. Grimmy had already devised her plan. I was to attend Monterey Peninsula College and live with her in Carmel so I could be monitored on a strict diet. She had to take forty pounds off of me before my debut in December. A new challenge!

My mother sat twisting her hands in her lap. Then, to my surprise, she spoke.

"She's my daughter. She's been away for four years, Mother. I want her living with me."

Grimmy dismissed my mother's request with barely a pause.

"You're not strong enough, Marjorie. She will trick you. She will fool you. We will never get this weight off of her. You can't control her. I can."

My mother put her hand to her mouth and began to weep.

"Oh, Mother," she said and stood up. She didn't look at me. She ran out of the front door crying.

I knew I should have gone after my mother and somehow made her feel better. I could have said, "It's okay, Mom. I will do this. It's only six months."

But I didn't. I stayed in my seat. In my shame, I let my mother get in her car alone and drive off. I couldn't defy Grimmy. I also felt relief that someone strong would be in control of my next steps in life, especially since I had no vision of what to do for myself.

I became Grimmy's prime project for the next 183 days.

That September, while many of my Santa Catalina classmates were enjoying their first year of dorm life in Ivy League schools, my roommate was fifty-two years older than me, and opinionated as hell.

Every morning, Grimmy would bake fresh bran muffins for breakfast. She would hand me a lunch she had packed to eat between classes. None of my meals included butter, cheese, chips, or anything containing sugar.

I went to boring 101 classes at the local junior college and managed to get good grades. I lived for the student union and spent all my time there, joining an ongoing rummy 500 game. It took my mind off my empty stomach. We didn't play for money. If we had, I couldn't have played. I had no money of my own and wasn't given a cent to spend. My grandmother allotted me only enough money for my schoolbooks and supplies. I had to bring her the change along with the receipts to prove I hadn't bought anything to eat.

Every evening I would go home to a diet meal prepared by Grimmy. One evening she declared that I "gobbled my food." Seriously? That's what really hungry people do.

The next night at dinner there was a metronome at my place setting and no silverware. I was to eat with a pair of chopsticks and chew in time to the click-clack of the metronome. The chopsticks didn't allow a full bite of food, and I had to move my jaw to a 4/1 tempo until the food in my mouth was liquid.

At the end of each week, Grimmy insisted that I weigh in so she could monitor my progress. When she would bend at the waist to look at the scale, I would lean on the bathroom sink to take a few pounds off the number.

I must have borrowed a quarter from someone at school, because I couldn't go another day without having a Mars Bar. I bought five, ate one while at school, and hid the others in my room. After Grimmy had gone to bed, I ended up eating the other four candy bars at the dining room table while doing my homework. One right after the other.

I folded the wrappers and put them in the pocket of my robe to hide them. I thought I could safely throw them away at school the next day, away from Grimmy's eagle eye. Very bad idea. I forgot about them.

I would always put a record on the stereo as soon as I got home from classes every afternoon. The next day I lifted the lid on the stereo cabinet and there, with the record needle piercing the paper, was an empty Mars Bar wrapper. My heart stopped beating. Grimmy had found me out. I went into my bedroom and there was another Mars Bar wrapper on my pillowcase. One more wrapper was taped to the toilet seat. I went into the kitchen and found a Mars Bar wrapper stuck on the door of the refrigerator.

I had no choice but to accept whatever would be my punishment. I timidly went to Grimmy's bedroom door. She was lying in bed, reading.

My voice shook. "I'm so sorry, Grimmy."

She wouldn't look at me.

"All that work. All. That. Work. Well, I give up. It's a waste of my time. You're on your own."

I stood in the doorway and pleaded, "Please, Grimmy. Don't give up on me. I'm sorry. I'll do better. I promise."

I guess she could have thrown me out of her house or ignored me completely, but she loved me enough not to do that. The diet drill sergeant resumed her post, and this time I followed orders.

Even though I was carrying a full load of classes at school, Grimmy decided that I should contribute to my own cause by earning some money. Every Saturday, I spent an eight-hour day folding towels at the Laundromat down the hill. On Sunday afternoons, Grimmy and I would walk to the movies. Buttered popcorn was out of the question.

All the debutantes had gathered earlier in the year for a fancy fashion runway show put on by Bullocks Wilshire. Each girl was given the opportunity to pick out the dress in which she would be presented. The dresses came in different styles, but they all had to be virginal white, floor-length, and worn with short white kid gloves.

I saw a runway model wearing a dress that I really loved.

Following the fashion show, each girl who had selected a gown was given her own dressing room and a Bullocks seamstress to take her measurements. The gown I had chosen didn't arrive, so my mother went to see what had happened.

She returned with bad news. "I'm sorry, darling. Peggy Rodi has already requested the same gown you chose."

My mother left me in the dressing room and returned about five minutes later with Mr. William Cahill himself, the famous gown designer, in tow. I couldn't believe my painfully shy mother had even approached him. I had never seen her overtly stand up for me. This time she had.

Mr. Cahill pulled out a sketch pad and charcoal pencil and sat down on the chair in my dressing room. "I will design a dress just for you, Sharon."

My debut dress would be a one-of-a-kind design by the famous William Cahill! It didn't get better than that, and my mother made it happen. That was the best part.

Thanks to Grimmy's determination—and my fear of disappointing her again—I was forty pounds lighter by the time December arrived. My mother and I went back to Los Angeles to attend the debutante parties being held around town before the actual ball. Grimmy bought me several new dresses to wear to each of the various teas and dinner dances. Mr. Cahill met up with my mother and me at Bullocks Wilshire to present my finished designer gown. It hung off my now much smaller body like a satin kimono. He called in a seamstress and had to rebuild the entire dress to fit me, with inches and inches of fabric removed.

I was the only girl who wouldn't have a father present to dance with her at the ball. My brother, Michael, would be there to walk me down the aisle.

The night finally arrived. My friend from boarding school Julie Cheesewright invited me to spend the night and get ready with her in the two-bedroom suite her parents had rented at the Beverly Hilton, where the ball was held. My gown was brought to the room. At eighteen, I was still considered too young to wear full makeup, except for pale lipstick and a little mascara.

Before the party, the debutantes gathered to be photographed as a group. No easy task to get that many young girls with layers of petticoats all into the same frame.

One of the matrons of the event came into the room following the photo session and said: "Girls, it is now adult time. Your parents and grandparents will be in this room next door having cocktails. We do not want to hear from you."

Grimmy had not yet seen my gown or what I looked like in it. I wanted her to have the very first look before I was presented.

I decided that I didn't care what the matron had said about not disturbing the adults. My grandmother and I had been through a lot—six months of my tears, deception, shame, and ultimate success. I went and boldly knocked on the door.

I was frightened that Grimmy would be angry that I was interrupting the "adults only" time, but I still had to risk it. For me, this was about something much bigger than the Las Madrinas Ball. Forty pounds thinner and in a beautiful white satin and lace gown, I waited for my freshman-year "roommate."

Grimmy came to the door. "You asked to see me?"

"Yes, Grimmy. I thought you'd like to see me in my dress."

She looked me up and down and smiled for the first time. "You look lovely. Very."

I said, "Oh, Grimmy, thank you!"

She nodded. "Run along now."

She slowly shut the door. But before it closed, I saw in her eyes a look of respect.

An hour later, each girl took the long walk down a staircase. The orchestra played "The Way You Look Tonight" for me. What I *didn't* look like was Moby-Dick, and I knew it. My brother Michael was so handsome in his white tie and tails. He could tell I was nervous, so he said through a mischievous grin: "Smile and say 'shit.'"

I did what he said.

We waltzed together, laughing because neither one of us remembered the steps despite five years of cotillion training.

The next morning the phone rang in the hotel suite. Julie's mother said it was my grandmother. I took the phone from her hand.

"Sharon? Grimmy."

"Hi, Grimmy!"

"I wanted to tell you that many people approached me last night, congratulating me on how attractive you looked. But why I'm calling is to say that the praise was misplaced. You were the one who did all the work. It was all you and I'm proud of you."

"Oh, Grimmy. Thank you so much."

She said, "That will be all." Then there was the dial tone.

⇒ • ⇐

Soon after, I was sent to live in the small Comstock cottage with my mother and little brother, Aric. With more freedom, I started to put the weight back on over the course of the next four months. I never thought about my second appearance as a debutante in the spring, when the Catholic debutantes were to be presented to the Cardinal in Los Angeles, close to Easter week. It was an event where we each wore our white gowns one more time. A seamstress was called. My dress had to be let back out almost as much as it had been taken in.

= Eight =

Sex Ed, Losing My Virginity 101 & 102

I was nineteen when doctors determined I should have my tonsils removed. A week later, I decided to get rid of my hymen, too. The surgeon took the tonsils; Phillip, a sweet young man I had been seeing for six months, took the other.

= • =

He wasn't all that good-looking. He wore his hair in a crew cut and had a nose like Karl Malden, but he was very funny. And, to me, funny is so sexy.

We met at an art gallery in Carmel.

Phillip was six years older than I was. His father was the head of art direction at Walt Disney Studios and had designed the Tinkerbell opening to Disney's *Wonderful World of Color*. Phillip's family had an art gallery in the Carmel Highlands and a gallery in Mendocino County.

He asked me out, and I said yes. He was very attentive and made me feel so pretty.

When he arrived to pick me up for our second date, Grimmy dropped the make-or-break question: "What do you want to do with your life?"

Oh my God! I could have died. It didn't seem to bother Phillip.

He would drive me to a bluff overlooking the ocean on his parents' property. We would neck. He woke me up, sexually. My body came alive in that car. He would make me come from outside my clothing—pretty impressive, I'd say—and then drive me home, still a virgin.

My mother had told me to save myself for my husband. She said that men wouldn't respect me otherwise.

Grimmy warned me, "There's only one thing in life that you can never get back once it is lost."

In response to my silence, she said, "Your reputation."

In the 1960s, where I came from, a young woman's reputation stayed intact as long as her hymen did.

One weekend Philip invited me to visit him in Mendocino, where he lived with his mom and dad. My mother insisted that I pack my flannel pajamas because I was recovering from having the tonsillectomy. It was her subtle message to me, flannel being the least sexy nightwear in the world.

Philip's mother, Libby, was so different from mine. She was young at heart, full of joy and laughter. His parents were both liberal and thought sex with love was great.

Phillip took me out to a lovely dinner. Before we went back to his parents' house, I lost my virginity on a rollaway bed in the middle of his father's art gallery.

I cried afterward. I was upset because I knew I was forever altered. I had lost something I would never get back.

"I want my mom."

I literally said those words! Jesus. Could I have been any less postcoitally romantic? Poor Phillip. He didn't know what to do. Luckily, he was not only kind. He was in love. He held me gently.

On Sunday night, when I got back to my mother's cottage, I did my best to act as if nothing had changed. My mother was different toward me, a bit cooler than usual. I could tell that she knew.

My mother never asked me about it, and from that day forward we never discussed any aspect of sexuality. Phillip left for his navy service that summer, and I was soon to be shipped out as well, though—once again—I had no say as to the direction of my future.

Grimmy had decided that I would enroll at Gonzaga University in Spokane, Washington, for my sophomore year of college. My mother had agreed. Because I had attended only all-girl schools seventh grade through high school, Grimmy wanted to make sure the university was coed. They were worried about my lack of maturity, with good reason.

Gonzaga has a fine Jesuit law school, which I'll bet factored into my grandmother's decision. My family is chock-full of attorneys.

Obviously, my grandmother held little aspiration that I might become a lawyer myself. Her hopes were for me to meet and marry a respectable and nice young man who could fulfill that role.

I was finally free. Free!! And I was in a city 975 miles away from Grimmy and my mother. No one monitored what I put in my mouth or what came out of my mouth. Restrictions were to be damned. Classes held little interest for me. Instead, I was more intrigued by the catalogue of real-life experience.

I soon met my new best friend, Cherie Orr. It was obvious to me that we were the only two girls in the entire dorm with a sense of humor. We made each other laugh all the time. We still do.

The girls' dorm had very strict curfews. On the weekends, every girl had to be signed back into the dorm by midnight. One of us would usually drag the other through the front door as the clock struck twelve. One night, Cherie and I got wasted on port in a pickup truck during a blizzard. I got sick on a snowbank and then all over my dorm room. I might have realized then that alcohol is not my friend, but it would take me many more colorful years for that to happen.

Eventually, curfew became an obstacle to our social lives. We wanted to throw all-night keggers in a motel room. Cherie figured out how to do it.

In the girls' dorm, if you were to be gone for an overnight, you had to "sign out" to an adult's house and leave their full name and phone number. Cherie's father was a doctor who had a good friend, also a doctor, who lived in Spokane. We would both sign out to his house and leave his phone number, though he had no idea we were doing this.

We would rent a cheap motel room, the graduate students would have a keg delivered, and we'd open the door for a party. There was one rule: That door stayed open. There would be no sex in our motel room. Cherie and I were still "good girls," just out for a bit of fun.

Halfway through the first semester I did meet a law student. I was sitting on the steps of the Business Administration building and he stopped to chat. His name was Carlos. He was intelligent and gorgeous. We decided to meet up. He couldn't really ask me out on a date since he was married—a fact he didn't try to hide from me. I still fell in love with him. Everything we did had to be a secret, but I had no complaints. Neither did he.

I lived in such fear that I would be considered "cheap and common" that I faked my virginity with him when we made love for the first time on the wide front seat of his car. He bought that I was still a nice girl.

I had very good muscle control.

I'm sure Grimmy thought a Jesuit university was a safe place for an immature nineteen-year-old girl. However, within three months I had become a weekend drunk and was having an affair with a married man. What can I say? I never let college interfere with my education.

I started doubting my Catholic upbringing more and more. The stringent rules of the church were becoming very inconvenient for me. I didn't want to walk around constantly knowing that if I had committed a mortal sin (a grievous offense against the law of God), i.e., having sex with a married law student, and I had no regrets or any intention of confessing that mortal sin to a priest, and I was hit by a bus and died, I would burn in hell for eternity. However, *if* you truly regretted having sex with that married law student and were on your way to confess that mortal sin to a priest and you were hit by a bus and died, then you were spared the eternal fires of hell. You see, it's all about intention. I was doomed.

Cherie and I continued our Saturday night motel parties after we signed out to her dad's friend in Spokane. My mother was the one who blew the lid off the whole thing. She called the dorm on a Saturday evening looking for me. They gave my mother the phone number of our "host" for the weekend. The response from the good doctor: "I've never heard of your daughter."

Two weeks before our final exams, both Cherie and I were suspended. We had to leave campus immediately. Grimmy refused to communicate with me. My mother wired money for a Greyhound bus ticket for the next day.

The week before, I had gone to a local fair with a young man who asked me out on a date. He played a carnival game of tossing baseballs in a bushel basket and had won a gigantic stuffed bulldog, which was the Gonzaga mascot. I couldn't leave it behind. I rode for twenty-four hours on a Greyhound bus with a huge stuffed animal in the seat beside me, mostly for protection, so no strangers would sit next to me. I stared numbly out of the bus window, mile after mile, in disbelief that I had to return to Carmel and leave Carlos, the man I thought I loved. And, I didn't know if I would ever see Cherie again.

My mother picked me up at the bus station. She told me that as soon as I got back to her house I should call Grimmy and apologize. I was petrified, but I did it.

"I may as well have flushed that money down the toilet," Grimmy snapped.

Then my grandmother let me know that there would be no future funding for my college education. I knew she meant it.

I lived with my mother and little brother in the small Comstock cottage. I found a job gift-wrapping in a lingerie shop. I learned how to tie elaborate bows, and I fell into a deep depression. I began to have debilitating migraine headaches at night.

At the end of the summer, I was the maid of honor in the wedding of my childhood best friend, Susan Binney, to her sweetheart, Tom Cole. The wedding was in LA.

When Grimmy decided to sell the Muirfield Road house, Susan's parents bought it. Susan's wedding reception was to be held in the formal living room. My mother and Grimmy were also invited. Though Grimmy maintained her stoic veneer when she entered the house, I tried to decipher a glimpse of what she must have been feeling. My grandmother had designed every inch of this house and had overseen its construction. She had raised her four children and then lost her husband to another woman . . . all in this house.

God only knows what my mother must have felt. She'd grown up in this house, and her own wedding reception had been here. She'd raised Michael and me here and brought baby Aric home from the hospital to this house. This was where she'd lost her own husband to other women, and finally, this was the house where she'd had to be the one to ask for a divorce. Here we were, three generations of women, back in the house that had shaped all of our lives.

That night, at Susan's reception, I wanted to feel lighthearted and have fun. I had drinks, I laughed, danced, and I hid my personal pain. At the end of the night, I returned to Grimmy's LA apartment, where my mom and I were staying. As Susan went off on her honeymoon and to start her new life, I was heading to a dead end. I felt trapped, immature, and useless.

It was pitch-dark when I stumbled into the bedroom. I could tell my mother was awake. I sat down on the floor, a crumpled pile of taffeta.

"Mom," I whispered, "I want to leave. Please, let me leave."

My mother knew I wasn't talking about leaving Los Angeles the next day. It was the bigger picture.

"You can't leave," my mother said sadly. "It will kill your grandmother."

I sat silent in the dark, my unspoken despair rising in my throat.

"You have to stay and do what your grandmother tells you to do," she continued.

Before I could censor myself, I whispered, "Well, you do whatever she says, and look where it got you."

I was met with silence.

The next day we went back to Carmel without Grimmy, who would be staying on in LA to visit with her other children and grandchildren.

About a week later, I woke up to an empty house. I thought my mother had gone to mass, but she was making other plans. When she came home, my mother said to me, "Sharon, you have two hours to pack your trunk and one suitcase. While you pack, decide what city you want to live in. When you're settled there, I will send your trunk. I only ask that you do not choose Los Angeles or Spokane."

My heart began to pound. Was my mother asking me to leave, or was she letting me leave? I didn't know how to respond. I was stunned.

My mother continued: "I've borrowed two hundred dollars from the neighbors. It's all I have to give you, but it's enough until you find a job. You'll have to leave by bus. I'll send your trunk once you find a place to stay. I would recommend you stay at the YWCA until you figure it out."

I was excited and terrified at once. I wanted to talk about it, but my mother held up her hand. "Do what I say, Sharon."

In complete silence, with my mother sitting in the living room pretending to read a book but never turning a page, I packed for my new life. My mother had tried to time it so that my bus would be gone before Grimmy's train arrived from LA. It would be too late for Grimmy to do anything about it. It became clear to me that my mother was giving me my best chance to figure out my future, on my own, and that she alone would face the consequences.

My mother was rushed for time when she dropped me at the bus station, kissing me goodbye on the cheek. She couldn't be late to meet Grimmy's train. I cried for a bit, but I also knew this was what I wanted, what I had asked to have. It was a gift. Still, I was shocked. And confident and hurt. And frightened. And thrilled.

Years later I asked my mother, "What did Grimmy say after you told her what you had done?"

She said, "Nothing. What could she say? I had to do it. You were dying."

Despite my mother's request, I bought a ticket to Spokane. I wanted to see Carlos. I found a pay phone and called him as soon as the bus arrived.

He only met up with me briefly in a hotel bar. He told me he would not be seeing me anymore. As we were talking, his wife came into the bar to find him. She had spotted his car in the parking lot. Pretending that I was merely a friend, he left quickly.

Later, I heard that my father had phoned Carlos at his home and said, "I'm sure your wife is sitting there, so just listen. I can have you thrown out of law school. It takes one phone call. So leave my daughter alone."

I never found out who told my father.

Unless you're a student, or having a clandestine affair with a married man, there's really no reason to be in Spokane.

I was always a big-city girl. I knew I couldn't go home, so off I went, on a Greyhound bus to the nearest big city: Seattle. I didn't have a single plan for my future.

≈ Nine ≈

Pink Suit and Paychecks

I knew no one in Seattle. I was twenty years old, but emotionally more like a tenth grader sent off on an unsupervised student exchange.

I checked in to the Y in Seattle, as my mother had suggested. I was given a bed in a room with three other girls. There was a large communal bathroom down the hall.

My mother had instructed me to look in the newspaper for a job. In the Help Wanted section I found an ad that read in bold type, "WANNA MAKE A LOT OF MONEY?"

The ad mentioned aluminum siding. I had no clue what that was, but I didn't question it. After all, if aluminum siding would bring me "a lot of money," then my independence would truly be possible. I put on the only interview outfit I owned, a pink linen suit with a white linen collar. I accessorized the look with a pink ribbon on my ponytail, white gloves, and heels.

I took a bus to the address, which was a large warehouse building in the bowels of Seattle. Even the office furniture was covered with grime and industrial dust. I went to a man at the front desk and said, "I'm here to apply for the job."

He did a double take, then said, "Hold on for just a minute. You wait right here."

He walked around a dividing wall behind his desk and I heard him say, "You guys gotta come out here and see this."

I'm sure it must have been pure entertainment for these men to hire this freshly scrubbed, ponytailed girl. It was decided that I should go out into the sales field with a trainer and test my skills, of which I had none.

At the first house, a woman answered the door with a baby in one arm, an iron in the other hand, and a toddler tugging on her leg. It was a scene out of a Dorothea Lange photography book.

I smiled brightly.

"Good morning! I was wondering if you'd be interested in buying aluminum siding for your house?"

She looked exhausted and sad. "No. Thank you."

I responded, "I understand. I'm sorry I took up your time."

I went to several more houses, apologizing profusely from door to door. Not a winning technique for someone working on commission.

I was walking up the driveway to the next house in the row when I heard a loud honk.

It was the car horn of the salesman who was training me.

I waved and smiled at him and continued on.

There was more honking.

I continued up the front steps, turned, and gave my trainer the "hush" sign, finger to lips. He kept honking.

Now I was irritated.

I stomped down the sidewalk to the car window and said, "What?!"

He snapped back at me, "It's a brick house!"

"So??"

"You can't put aluminum siding on a brick house!!"

He put his head down on the steering wheel and groaned.

Years later, I told this story on *The Tonight Show*. Johnny Carson howled with laughter. The producers had told me that Johnny loved a good aluminum siding story.

The pink linen suit next got me hired as a switchboard operator at the Seattle Credit Union, without even one incredulous double take from anyone in the company. I worked in a large room with about fifteen other people. There were no desks or chairs, only hundreds of connection ports along the wall. I wore a headset and I'd plug in wherever there was a blinking light on the wall.

"Seattle Credit Union. How may I help you?"

All day long.

Once I had a few paychecks to my name, I was able to afford a private room at the Y. I still didn't have my own bathroom, but I did have a sink. Simple luxuries took on a whole new meaning.

It became clear to me that I lacked the technical skills to upgrade to a better job. In the 1960s, a woman had to know how to type to advance in the corporate world. I had no idea what I wanted to advance *to*; I only knew that any retreat back to Carmel was out of the question, so I worked all day and took typing and shorthand classes for three hours in the evening.

I soon turned twenty-one, and that opened a whole new world for me. The bars! Drinking! Dancing! It was so much fun, and I would stay out all night long. I was having the time of my life. I was free to do what I wanted. I'd go back to my room at the Y in time to take a shower and put on clean clothes for work. I would test my stamina to see exactly how long I could go without sleep. I could repeat this schedule for three nights in a row and run on adrenaline during the day, until I could no longer focus.

The film *West Side Story* was showing in a movie theater close to the Y. I went countless times during the weekends, walking down the hill to the movie house, as the never-ending Seattle rain fell, wondering if Carlos ever thought about me. I related to Natalie Wood's character, Maria, and her tale of forbidden love, except my real-life situation was reversed. Caucasian girl falls for Latino man. Oh my God, the drama in my head!

One evening I used the pay phone booth in the hallway of the Y to call my brother Michael. I missed him and wanted to hear his voice. We hadn't talked since I left California. Suddenly, the door of the phone booth slid open and in stepped a young woman who was also staying at the Y. We had chatted in the hallways over the months. I knew she was gay, but thought she understood I wasn't.

"I'm in love with you," she whispered.

Always taught to be polite, I told her, "I'm so sorry. Um . . . I'm on the phone? Um . . . could you, yeah, could you possibly give me a couple of minutes?"

She stepped out of the booth but stood staring at me, her face inches from the glass door, like I was a goldfish in a bowl. I had no idea how to handle this. It was a first for me.

The encounter made me realize that no one in Seattle really knew me. I was lonely for my family. My older brother was in Los Angeles. My dad was there, and so were Aunt Hoonie, Uncle Jack, and my cousin Lizzie.

I clutched the phone. "Michael, I want to come home to LA."

"You can come back anytime, as far as I'm concerned," he said.

A feeling of relief came over me.

Why hadn't my brother let me know that before? It hadn't occurred to me that it could be that simple. After all, if I could support myself, I had the right to live anywhere I wanted.

I gave notice at my job, packed up my few belongings, and left Seattle the next week, ten months after I had arrived.

Aunt Hoonie and Uncle Jack let me move in with them until I could save enough for my own place. I was soon hired at the Bank of America on Hollywood Boulevard, as a receptionist in the trust department, where I would entertain myself by reading the wills of famous movie stars.

I was on my way. I was happier. Having a job and supporting myself was what mattered the most to me. It guaranteed my independence. No one could criticize me.

A couple weeks later, Grimmy came to Los Angeles for a visit. She knew I had come back. I dressed up and went to the Glendale train station with Michael to meet her. I had not seen her for a year. She had suffered a heart attack during that time and seemed slightly diminished. I was afraid to see her again, because I knew I had hurt her deeply.

She nodded a hello. It was awkward at first.

Eventually she warmed up, recognizing that I wasn't the hapless girl who'd secretly left home on a Greyhound bus the year before. I could stand up for myself.

To my huge surprise, Grimmy offered me the use of her Park La Brea garden apartment, since she rarely visited Los Angeles anymore. I was also given permission to use her Mercury Comet that she kept parked in the garage, with the stipulation that it was only to be used for driving to work and back home.

Then, one weekend, some fellow bank pals and I decided to go to Tijuana for a day. Taking a bus would be a big hassle, and the Comet was just sitting there—perfectly good, unused transportation. I figured it was one short trip into Baja for eight hours. Who would ever know?

On Monday, Grimmy called to inform me that since I'd broken her rules, if I wanted to continue to use the car I would have to buy it from her at high blue book pricing. It was five hundred dollars. That was a fortune to me. She would not take a dime less. I have no idea how she knew that I had driven the damn car into Mexico, but I was busted. I took out a loan from the bank where I worked to buy Grimmy's car. That was one fucking expensive day trip.

Soon after, I made a more creative employment move, over into the world of advertising, starting as a secretary at the ad agency Young & Rubicam. The craziness on the show *Mad Men* was mild compared to what really went on in our LA office.

I worked as a secretary for two major account executives on the Frito-Lay account. Another executive at Y&R, Patrick, began to flirt with me. He was smart, funny, tall, thin, and handsome in a very Brooks Brothers way. Like many men in the industry, he was a heavy drinker. He was also married. Neither of those things bothered me. I delighted in my freedom and in not having to answer to anyone.

I enjoyed being wanted. Commitment was not my objective, but it didn't stop me from falling in love with him.

At the end of almost every workday, the executives would invite me downstairs to drink with them in the bar that was on the ground floor of our building.

My drink of choice at that time was J&B on the rocks. We would have two or three drinks and then we would all get in our cars and drive home. No one thought twice about it in the mid '60s.

The men at Y&R understood that I wasn't the type who was only working long enough to find a husband. I loved having a job, supporting myself, and making my own decisions.

I didn't grasp until much later that I had a severe marriage phobia. Marriage, from my young perspective, was an institution that caused only pain. Grandma Nellie, Grimmy, and my mother had all ended up alone. With the exception of Aunt Hoonie and Uncle Jack, I had no role model for a lasting marriage.

I had grown up watching my mother, underappreciated and always left to wonder if her husband was coming home. Both of my grandmothers had similar experiences. I had no intention of repeating that pattern in my own life. Freedom to me meant making my own living and enjoying a man who wasn't technically available. His being married was the perfect aphrodisiac. I did not want to be the one wearing the ring.

All of this meant that my chances of making Grimmy proud were getting more remote. Her health had now deteriorated and she made the decision to move in with my mother.

The last time I saw my grandmother, I sat on the end of her bed. She wasn't speaking much, so I stayed quiet. My heart was aching. I so wanted to make her proud of me. I knew I wasn't doing that.

So I made up a scenario that I thought would please her. I told her I had gone out on two dates with a single attorney whom I'd met in the elevator of my downtown LA office building. I said that he had his own office. I told her I really liked him. It was all a lie, but I wanted to make her happy.

My mother came in the room. "Your grandmother needs to rest. Leave her alone now, Sharon."

Before I left, my grandmother looked at my mother and said, "I think she's growing up, Marjorie."

I had to go back to LA for work, but I didn't want to leave.

A short time later, my mother called to say that Grimmy had died peacefully during the afternoon. I was ambushed with sorrow. I went back to my apartment and found one of the cookbooks she had written. I looked at her author photo on the back cover, sat down on the floor, and wept. She had been my main motivation to succeed, and now she was gone before I had a chance to prove myself to her. I never got to say goodbye.

That night at around one in the morning, I woke up abruptly to the sound of the phone ringing. I flew out of bed and rushed to grab the receiver.

"Hello."

"Sharon? Grimmy."

That is exactly what she said on every phone call. I knew she had died, but it was my grandmother. I swear.

"Hi, Grimmy!"

There was silence. Then the dial tone. I stood and listened for a minute. Was that real? I knew it was. My grandmother had called me. I'd needed to hear her voice once more. And she'd come through.

Many years later, when I was starring in *Cagney & Lacey*, I paid a visit to a psychic medium. I asked her to contact Grimmy.

Considering my success as an actress, the awards I'd collected by that point, and the salary I was commanding, I asked the question, "Is Grimmy proud of me *now*?"

The psychic told me, "Your grandmother wants you to know that she's proud of you . . . *still*."

≡ Ten ≡

You've Got $150. Now What?

A few days after Grimmy's funeral, I came home from work to complete darkness. Every lamp in the apartment was gone. The only sources of light were the bulbs over the stove top and the bathroom sink. I didn't call the police. I knew what had happened. Aunt Rosemary, my mother's younger sister and my least favorite relative in the entire world, had used a spare key to enter Grimmy's apartment while I was away at work. She had taken whatever she wanted, including every lamp.

Very soon after, I was given notice that I was to vacate. Grimmy's apartment was going to be sold.

I moved in to my own apartment in West Hollywood and on to a new job at Grey Advertising in Beverly Hills, in the creative department. I worked for three copywriters who were completely wacko guys. They loved making me laugh. I had the sense of humor to get their nonstop shtick and was like their kid sister, the one who kept their secrets.

I had ended the affair with Patrick months before and had fallen in love with David Lockton, a first-time film producer. Unlike his predecessors, David was separated from his wife! He offered me a job as the production assistant on his current movie project. On location, I also took over as the script girl. I learned a lot about behind-the-camera jobs, one mistake at a time.

One day Patrick contacted me. His marriage was officially over, and a divorce was underway. He wanted to see me. I broke it off with David, convinced that I was still in love with Patrick. We dated for a number of months, and then he proposed. He even asked my father for my hand in marriage. My father liked that.

My mother loved Patrick and was always impressed by his "impeccable manners." I was sure Grimmy would have approved of Patrick's career ambitions. He got along famously with both of my brothers. My grandfather liked him very much and wanted our wedding ceremony to take place in his Sunset Boulevard mansion. Grandpa had expressed wanting to walk me down the long curving staircase in his elegant foyer to "give me away."

Everyone in my family was so enthusiastic about Patrick, and I was crazy about him. All I had to do was talk myself into wanting to be married, to be a wife. I was proud of the woman I had become in four years. I was enamored with my independence and liked making my own money and choices. I even had my own credit card, which was not a standard practice for women in the late 1960s, as women usually needed a husband to cosign. I was oblivious to the rising women's liberation movement, probably because I didn't see myself as not being liberated.

Yet I still felt pressure to marry, due to both societal expectations and the expectations of my own family. As much as I loved my single life, I didn't want to disappoint my family. Their approval held sway over me.

My brother Michael had told me on the eve of his own wedding, "If you're not married by age twenty-five, you may as well forget it."

The label of *spinster* was looming in my not-so-distant future.

I knew Patrick had a serious drinking problem, but he was never anything but kind, even when drunk. I thought I could change him. It never occurred to me to take a long look in the mirror at my own habits with alcohol. I asked Patrick to stop drinking for six months before we planned a ceremony. He agreed. On that basis, I said yes to his proposal.

About three weeks later we were at a restaurant in Hollywood, having dinner on an outside patio. Patrick ordered a carafe of red wine for the table.

When I asked why, he shrugged it off, saying, "I thought you would enjoy a little wine with dinner."

I'm not a wine drinker. He knew that. The wine wasn't for me. I knew that.

I watched as he poured himself a glass. He was breaking his promise to me, and I lost control.

I picked up the carafe of red wine with both hands, tipped my head back, and poured the wine directly into my mouth. Cabernet ran down the sides of my neck and through my hair. It stained the shoulders of my yellow suede jacket. I stopped long enough to catch my breath and then guzzled more. When the carafe was empty, I slammed it back down on the table. Patrick sat staring at me, his mouth open in shock. I'm sure the other diners were stunned, but I didn't see it, as I was blind with rage and red wine. I left the restaurant and had a cab take me home, alone. (Years later, I had the *Cagney & Lacey* writers replicate this when Christine confronts her father's alcoholism in an Italian restaurant. We went through five yellow suede jackets to shoot it.)

Patrick offered to start over with our agreement, promising me he wouldn't drink at all. Five months into our engagement, we drove to Carmel to see my mother and make wedding plans.

As soon as we entered the house she said, "Patrick, darling, how lovely to see you. May I offer you a libation?"

And he answered, "I'd love one, Marjorie."

My heart stopped beating. At that moment, I knew there would be no wedding.

The next morning Patrick and I drove back to LA together in silence. He couldn't fight for me. Booze was his mistress. It was over.

A number of months later, I found myself sitting in my small, one-bedroom apartment in West Hollywood, contemplating what my life had become. I had been working for an independent film company as a production assistant for about nine months, handling everything from finding the office space to scheduling auditions.

When an actress would come in to audition, the producer would ask me to read the scene with her. I wouldn't blandly recite my half of the dialogue. I would throw myself into the role I'd been given to read in order to support the auditioning actress.

Then I would return to my desk in the front room. I could tell by the reactions that I had given a good performance. With each reading, my confidence would grow. Though I never voiced my feelings, I had an increasing conviction that I could act, that I was good at it.

As the company began to struggle financially, I tried to help out by letting them postpone a few upcoming paychecks. Then, without any advance notice to me, the producers filed bankruptcy and fled their debts, including my back pay. I had no job and no savings. Worse still, creditors were hounding me to pay off the Xerox machine my fleeing bosses had abandoned. I was adrift in my career and my personal life and had no idea what to do next.

The phone rang. It was my grandfather. He had bought a ranch in Scottsdale, Arizona, as a second home and was calling to say he needed a favor.

"Look. I need my station wagon," Grandpa insisted. "Go to the house on Sunset, pick up my car, and drive it to Scottsdale. Then stay a couple of weeks and hang out with Mary. Keep her company."

Mary was my grandfather's second wife. He had remarried after Grimmy passed away.

I had nothing else going on. I packed a suitcase, picked up Grandpa's station wagon, and headed east. When I was almost there, I rear-ended another car at a traffic light. The front of the station wagon was all crumpled, yet the car was still drivable. An occasional cloud of steam would rise up, probably from a cracked radiator, but I limped along to my grandfather's ranch. I was terrified to see him now. I had failed in my one mission: to bring the car safely 380 miles from Beverly Hills to Scottsdale.

My grandfather came out of the house and stood, arms crossed over his chest, on the front porch.

"What the hell?"

"I'm so sorry, Grandpa! I have insurance. I'll pay for it."

He broke out in laughter. I stood by the car in disbelief at his reaction as he walked around it, shaking his head and then laughing all over again. He was probably thinking how pathetic it was. Lucky for me he had a sense of humor. I'd lost mine.

Whenever I had visited Grandpa, we would always go out to dinner. For some reason, that night he announced that he wanted to go to bed early after Mary made us all something to eat. Mary and I stayed up late, sitting in the solarium on the back of their house, and polished off a bottle of champagne.

Both of us were more than a little juiced when Mary said, "Sharon, you're twenty-six years old and you have nothing to show for your life."

I thought it was kind of rude of her to point it out. But she was right.

I looked out at the night sky.

Mary didn't let my silence stop her. "What do you want to do, Sharon?"

I tried to quickly think up an appropriate answer. She didn't wait.

"Just say it," Mary persuaded. "Don't judge it. Don't censor it. Just open your mouth and say it. Even if it seems impossible to accomplish."

"I want to be an actress."

Mary smiled. "So? That's great. When I was your age, I was under contract to MGM."

"You were?"

"Well, I only lasted a year. I wasn't very good."

She didn't seem embarrassed.

"Tell me. Why don't you pursue acting?" She tipped the last of the bottle's contents into her glass.

I said, "Oh, Mary, I'm too old to start now."

She shook her head in disagreement.

Although I was twenty-six, I looked and often acted like I was just out of high school. It wasn't really about being too old. I had never given myself the permission to seriously consider acting as a profession. After all, Grandpa had told me to stay away from the "filthy business."

"Please don't tell Grandpa that I want to act. Please."

Mary said, "I won't. But I think it's crazy not to try. I always thought you had a Carole Lombard quality. Do you know who that is?"

Of course I knew. I adored her.

The next morning I woke up in the guesthouse. I got dressed and went over for breakfast.

Mary turned to look at me from the kitchen counter.

"Your grandfather would like to see you."

It was clear that she had told on me.

I went into his bedroom and Grandpa was sitting up in the bed, reading a newspaper.

"Grandpa, Mary said you wanted to see me."

"Yes I do," he said. "That's ridiculous."

I was crestfallen.

"I knew that's what you would say. I asked Mary to please not tell you."

He said, "I mean it's ridiculous you thought I would stop you. So you want to be an actress? What are you going to do about it?"

For the first time, I felt no fear of what my grandfather might think.

"Well, I have to get into an acting class and study."

He said, "How much is that?"

I knew the answer because my cousin Lizzie had taken acting classes.

I continued on as boldly as I could.

"The acting class I'm looking at is one hundred and fifty dollars for three months of training."

"Okay," he said, "you've got one hundred and fifty dollars. Now what?"

That was a fortune to me. I couldn't believe he was going to pay for my classes. "Oh, thank you, Grandpa!"

Then he said, "You're welcome. Now what are you going to do? How do you plan to support yourself while you take these classes?"

I said, "I'll get another secretarial job."

"Good. Is that a plan, then?"

I couldn't believe this was happening.

"Yes, Grandpa."

He said, "Do you want to go home now?"

I hadn't even been there twenty-four hours, and I had intended on staying for two weeks. It seemed very rude to leave, even though my heart was racing with excitement at my new prospects.

"No, Grandpa. I came to visit you."

He repeated, "I understand. Do you want to go home now?"

My grandfather, a man who bought and bred winning racehorses as a hobby, always knew when a filly was ready to race.

"Yes, Grandpa."

I would be starting a new life. I had won approval from my grandfather, which meant the world to me.

"Good. Go tell Mary to get you an airplane ticket."

I flew home that evening.

I looked out from my window seat as the plane left behind the barren desert of Arizona. Soon I was flying over the vast urban sprawl of LA. It's a city where people still come with a dream and no small amount of hope. It has always been my home.

I had an epiphany as my flight descended into the City of Angels. It was an intense feeling, a deep confirmation: I would not fail.

I knew I had no experience. I wasn't fresh out of high school. I wasn't a great beauty. I was starting from scratch.

But still, I knew I would not fail.

Eleven

I Got Seven Years for Being in a School Play

The most famous acting teacher in Hollywood in the 1970s, Estelle Harman, judged my audition to be in her class as "the worst performance" she'd ever had to sit through in her entire career.

I didn't hear that brutal complaint until two decades and two Emmy awards later.

Even though she wasn't impressed by my audition, Estelle accepted me into one of her acting classes. She may have done so out of deference to my uncle Jack. He had probably made a phone call to her on my behalf.

I was about five years older than most of the other students in her beginner class. I didn't care. I just wanted to start my training. The class met on Thursdays from 2 to 6 p.m.

Now that I had the acting class, I knew a secretarial job wouldn't work out, as Estelle's classes were during daytime hours. I needed some type of evening employment. My idea was to apply to be a bartender at the Bel Air Hotel, despite the fact that female bartenders were rare in the early '70s in LA.

I certainly knew how to enjoy drinks; I only had to learn how to make them.

The next morning my phone rang.

"Sharon. This is Arthur Marks."

Arthur Marks was a producer who had a prolific and rising career as a film director. I had met him through a previous job of mine.

He said: "I'm starting a new company, and I want you to come and work for me."

I said, "Mr. Marks, thank you, but I can't."

He said, "Why not? You're the best production secretary around."

"You'll laugh when I tell you."

He said, "Go ahead. Tell me."

"I'm going to be an actress."

He said, "I'm not laughing. How will you support yourself until that happens?"

I told him, "My acting class is on Thursdays from two to six. I'll have to get a night job."

He said, "So, you've got Thursday afternoons off. And I'll still pay you for the full week. Now what?"

I went to work for Arthur Marks's new production company at General Service Studios in Hollywood on Las Palmas Avenue. He stayed true to his word. I took my acting class every Thursday afternoon for the next full year.

When Estelle passed away years later, I was starring in *Cagney & Lacey*. Her daughter Eden told me that her mother had changed the way she taught acting because of me. I was floored. Estelle believed in working from the outside in—through mannerisms and costuming—to develop a character. I instinctively worked from the inside out. It was all I had.

In 1972, a young playwright, Candy Carstensen, had written a two-act comedy called *What's What*. It was a play within a play. She cast me in the ingenue role. There was no pay involved, and we only performed the play twice, at the Encino senior community center. The audience, composed of our family and friends, sat on folding chairs. We didn't charge anybody.

I played a visually challenged actress who is playing a nurse who cares for an elderly male patient. On our opening night, I exited for a quick costume change. Too late, I realized that I was supposed to remain in my nurse's uniform for the next scene. I tried to hurry back into the costume, but when my cue came, I was only half dressed. I didn't have time to button up, so I held the nurse costume closed in front with my hands and made my entrance, my hair now a disheveled mess. It looked like the old man had had his way with me. The audience burst into laughter. The rest of the cast tried to hold it together. It was a big mistake that couldn't have worked more in my favor if I had planned it.

My entire Los Angeles family came to see my first stage appearance. They called it my "school play."

At one point, Candy came backstage and said, "There's some man in the front row who keeps yelling out, "Bravo! Bravo!"

I peeked through the curtain.

It was my dad.

I had no idea who else might be in the audience. I certainly didn't expect the phone call I received Monday morning while at work.

"Sharon, my name is Orin Borsten, and I'm in publicity at Universal Studios. I saw you in your little play over the weekend. You'd be perfect for the lead in John Cassavetes's new film, and I want you to meet Monique James, the head of our talent department."

Every wannabe actor knew who Monique James was, so I thought it was a prank call from an acting classmate.

I laughed, saying, "Okay. Cut the bullshit. Who is this?"

He said, "I understand why you're skeptical. Why don't I have Miss James call you."

I said, "Yes. Do that."

I hung up the phone, incredulous that a classmate thought I would fall for that shit. I mean, please!

Five minutes later Monique James's assistant called. She requested that I come to Universal Studios and meet with Monique, in person. I couldn't believe it. I set the appointment and immediately called Orin Borsten to thank him for the connection. He asked me to please stop by his office after my meeting.

My first encounter with Miss James was brief but significant. Her short physical stature, owl-eye glasses, and sensible shoes belied the powerhouse confidence she exuded. I was both intimidated and in awe.

She requested that I prepare a short scene from a play for her to see, "preferably with a male actor." Then she tapped her cigarette out in her full ashtray and stood up, signaling that it was time for me to leave.

I didn't ask her what type of scene she wanted. She just said, "Call me when you're ready and bring it in."

As I promised, I went by Orin Borsten's office.

He told me, "You're a comedienne, but forget doing anything by Neil Simon. She has seen it all."

Neil Simon was the most prolific Tony-winning playwright of my generation.

Orin gave me a play, *After Haggerty*, which was a recent comic romp he had seen onstage in London. "This has never been done in the US. Do act one, scene one."

I went home and read over act one, scene one, and gave him a call.

"Mr. Borsten, I can't do this scene."

"What? Why not?"

I told him why. "Every line has the word *pussy* or *fuck* in it."

He laughed. "The hell you can't do it. Find an acting partner and rehearse."

I said okay. I found a very good actor, an older British man, who was working at General Service Studios. We rehearsed together for four months.

My phone rang at work one morning.

"Are you ever bringing in that scene?" It was Monique James.

I told her, "I want it to be letter perfect, Miss James. My uncle told me that you occasionally remember when it's good. You never forget if it's bad."

I could almost hear her rolling her eyes on the other end of the line.

"Just bring it in," she insisted.

Good or bad, she wanted to see the scene soon. My acting partner was available and graciously showed up to the audition, which was held in Claire Miller's office. Claire was Monique's assistant. I had heard through the grapevine that Monique held all auditions there so she had the option of getting up to leave whenever she wanted. Seated next to Monique was Eleanor Kilgallen. Monique and Eleanor had started the only female-owned talent agency in all of New York. They had signed Grace Kelly and Warren Beatty early on. Lew Wasserman at MCA talent agency bought them out and placed them under the MCA banner. A few years later MCA acquired Universal Studios. Monique James was given the title of Vice President, Head of Talent on the West Coast, and Eleanor was given the same title on the East Coast. They became the first two female vice presidents of MCA/Universal. They were magnetic and intimidating, each on their own, but even more so as a duo. Eleanor was tall and thin and sat with a straight spine, her hair perfectly sprayed into place, white gloves on her hands, a crucifix around her neck.

I announced the name of the play, and we did our scene. Since it had not been done in the United States, I took the liberty of changing some of the words in the scene to make them flow better from my American mouth. I thought it was a crafty thing to do and that no one would be the wiser about my rewrites.

Afterward, Eleanor Kilgallen said, "I saw the play last month in London, starring Billie Whitelaw."

Oh, fuck.

I thought it was all over. I had taken liberties with a script and been caught. Monique and Eleanor stood up and walked toward the door.

Because I was so naïve and had no experience outside of acting class, I didn't realize that professional auditions were often yes or no. They like you. They don't like you. You never get helpful notes. No one has that kind of time. I called out to Monique before the door closed, "Excuse me, Miss James. No critique? Nothing?"

She turned only her head, momentarily, toward me, "No. I will speak with Orin."

I thanked my acting partner and he left. Any hope I had of

making an impression had dissolved. Claire was silent as I collected my belongings.

"I guess I blew it."

"Go home and wait by your phone," was Claire's only response.

About a year later, I had the courage to ask Claire how she'd been so certain that Monique would call me.

She said, "Monique always carries a pencil with her. During most auditions, she turns the pencil over and over in her hand. But while you were doing your scene, she held the pencil still."

It was interesting to hear in retrospect. But on the day of my audition I had no clue. I also had no choice but to go back to my secretarial job that afternoon. I walked in and Mr. Marks said, "Monique James just called. She wants you to come back this evening and meet with her."

Right after work, I drove back to Universal. Monique wanted me to go to a producer's office and read for a series role that night.

She said, "Whether or not you get this part, we'd like to offer you a seven-year contract."

I was floored.

Monique James, the head of talent, wanted to sign me to be one of fifteen contract players for Universal Studios! She held one of the most powerful and influential positions in Hollywood in the 1970s and '80s. You couldn't buy her attention for any price. She wasn't about to squander her reputation on a poor bet. She was counting on me to succeed. Me! Holy shit!

I went to audition for the producer. I'm pretty sure I was in a dreamlike state. I found out years later that he told Monique that I was dreadful.

Well, you know me. Go big or go home!

Thankfully, I was none the wiser to his response regarding my audition, and Monique James let his apparent complaint go in one ear and out the other. She had made up her mind to sign me. I would be making $186 a week, guaranteed, whether I worked or not. My life had changed in a matter of hours.

I thanked her over and over. She responded by saying, "I have a feeling you've been acting your entire life. Now we're just going to pay you for it."

I completely forgot that I was supposed to meet my grandfather at the Los Angeles Country Club for our weekly scheduled dinner. He was very pissed about my no-show. You don't stand up Neil S. McCarthy without a really good reason. I thought I had one.

I apologized to Grandpa and met him for dinner the following evening to tell him my good news.

Halfway through dinner, I went to the ladies' room and sat in the outer lounge area at the vanity counter. I stared at myself in the mirror, something I rarely do, thinking, "This is what an actress looks like."

A woman said from behind me, "Well, that's a happy face. Did something wonderful happen to you?"

"I don't know if I'm supposed to say this, but I just got offered a contract at Universal Studios. I'm an actress now."

"You are? Well, you're certainly pretty enough."

I was embarrassed and flattered.

Then she added, "My brother is an actor. You may have heard of him. Robert Wagner?"

"Oh my God!" I almost shouted. "I love Robert Wagner!"

"Well, I'm his sister, Mary."

I never could have anticipated that years later I would be in *Switch*, a hit series with Robert Wagner.

When I returned to the table, flushed by Mary's compliments, I asked, "Grandpa, do you know Lew Wasserman?"

Lew Wasserman was the executive mogul heading up MCA/Universal.

He said, "I know Lew very well. Why?"

I had a complaint. I thought Grandpa would sympathize.

"I'm making two hundred dollars a week as a secretary. This contract is for only one hundred and eighty-six dollars a week. I thought actresses made a lot of money."

He said, "Let me see it."

I handed it to him and he burst out laughing.

"This is *my* contract. I drew up the first contract between a player and a studio forty years ago. They're still using it."

Since Uncle Jack had made a call to get me an audition for my acting class, I thought surely Grandpa could make a call and get me another fourteen dollars a week.

Completely guileless, I plunged ahead. "Will you talk to Mr. Wasserman for me, Grandpa?"

He paused, put the contract back in my hands, and said, "Do you want to be an actress?"

"Yes, Grandpa."

"Then sign it. You have to be coming from a position of power from which to negotiate. You are not."

I was rightfully humbled. But I was also proud. I knew that Uncle Jack had helped me get into Estelle's acting class and that Grandpa had paid for it, but any nepotism ended there. I had secured a contract with Universal Studios on my own. It was completely up to me now. Make or break, fly or fall.

By the time the dinner check came to the table, I understood that being Jack Baur's niece and Neil McCarthy's granddaughter would get me only two things: a lot of love and a plate of breaded veal cutlets at the Los Angeles Country Club.

Twelve

Something Happens

My first day on the Universal lot, I was absolutely spellbound. I was so full of gratitude to be an exclusively held player, one of the chosen few. I could now drive up to the main gate, wave to Scotty, the guard, and be let onto the studio lot. I was a professional actress.

I was the property of Universal Studios, the largest motion picture and television production studio in the world, for seven years, or as long as they wanted me. Some actor friends warned me against signing an exclusive contract. They told me that I would be absorbed by the system and never heard from again.

My response was, "Nobody has ever heard of me now!"

Most warnings came from struggling actors. Sure, they were unrestricted. They were also unemployed.

I now had a steady income, whether I worked or not. I was sent to auditions where the producers and directors had requested to meet me. As I saw it, I had won the lucky-actress lottery. I was twenty-seven years old. I was in good hands and the possibilities were endless.

On that first day, as I was crossing the lot, heading toward the Westmore makeup building, with its signature large red doors, I heard a man's voice behind me say in a staccato manner: "Don't. You. Ever. Think. That you. Are not. A pretty girl."

I turned around to get a look at the woman he was complimenting. I couldn't see her. But I did see him. It was actor Walter Matthau, who was on the lot filming *Pete 'n' Tillie* with Carol Burnett.

Mr. Matthau pointed at me and said, "'Cause you are."

I was thrilled! I had been there only four hours and look at that! A compliment from a very famous actor!

After I had signed my contract, Orin Borsten told me the reason he'd wanted me to meet Monique James was "You're the blonde Susan Saint James."

Susan, a contract player since 1966, had already won an Emmy and was costarring in *McMillan & Wife* with Rock Hudson. She had it all going on. Monique James had taken her there. I was always a great fan of Susan's.

Orin explained that Susan and Monique were in a bit of a rough patch and that Susan had fallen out of favor.

Was that what had gotten me in the door? Jesus! Well, welcome to show business!

Monique always took her newest signed contract player to eat lunch in the executive dining room. She had her own booth, in a prime location, right where casting directors would walk by.

I was so nervous about eating in front of her. I bypassed ordering any type of food that could fly across the table with one misplaced stab of a fork. I went for a very thick soup. It gave me the least chance of embarrassing myself. As I ate, I looked around the dining room at the huge photo portraits of current Universal stars that lined the walls. It was impressive. They had years of experience, good looks, charm, wit, and success. I only had one year of weekly acting classes and one play that had run two nights.

After a bit of small talk, I finally worked up the courage to ask Monique why she had signed me.

She said, "I'm not going to tell you. If I did, you'd become aware of it."

I went back to my bowl of soup. I wasn't about to challenge her. There was a silence that lasted a few minutes.

Then she said, "All right. I'll tell you."

I held my breath.

"Nothing about you fits," she said. "Your voice doesn't match your face. Your stride belies your lack of confidence. You're as soft as a puppy, but you talk like a teamster. Absolutely nothing fits. However, you put it all together and it works. Something happens."

Monique took that "something," whatever it was, and made it "happen" for me. The story of my early career was conceived and authored solely by Monique James.

Thirteen

America's Sweetheart (Not Me)

I got my first TV acting job within days of signing my seven-year deal. I take no credit for a brilliant audition. There wasn't one. The role was handed to me.

David J. O'Connell, the executive producer of *Marcus Welby, M.D.*, had an agreement with Monique James to always give the newest contract player his or her first job. He did it for me. It qualified me for my Screen Actors Guild card.

Per SAG rules, producers are to only hire a nonunion actor if there are no current union members who could possibly play the role. Apparently, the Screen Actors Guild was short on inexperienced husky-voiced blondes in 1972. No one disagreed or complained otherwise. I got the part and my card.

I was cast in a guest-star role as a young secretary who has an affair with her married boss. I was pretty confident I could pull this part off.

Actress Margaret O'Brien, arguably the most famous child star of the 1940s, played the boss's distraught wife. Three decades after costarring with Robert Young in *A Journey for Margaret* and, of course, *Meet Me in St. Louis* with Judy Garland, she was making a very rare TV appearance. The press was buzzing. Generations of fans loved Margaret O'Brien. She was exceptionally kind to me on the set.

I didn't have much dialogue, but they used many close-ups of me, the seductress, watching sweet Margaret from across the room, waiting to steal her spouse.

Marcus Welby, M.D. was the number one show on ABC in 1972, with millions of viewers. My first ever television role, my debut, was playing the person who wrecks the life of "America's Sweetheart."

Fourteen

No One Messes with Sweet Pea

"What's your favorite flower?" Monique asked me one morning in her office.

I had no idea why she wanted to know.

"Sweet peas."

I was thinking of the photo of my mother's bridesmaids, each carrying a long, draping bouquet of full-bloom sweet peas.

"Sweet Pea it is."

From that day forward, Monique rarely called me Sharon. It was "Sweet Pea" if it was the two of us, and "Miss Gless" if anyone else in the business was present. The nickname made me feel special. It was pure affection.

I trusted Monique. In a very short time she became my teacher, mentor, adviser, friend, and confidant. She knew I was inexperienced but pliable and always eager to improve. She knew how to prod my self-esteem sky-high for each acting job and then reduce it in a persuasive manner so I would never stop improving.

In my first year as a contract player, I got a number of guest-star spots on TV shows that were popular—*Emergency!*, *McCloud*, *The Sixth Sense*, *Ironside*, *Chase*—and I had a starring role on the series *Faraday and Company*. I was so happy to be a part of any production! I'd show up early and stay late, whatever was needed. I had a great attitude, which is a good thing, since I had no technique. I was so green.

Every few months, Monique would set up an afternoon in one of the huge screening rooms at Universal so she could give me notes on improving my work. It was how she trained me. She and I would sit next to a console in the center of the darkened theater. She would press a button, lean toward a microphone, and say, "Run Miss Gless's scenes, please."

A projectionist would run a compilation of my guest-star spots. Then Monique would critique my performance as we watched.

"See *that thing* you're doing with your mouth?"

"Yes."

"Don't do it."

There are photos of me as a toddler with that same lopsided half grin. I've never done it on purpose.

She would say something along the lines of, "I want you to watch yourself in this scene. It looks like you're waiting to say your line."

"I *am* waiting to say my line," I would agree.

Monique would close her eyes behind her oversize glasses, lean back in her seat, and sigh. "Yes. I know."

She often asked the projectionist to rewind the scene one more time so "Miss Gless" could see it for herself.

"You're not really listening to what he's saying. You're just waiting for him to finish so you can say your line. I want you to learn to really listen. I'm teaching you a lesson."

I could see it. She was right.

"You must know your dialogue backward and forward so you don't have to think about it anymore. I want you to learn it so well that you could juggle the props, move the furniture, or whatever and still be line-perfect."

She continued. "When your partner is speaking, really *listen* to every word he or she is saying. I promise you, when you're really listening, your face, in particular, comes alive. The director and editor will cut to you, whether you are speaking or not."

It was the best piece of acting advice I was ever given.

I left that meeting and made sure I became the best listener on the lot. I listened to every vocal nuance of every line, delivered by every actor, in every scene I was in, *ever*. That's when my job really became fun.

As long as Monique was happy with me and I'd hear good reports from her, I was fine. During my first year as a contract player, I was mostly cast as an unknown guest star, but Monique would treat me as if the show could not go on without me, and she would presume that the show's director and crew would treat me with the same regard. She expected the same of casting directors.

One casting director called Monique and said, "We liked Sharon quite a bit. We have a small role for her."

"What's the part?" Monique asked.

"Well, it's . . . um . . . a nurse."

Monique responded, "Miss Gless doesn't do nurses."

When she told me that, I burst out laughing.

That didn't spare me from playing my share of stewardesses (that was the job title then) in various near-death plane-disaster productions. When Universal Studios needed the supporting players but didn't want to pay much, they used all the contract players. It was unquestioned.

I don't remember my dialogue in the first one, for a series called *The Sixth Sense*. I was the new attendant on the flight. I think the part called for a lot of screaming, "What's happening???" and looking absolutely terrified.

I was also a stewardess in the movie *Airport 1975* with Gloria Swanson, Myrna Loy, Charlton Heston, and Karen Black. Monique somehow worked it so I stood out from the other attendants and was in half of a "two-shot" with Karen Black, the female lead, before she was almost sucked out of a broken cockpit window.

The last time I played a stewardess was in the TV movie *Crash*, about the true-life tragedy of Flight 401, traveling from New York's JFK International Airport to Miami in 1972. The plane went down in the Everglades. My character survives the crash, manages to get out of the crumpled aircraft, and swims away. No one explains where I am swimming *to*, but my character comes across the head stewardess, played by Adrienne Barbeau, who is badly injured and stuck in the branches of a tree. She asks me to say the Lord's Prayer with her. It's a very poignant moment preserved somewhere in film history, with Adrienne dangling from a limb overhead as I tread swamp water and pray out loud. Come on! It was crap, and I knew it. It didn't matter. I loved to work, and I liked Adrienne.

I hadn't been in the business long when I landed the guest lead on James Garner's hit series *The Rockford Files*.

I spent my first hour on the set of that show leaning against the soundstage wall watching Jim. I saw how he interacted with the crew. They seemed to love him. He was tall, handsome, confident, and clearly nobody's fool. I was instantly besotted and very nervous about meeting him.

I must have been pointed out as his guest star for the episode. He walked over and extended his hand.

"Sharon? Hi. I'm Jim Garner."

"I know. Hi."

Could I have been any cleverer? Dear God.

Obviously, it didn't take him long to see that I was completely starstruck, so he made gentle conversation that put me at ease.

After a few more minutes he asked: "So. You married?"

"No."

"You going with anybody?"

"No."

"Really? Do you want to . . . fool around?"

"No."

"Well, do you mind standing still while I do?"

I started laughing.

He grinned. He had dispelled my nerves.

I'm sure that would be considered sexual harassment today, but I never felt threatened, and Jim would have been horrified if I had. He was a very funny guy. I learned a lot from Jimmy. I miss him.

Societal and cultural rules have changed since the 1970s, especially with the #MeToo movement. I was fortunate. As a contract player under Monique's powerful authority, I was spared the sexual harassment that I'm sure many actresses suffered.

None of the casting directors, producers, or even executives messed with me. They knew exactly how much influence Monique held in our industry, and they treated her, and those she staked her reputation on, with nothing but respect. It was either that they feared Monique, or that they just didn't find me attractive. I choose to believe that they were afraid of her.

Fifteen

Wunderkind (Not Me)

Richard D. Zanuck, a well-known film producer, had phoned Monique and asked her to send over headshots of the current young female contract players. He needed to find a date for his hottest upcoming wunderkind director to the first-ever American Film Institute dinner. Mr. Zanuck looked through the stack of headshots and picked me.

And so I went on a date with Steven Spielberg. His directorial debut, *Duel*, an action-thriller TV film starring Dennis Weaver, had impressed the executives.

I had no idea who Steven Spielberg was, and he certainly could say the same of me. The studio loaned me a floor-length black velvet coat to wear and they did my makeup and put a long black ribbon in my hair.

He arrived to pick me up at my little apartment in West Hollywood. He was wearing a tuxedo with a Road Runner T-shirt and sneakers.

I opened the door. He held his jacket open and said, "Beep-beep."

Looking back, the shirt was pretty metaphoric for how quickly Steven blazed up the road to success.

Grimmy had always advised me, "If there is a lull in the conversation, always ask the other person about themselves."

Once we got in the car, that's what I did.

Steven told me about sneaking onto the Universal lot, maneuvering his way onto the set of every production he could, and setting up an office space in an empty bungalow, even though it wasn't his. He didn't have an ego about it. He was very polite, though once we got to our destination, a pre-event cocktail party, he didn't speak to me again.

The pre-event party was at the home of George Roy Hill, best known for directing *Butch Cassidy and the Sundance Kid*. He was putting the finishing touches on his next movie, *The Sting*. He played the soon-to-be-famous title song music on his piano for us. Not exactly Scott Joplin, but not bad.

The American Film Institute event was to honor John Ford, director of such classic movies as *The Quiet Man* and *The Grapes of Wrath*. I was seated at a table with Steven on my left and no one to my right. George Roy Hill sat next to Steven and it became obvious that they would be engaged in conversation all evening. I didn't mind. I had plenty to look at. The room was full of notable actors and performers: Henry Fonda, Charles Bronson, Bob Hope, and Cary Grant. President Richard Nixon was in attendance, so there was a lot of security around. The funny Danny Kaye was the master of ceremonies.

Right before dinner was served, a waiter squeezed two more chairs beside me on my right and quickly followed with place settings. They were for Richard Zanuck's mother and her guest. Mrs. Darryl Zanuck had arrived unexpectedly, escorted by Mr. Frank McCarthy, who sat in the chair next to me. He introduced himself to me, and I said, "I'm a McCarthy, too."

"Are you?"

"Yes. My grandfather was a show business lawyer."

"You're Neil McCarthy's granddaughter!?!"

He was thrilled. For the first time that evening, I felt I belonged there.

Thank God I didn't ask him what he did for a living. Frank McCarthy had recently won the Academy Award as producer of the best picture of the year for his pet project, twenty years in the making, *Patton*. Frank McCarthy was a former brigadier general in the US Army, a closeted gay man who had a Beverly Hills home right next door to his longtime partner, Rupert Allan. Rupert was a Hollywood publicist who represented Grace Kelly, Steve McQueen, Bette Davis, and even Marilyn Monroe at one time. To protect their reputations, each would always escort a woman to any event he attended. Even though it was the 1970s, homophobia was still the norm and very few people felt comfortable being out about being gay.

I liked Frank right away. He was a perfect tablemate for me. Mrs. Zanuck dozed off in her chair before the soup even arrived, so Frank and I were left to entertain one another. The whole evening was so terribly serious in every way, each tribute more saccharine, sincere, and overblown than the one before. Frank started in with some sardonic running commentary under his breath, and I couldn't stop laughing. Then he made a joke about everything that was happening on the stage. We were like two naughty children.

At the end of the evening, Steven walked me to my door and then asked if he could use my phone. I invited him in. He dialed and said, "Hi, Susan. It's me. Can I come over?" Clearly, Susan was a much more interesting woman than I. He said good night and left. I don't know if Steven complained to Richard D. Zanuck about the date he had chosen for him or not.

Years and years later my husband Barney and I attended a party, and Steven was there. Barney reminded him of his long-ago date with me. I tried to make a joke as I shook his hand. "So, whatever happened to your career after that?"

He laughed. Thank God. Beep-beep.

Sixteen

Bitch (Still Not Me)

Before I played a single professional woman named Christine Cagney, I got to work with Suzanne Pleshette, the actress who gave new definition to the role of sitcom wife. Actually, I think she shattered the traditional role and left it for the history books. Suzanne played Bob Hartley's better half, Emily, on *The Bob Newhart Show*, a major hit show on CBS. Bob's natural comic timing was his iconic "stammer and pause." Suzanne's was sardonic and came with a sting. What a pairing!

I guest-starred in one episode playing the young date of Bob and Emily's neighbor, Howard, the airline pilot. It was my first time ever filming before a live audience. It was also the first time Universal had loaned me out to another studio. It was 1974 and I was making $210 per week. I've no idea what Universal Studios charged CBS for my "services."

Suzanne was the only actress I had ever met whose voice was huskier than mine. Her personality matched her voice far better than my own. For the most part, I was still very quiet and reserved with my opinions. Not Suzanne. At the table read for our episode, she arrived wearing a tight-fitting black T-shirt with the word *BITCH* spelled out in rhinestone capital letters. I was intrigued.

After we were introduced, she announced to the room, "I just got a call from my agent to be in some feminine hygiene commercial."

Wide-eyed, I asked, "Are you going to do it?"

"Are you joking?" she answered. "Dorothy Provine went on national television and told everyone in the country that her cunt smells. Now they want *me* to say mine smells *worse*! Hell NO! I'll pass."

Suzanne was a living paradox: a gorgeous blue-eyed brunette who smoked and swore like a pirate. She made me laugh. She was fearlessly herself. And she was a motion picture actress, too. If you want to see a star rise, watch the movie *Rome Adventure* from 1962. God, she was sexy and strong.

After I filmed my one and only scene, Suzanne put her arm around me and said, "You were wonderful." Her compliment meant the world to me.

Three months later, I was meeting for a ladies' lunch at Ma Maison, which was a very popular industry hangout in West Hollywood. It was exactly the type of place I avoided, if possible. Patrick Terrail was the owner and Wolfgang Puck was making his debut as a master chef. I was early, so I decided to wait in the bar. Patrick body-blocked me at the entrance. It was momentarily embarrassing, until a husky voice shouted from the dark bar behind him, "Stop being such a twat, Patrick! She's a wonderful actress. Let her in."

He turned to me and asked, "Was I being a twat?"

"Yes. You were," I answered.

He let me in. I went over and thanked Suzanne Pleshette.

After that, I would run into her at peripheral events, CBS functions, or cocktail parties.

One afternoon, I was at my dentist's office. As he finished up with me he remarked, "You know Suzanne Pleshette, don't you?"

I nodded.

He continued, "She's in the waiting room and wants to interview me to be her dentist. I understand she can be tough. So if you want to say anything positive about me on your way out, I'd appreciate it."

He didn't need my recommendation. He had a waiting list that went on for days. I decided to have fun with it. I bunched up some tissues and put them in the side of my mouth to make my cheek stick out. Then I went by the waiting room, pretending I didn't know Suzanne was there.

I held the side of my face and moaned as I walked, saying just loud enough for her to hear, "Oh, fuck. What a butcher!"

I looked over at Suzanne's horrified face and started laughing. I pulled the tissues from my mouth. "Just kidding."

I'm pretty sure she called me a bitch. You know, in a friendly way.

⇒ • ⇐

During season four of *Cagney & Lacey*, I invited my family out to dinner one night in Malibu.

We ate at a local restaurant. There was a big round table next to ours that was occupied by Bob Newhart, his family, and close friends.

I went to Bob's table and said, "Excuse me, Bob. I don't know if you remember me. I guest-starred on your show years ago."

He graciously introduced me to those around his table. It was my first time meeting the famous insult comic Don Rickles, known for his caustic jabs that spared no one.

As I returned to sit with my family, Mr. Rickles said in a loud stage voice, "Personally, I like the brunette better. Now *there's* an actress!"

I thought my brother Michael was going to fall out of his chair, he was laughing so hard. It was hilarious. I was so honored to be the subject of Rickles's acidic humor.

Both Don Rickles and Bob Newhart developed their comedy chops with their memorable styles, playing their gimmicks brilliantly. Their longevity in show business is a testament to their talent. But in the case of the Bob and Suzanne partnering on *Bob Newhart*, I would agree with Don Rickles. I preferred the brunette, too. Now *there's* an actress.

Seventeen

Hired, Fired, Hired, and Canceled (All Me)

It was season six of the show *Marcus Welby, M.D.* The popularity of medical dramas on TV was starting to wane by 1975. The young and single Dr. Steven Kiley, played by James Brolin, wasn't quite so young anymore, though he was still very handsome. The executive producers thought a love interest for Dr. Kiley might be the defibrillator that would give the show a heartbeat for a few more seasons.

I had already done a prior guest appearance and also two TV movies with Robert Young, the star of the show. He liked me and would invite me to lunch with his wife in their beautiful home. Soon, Monique let me know that the regular series role of Kathleen Faverty, assistant program director of the family practice center, had been offered to me.

Right away the producers decided to alter my current look by having my long straight blonde hair cut into a short curly bob. That was the first mistake. Then they outfitted me in stiff business executive attire, one more step in the wrong direction. There was nothing sexy about any of it. I wouldn't have wanted to date me either.

No one did a test run to see if James Brolin and I had any on-screen chemistry. (We didn't.) The humorless scripts didn't help. It was a lot of dry hospital jargon, all centered on the treatment of a severely ill patient. Nothing sets the stage for romance like a kidney dialysis machine. I had no idea what to do with my character. James

Brolin was very quiet off camera, barely speaking to me. He wasn't unkind—he just wasn't anything at all.

I knew that I had been miscast. Between the haircut, the wardrobe, the lifeless dialogue, and the lack of chemistry, whatever pulse-racing romance the executive producers were hoping for became a minor bleep on an otherwise flat line.

My saving grace on the set was Elena Verdugo, who played Dr. Welby's office manager and RN. I had followed Elena's TV career since I was a child. She had had her own sitcom. I found her brilliantly funny.

When I was a fourteen-year-old at boarding school, I got a package from an E. Verdugo in the mail. It was my little red wallet with my student ID. I had lost it in the Park La Brea complex. I couldn't wait to go back to LA for Easter break to see if it was *the* Elena Verdugo who'd found my wallet and sent it to me. I went to the apartment on the return address label to thank her personally. Well, it was the polite thing to do, after all.

The voices on the other side of the door were engaged in a heated argument. I was afraid to knock, but eventually I did. The door swung open with force and there she was, actress Elena Verdugo, standing before me. I stammered out my greeting.

"Miss Verdugo, I'm Sharon Gless. You found my wallet and sent it to me. I wanted to thank you."

I thought she would be impressed that I had come to thank her in person. I was hoping she would invite me inside and that we would talk for a very long time and become really good friends. God, I was so young.

She said, "You're very welcome." Then she shut the door.

I finally had my second chance to have Elena Verdugo as a friend. This time it went better. She became my refuge on the set. She encouraged me and mostly made me laugh.

One day, a group of us went for lunch at the Polynesian restaurant across the street from the studio. Elena was enjoying a number of umbrella drinks with her entrée. I had one myself. When we got up to go back to the studio, it quickly became clear that Elena was smashed. She was too drunk to walk. Two of the larger crew guys held her up between them and we left the restaurant. Elena's feet dangled in midair between the two men as we all hurried back onto the studio lot. They deposited her in the makeup chair for a touch-up. She was due back on the set within minutes, and her close-ups were the first thing on the schedule for the afternoon.

I was panicking for her, but I seemed to be the only one. No one else appeared to be at all concerned. I watched from the sidelines, anticipating the disaster that was about to take place.

The director yelled, "Action," and Elena snapped into character as if she had not had one sip of one drink. She didn't miss a line, a cue, anything. She was flawless.

I guess the crew had been through this before. They knew she would be fine. I have no idea how she did it. She was the ultimate pro. Production would never shut down due to her. She was in every single episode, all 172 of them.

Every Sunday morning Elena would call me at home.

I'd say, "Hang on a minute."

I'd go into the kitchen and make myself a screwdriver. She would have her drink ready on her end of the phone, and we'd talk and laugh for an hour.

At Christmastime, she and I would drive to LA's downtown train yard in my little station wagon to pick out fresh-cut evergreen trees, stopping along the way to get some cold canned cocktails at a liquor store. At the train yard, Elena would charm a willing young man into holding up and rotating any tree she wanted to inspect. She would keep everyone laughing with her one-liners. Then, two or three mesmerized guys would happily tie our chosen trees to the roof of my car. How we made it home, as drunk as we were, I don't know.

Elena and I remained friends for the rest of her life. Anytime I was in Los Angeles, I would visit her. In her last years, following our decades-long tradition, I would have a fully decorated small

Christmas tree, filled with lights, sent to her room in her retirement home.

At the end of season six of *Marcus Welby, M.D.*, I was fired from the show. I'd known it was coming. I didn't blame them. I had been trying to call Monique for weeks to ask her advice. She wouldn't return my calls. This concerned me even more than the idea of being let go from the show. Every six months, a contract player's work comes up for review by the top executives at Universal. If Monique couldn't or wouldn't defend my value to them, why would they keep me? I was very depressed. I thought I would lose my contract with Universal as well.

About a week after the season wrapped, I got a call that I was being considered for a new show that was starting up called *Switch*. It would star Robert Wagner as an ex-con and Eddie Albert as an ex-cop who become partners in a detective agency. They needed a young actress to play the office receptionist who also acted as an undercover decoy when needed.

I was trying to grow out the bad *Marcus Welby* haircut, but it was still very short. Charles Ross, my hairdresser for forty years, did his best to fix it by cutting it into what would become the "wedge" that Dorothy Hamill wore in the Olympics the next year. No one had seen the cut yet.

I went in to read for the part on *Switch*, which was described as "a Natalie Wood look-alike." Well, check me out. I was far from being a gorgeous, petite brown-eyed brunette. The show's creator, Glen Larson, and Robert Wagner were both at the audition. Glen Larson was often referred to as Glen "Larceny" in the TV industry, a producer who would shamelessly lift the story line, characters, and even dialogue from famous movies or TV shows, do a slight rewrite, and slap his name on as "creator." Universal seemed to like that he got shows made, even if most people on the lot didn't care for his style of producing.

I once overheard Monique on a phone call saying, "Well! I finally met a bigger asshole than Glen Larson!"

Now I was auditioning for that asshole.

I could barely make eye contact with Robert Wagner during my interview. I mean . . . it was Robert Wagner! He's gorgeous! He smiled at me warmly.

The style of scene they had me read was easy for me. I nailed the reading, and the interview went pretty well, too.

Glen Larson crossed his arms, saying, "But that short hair. How can she do undercover?"

Robert Wagner said, "Glen, that's why they make wigs."

My phone rang the next day. It was Monique. She didn't bother with hello. She said, "Well, saved by the bell."

It was her way of letting me know that I'd have been out on the street if I hadn't been cast in *Switch*.

"They're fuckin' lucky to have me," I snapped back at her.

She was quiet for a bit and then she said, "Well, yes. Yes, they are."

It took a while for me to get past the lashing my self-esteem had taken, not on *Marcus Welby*, but from Monique shunning me for almost two months.

A short while later, I was in her famous booth at the commissary, back in her good graces, having lunch with her.

"Why didn't you return my phone calls?" I finally asked.

She replied with a bland expression and an exhale of cigarette smoke: "Because you were *so* boring."

I burst out laughing. I couldn't believe she had said that.

"I've never had anybody say that to me in my entire life."

For the first time in months, we laughed together.

After a few *Switch* episodes had been shot and I knew Robert Wagner well enough to call him R. J., as his friends did, I asked him: "Did you know that I was about to be fired from Universal when you hired me?"

"I did."

I had to ask: "Is that why you gave me the job?"

He acted a bit offended: "I'm not running a charity. You were the best one for the part."

To this day, whenever I see my friend R. J., I make a point of telling everyone within earshot about how he saved my career. I think he's tired of hearing about it now, forty years later. But I won't stop.

R. J. didn't have an ounce of arrogance, even though he was as physically beautiful in person as he was on the screen. He went out of his way to make fun of himself. He always tried to let his fellow cast members have the spotlight.

One afternoon on the *Switch* set, we were rehearsing a scene, and R. J. whispered to me, "You get a look on your face when you're fed up with me. Do that expression during your close-up. Even though it's my dialogue, they'll cut away from me to you."

When the cameras rolled, I was caught up in the scene, and I missed my chance to give "the look." R. J. noticed. He dropped a prop, making noise on purpose, so the scene would have to be filmed again.

R. J. said, "Sorry, guys," to the crew and came over to me while they reset for the next take.

"Sharon, you didn't do the look. Put it in this time."

He looked out for me from the beginning.

It took a while for Eddie Albert to warm up to me, probably because I was still green in the business. Eddie had a long professional history. He had played on Broadway, in musicals, in movies, sitcoms, and hour-long TV dramas. At first, I felt intimidated.

When his character was at his desk in the office with me, Eddie always wore a very bright red cardigan sweater.

One day I joked, "Are you trying to upstage me?"

He replied, "I don't have to wear a red sweater to do that, honey."

Eddie smiled and winked at me after he said it, but there was no question he meant it. And he was absolutely right.

In the beginning of the show, most of my scenes took place in the office. One day, I was sitting at my desk, getting ready for my close-up. Behind the camera, sitting in a director's chair, was a petite figure wearing a dramatic Russian fur hat, cocked to the side, and holding a fur muffler at her waist. She wore a beautiful black suit and high-heeled boots. Once my eyes focused, I realized who it was.

My mouth flew open in surprise and the words spilled out: "Oh my God! It's Natalie Wood!"

It was. It was really Natalie Wood. She was married to Robert Wagner and had come to the set because they had an event to attend that night. She laughed at my speechlessness. I had to return to the scene. I was self-conscious acting in front of this icon I had watched hundreds of times in some of my favorite films. She visited the set a few more times, always looking like a million bucks. She was a lovely woman. And, like R. J., she was always sweet to me.

With the money I earned on *Switch*, I bought a small house in Studio City, close to the Universal lot. I had to borrow the down payment. I own it to this day.

When the final season of *Switch* concluded in 1978, R. J. gave me some good advice. "Now that you've been on this series, you should never appear as a guest star on other TV shows. Before you know it, you'll have a series of your own."

Months after the *Switch* finale, I did have my own series, just as R. J. had predicted. I was the costar of an NBC sitcom, *Turnabout*, with John Schuck playing my husband.

The pilot was based on Thorne Smith's best-selling book. It was about a young married couple who buy a magical statue. They inadvertently make a wish on it to change their lives, and they wake up the next morning to discover that the wife's personality has transferred into the husband's body and vice versa. I played a man trapped inside a woman's body. I had the best time!

I called Monique from the set one day. "This is the happiest I've ever been in my entire life! Thank you."

Every night, I met the producers Sam Denoff, Michael Rhodes, and Arnie Kane for drinks in Sam's office. We never stopped laughing together.

Unfortunately, viewers had to watch the animation that made

up the opening titles of *Turnabout* to understand the premise of the show. Even then, it was too complicated to explain in every script.

I knew we were sunk when my mother told me that she liked the show but didn't understand it. Apparently, no one else did either. NBC canceled the show after seven episodes.

I called Monique. "This is the most unhappy I've ever been in my entire life!"

I got over it. Thank you.

≡ Eighteen ≡

Barefoot in Brooks Brothers

Jack Colvin. The man stirred me up. He pulled my attention.

He had been cast as a police investigator in a two-part episode on *Switch* that we were shooting in Las Vegas. I couldn't stop staring at him. If I wasn't on camera, I was preoccupied with Jack Colvin.

Jack was also a Universal contract player, but he already had decades of acting experience, mostly in the theater. As a teenager, he'd been a protégé of Michael Chekhov, the famous Russian actor, director, and teacher.

I tried to play my cards right so he would notice me. When we wrapped, I was supposed to fly back to LA on a commercial airline along with R. J. and Eddie. The rest of the cast and crew were required to ride in a chartered bus. I turned in my airline ticket and rode the bus back for one purpose only.

I sat up front with R. J.'s longtime assistant, my dear friend to this day Peggy Griffin. All week I had been confiding to Peggy about my obsession with Jack, so she knew what was going on. Jack sat way in the back of the bus by himself. I was hoping he would make his way up front to talk to me. He didn't.

Finally I turned to Peggy and said, "Here I go. Wish me luck."

I walked down the narrow aisle and sat next to Jack.

I said, "Would you like to have coffee sometime? Some . . . day? Somewhere? When you're not busy?"

"I thought you were seeing someone," he replied.

"I was."

Jack burst out laughing at my lack of guile.

I went home and severed my relationship with a photographer I had been seeing for five years, never knowing if I would ever hear from Jack.

A couple of days later he called me. We didn't date for very long before he insisted on moving in with me, telling me that it had to be that way or we couldn't see each other anymore. I had never lived with a man, nor did I want to, but I didn't want to lose Jack either. The sex was wonderful, and we laughed all the time. It was new terrain for me. And he changed the terrain of my little Studio City house. He landscaped my entire yard, lining the borders with river rock and planting trees, native shrubs, and flowering plants. To this day, I still have the most beautiful garden, completely landscaped by Jack.

His biggest TV success came from playing the frustrated reporter on the TV show *The Hulk*. He was dubious about it. When he appeared on *The Tonight Show*, Johnny Carson asked him, "You've acted in Shakespeare and Chekhov, directed plays, taught at the American Academy of Dramatic Arts. Why are you now on TV chasing around a big green man, Jack?"

He answered, "For the big green buck, John."

He despised the turn his career had taken. It eventually sent him spiraling into a depression.

I could make him laugh, though his moods were unpredictable. He was very sensual, charismatic, a vast appreciator of aesthetics, and yet he could be occasionally sharp-tongued and cruel.

In our second year of living together, in a moment of weakness, I asked Jack Colvin to marry me. He declined. A year later, he asked me to marry him. I declined. I think we both knew better.

One afternoon my father called me with a complaint. At that time, he was a vice president for Catalina sportswear. Jack and I had gone to their employee store, which was open to family members. We'd each written a check for what we bought. That's where this phone conversation started.

"Are you living with Jack?" my father asked.

I was silent.

He continued: "I saw his check. I wanted to be sure he was good for the money. You have the same address."

I choked. There was no good answer.

My father called me a whore and slammed down the phone.

I was in shock. My father had never spoken to me like that in my entire life.

In tears, I called my aunt.

Aunt Hoonie phoned my father and told him, "Dennis, you just lost your daughter! With all the mistakes you've made in your lifetime, this one is the worst. You better do something to fix it. I can guarantee you'll never see her again."

Within a couple of minutes, my phone rang once more.

"I'm so sorry," my father said.

I was numb. I had gone to my dead place, shutting down. So I just told him it was okay.

It wasn't okay, but the rules for his daughter had always been different than the rules for himself.

He had cheated on our mother and hadn't financially supported my brothers or me since the divorce. He had met other women, made promises to them, and left them devastated. One woman had a nervous breakdown after my father promised to marry her. She made plans for a wedding only to have my father abandon her before the date.

Ironically enough, at this same time, Monique called me into her office with an offer to play a wealthy young manipulative seductress in a new miniseries for NBC.

The Last Convertible was developed from a hugely popular 1978 best-selling book written by Anton Myrer. The story follows five Harvard boys from their freshman year, pre–World War II, through the next thirty years.

As Monique explained to me, "Your role is different from the other parts. You play the Vassar coed who sleeps around and

destroys lives. Your character, Kay, is a little older, more sophisti-
cated, and a very sexy vamp."

I never considered myself sexy. I wouldn't wear a tight-fitting
dress, hose, or heels in real life unless I had to for an occasion. I
didn't own lingerie. At home, I could usually be found padding
around barefoot in a man's Brooks Brothers shirt. I'm still that way.
More than once, people have had to remind me to put on pants to
leave the house.

I told Monique, "I don't know how to do that va-va-voom stuff.
I'm not comfortable. They should get somebody else."

She firmly suggested that I go talk to Jo Swerling, the executive
producer.

I kindly explained to him, "Mr. Swerling, I'm not your girl. I can't
do the Marilyn Monroe poochie-lipped, sleepy-sex-eyes thing."

He told me, "You don't have to be Marilyn. Do *your* version of
sexy."

And that's what I did.

After the miniseries aired, I got a letter from the novelist Anton
Myrer.

He wrote that he had originally watched my character, Maggie,
on *Switch* and didn't think that I was right for the role of Kay. From
the start, he had argued with the producers about casting me. Then
he wrote, "It took two minutes in dailies for you to convince me
about how wrong I was. I'm writing to thank you for the brilliant
Kay you gave me."

I know that fiction writers envision their characters in their
imaginations as they put the words on the page, so I understood the
generosity of his letter. There were no complaints from Anton Myrer.

≡ • ≡

It seemed the more successful I became, the more depressed Jack
became. He would spend hours sitting in his chair in the living
room, staring out of a window. It wasn't that he was jealous of my
success, it was simply that he was bored and disappointed with the

direction his own career had taken. Still, every night, he would help me run lines and coach me for the next day of shooting.

One evening, at home, I decided to try out a little of the seductress I had just played on-screen. I was hoping to bring Jack back to the funny, sexy man he'd been when we met. I bought a floor-length midnight-black satin nightgown with spaghetti straps. I put it on and stood in the living room doorway, my arm raised up and leaning against the frame. Jack did a double take from his chair and burst out laughing for the first time in months. He couldn't stop. That was not what I'd planned.

"Fuck you, Jack!" I yelled. I went into the bedroom and slammed the door. I was so hurt.

A moment later, Jack came in, trying to suppress his amusement.

"I'm so sorry," he said, sitting on the edge of the bed. "Listen. Nothing is sexier than you walking around in one of my shirts, naked underneath and barefoot. But slinky lingerie is just not you."

I can still hear him laughing.

We often had the best sex after a good argument. I think that was the last time. Our intimate life disappeared completely. It took me another two years to face that reality. During those years, we never talked about it.

One afternoon, I was sitting on the floor of the den, going through the mail. Jack came to the door to see what was going on. It seemed to be as good a day as any to end it.

"Jack, I think it's over. Our relationship has deteriorated into nothing. It's time to move on."

He asked quickly, probably thinking I'd change my mind. "Should I go and pack up my things?"

"Yes. I think so."

He looked devastated. He turned to leave the den.

I called after him, "Jack, before you go, will you make love to me one more time?"

He stepped back into the doorway. "Do you know the part of a man's body that turns you on the most?"

"No," I said.

"His back when he's leaving."

Perhaps he was right.

Jack and I eventually became friends again. In 2004, he suffered two strokes in a row and lost his ability to speak clearly. His wit and voice were so much of his presence. I knew he wouldn't be interested in living without them. He passed away soon after his second stroke.

I prepared the eulogy for his funeral. Another woman with whom he had been in a relationship also spoke. She was still in love with him.

At the end of her eulogy, she said, "My only regret is that I wasn't Sharon Gless."

I think I never realized how much he loved me until she said that.

Years later, a young man who had been like a son to Jack called to tell me he had Jack's ashes.

He told me, "Sharon, the only place Jack ever wanted to be was at your house with you."

I told him, "Yes, it's time. Please, bring him home."

The young man came over. We each poured a drink and toasted Jack. At sunset, we spread Jack's ashes in the garden he had created.

Nineteen

Funny or Die

Funny men like women who laugh. That's how I became friends with Andy Griffith. He was very funny. I love to laugh. He liked having me around.

After *Roots* became the archetype for "event" television, miniseries became as trendy as leisure suits, and usually about as regrettable and embarrassing.

I was cast in *Centennial*, a colossal, twelve-episode TV western based on an epic novel by James Michener. It was promoted as *the* major television event of the season. Many TV, film, and even stage actors vied for a role, and it would appear from the cast list that they all got one.

Centennial was a grab bag of personalities, ranging from David Janssen, Richard Chamberlain, and Dennis Weaver to Chad Everett, Merle Haggard, and an NFL football legend thrown in to appeal to the masses. The series spanned centuries of life in a Colorado town. My episode was modern-day. I played a young reporter getting the scoop on the history of the area. Andy Griffith played a college professor on a research project. The two of us met filming this miniseries.

We were filming in eastern Colorado because they needed a place big enough to build a small town that could be continuously updated. It was the dead of winter. Frostbite cold.

In most of my scenes, I fly around in a two-seater plane with

David Janssen, who played the heir to the world's largest cattle ranch. He recounts the history of the town to me in long, detailed monologues. I did my best "listening," as Monique had taught me to do.

David Janssen and I were in the makeup trailer at the same time each day, early in the morning. David would have a large pewter mug full of vodka and ice in his hand—and would have chugged down two or three of them by the time we began shooting. He had to have been pretty drunk when the cameras rolled, but you'd never know it. He had every line down perfectly.

After a few days, I had to ask him, "David, forgive me, but it's amazing the amount of dialogue you have. You start knocking back that vodka pretty early. How do you remember it all?"

He said, "Oh, kid, I don't remember any of my lines. I have a photographic memory. I can see the script in my mind, so I read it from the page."

Impressive. Lucky for me he didn't actually fly the plane, since he was plastered.

Being a relatively new actress, I didn't have high billing or any special "perks." My dressing room was in a "quad," one long motor home divided into four small dressing rooms. Every morning someone would turn on the heat and lay out my costume for the day. It was freezing out.

I would get dressed and then, not knowing when I'd be called to the set, I would lie down on the couch and quickly fall asleep. Andy Griffith's personal driver would invariably knock on my trailer door and wake me up minutes later to ask if I wanted to come hang out with Andy.

I'd follow the driver to Andy's large motor home, and I'd sit on his couch each day for the two weeks we were on location, be his personal audience, and laugh all day long. He would do character voices, tell stories, and imitate people he knew.

If Andy would be called to the set to shoot a scene, he'd tell me, "You stay right here until I come back."

I would never go back to my trailer until I changed out of my costume at the end of the day.

Weeks later, when I was back in Los Angeles, I heard from Monique that an actor had died very unexpectedly while on the set of *Centennial*. His name was Richard Kelton. He was thirty-five years old. At first, they thought he died of a heart attack. Then the autopsy revealed that carbon monoxide poisoning from a faulty heater in his trailer was the cause of his death. He had occupied the exact same quad of the trailer that had been my dressing room. He must have put on his costume and become sleepy, the same way I did. When they came to get him for his scene hours later, he was dead. That would have been my fate. There but for the grace of Andy Griffith go I.

When filming was over, Andy and I went out to lunch three or four times in LA. He always picked me up in one of his many vintage cars. I could tell he had become interested in me. When he dropped me off at my Studio City house one afternoon, he said, "You want to go out to lunch again sometime?"

"I'd love to," I replied

"At night?"

Clever and charming man.

I knew he wouldn't put the moves on me without encouragement, and I didn't want to mislead him.

I still heard from Andy over the next couple of years. He would send me handwritten letters every so often from his alter ego, "Dink" Taylor, a good ol' country boy.

Dear Miss Gless,

Well, our Sunday school class is up here in the Poconos . . . we eat lunch and at 1:30 we see a film show. Sometimes it's funny and sometimes regular like how to grow different kinds of ducks and chickens and stuff and one day it was about VD and how to not get it. But the one I liked best was a show about some doctors called *House Calls*. Afterwards, we had some free time and me and Garret Steele and Jim Forrest got together and got to talking about you and how pretty you are and your voice is husky and nice and special and about your figure and how your eyes and hair are pretty and all and Garret Steele had to run out the room. We started a chapter of the Sharon Gless fan club and while we were writing out our charter and rules and all, the preacher came by and we told him what we were doing and he said he wanted to be a member. . . . When you have time, send us a picture so we can put it up on our wall.

Sincerely,
Dink Taylor

Andy's birthday was June 1. Every year he would call me on my birthday, May 31. He would send me a Christmas card, too. We had an odd and sweet friendship, one that lasted until the day he died. My one regret is that I didn't send a signed headshot to Dink Taylor. What was I thinking?

=⸳=

In the early '80s, I seemed to be in demand as a made-for-TV movie and miniseries actress. I played a lot of roles, but my favorite in the long string of one-off characters was Carole Lombard in *Moviola: The Scarlett O'Hara War*. I had always been a Carole Lombard fan and as a girl found it significant that she died in that Las Vegas plane crash one year before I was born. Lombard was funny, foulmouthed, tantalizing, had great style, and was quirky as hell. I'd sign up in a heartbeat to carry that torch forward.

Before I actually portrayed Ms. Lombard in the miniseries, I was invited to be on Johnny Carson's *Tonight Show*. It was my first appearance, and I didn't know enough about talk shows to stick to the subjects the producers wanted me to talk about.

Johnny was trying to make me feel comfortable. "Your bio says that you're a fifth-generation Angeleno. Is that right?"

"Yes, my family were Basque sheepherders," I said. "Actually, I'm part sheep."

Johnny howled. He kept me on for another segment, booting his final guest from appearing. After the show, I was getting into my car at the same time Johnny was leaving.

He stopped in his tracks, turned and pointed to me, and said, "Carole Lombard. That's who you are."

At that time, I didn't think there was a better compliment.

Johnny was a very funny man, but the most hilarious person on his show worked behind the scenes. He was Jay Michelis, the head of talent relations for NBC, who handled the PR for *The Tonight Show.* He was a stocky, balding, closeted guy. He walked around in brightly colored Hawaiian shirts and had a very wry and dark sense of humor. He was as irreverent on any given subject as a person could possibly be. Of course, I instantly loved him.

I had met Jay at a party through my cousin Lizzie, who was on *Ironside,* which was an NBC show. It was a network party, so I was supposed to mingle. Instead, I stuck with Jay Michelis all night.

He called me Miss Gless. Always Miss Gless. Judith Ann, my best friend from childhood, signed on as the third side of our Bermuda-triangle friendship. On weekends, the three of us would completely go off the radar and disappear for two days, sucked into a haze of booze and cocaine. I'd bring my cocaine grinder and some coke, Judith Ann would bring snacks and mixers, and Jay would bring liquor and *Tonight Show* beach towels or some other "gift" meant for guests of the show.

We thought we were so fascinating that we wouldn't sleep for forty-eight hours straight. The cocaine helped with that. Hey, it was the '80s.

Like Andy Griffith, Jay sent me the most memorable and funny correspondences, always unexpected.

One night Monique called me at 10 p.m. Angie Dickinson had

dropped out of a TV movie, *Revenge of the Stepford Wives*, due to the unexpected death of her mother. It was scheduled to begin filming the following morning.

NBC sent out the call for me to step in. I had never even seen the original *Stepford Wives* feature film, so I didn't know what it was about. I had to meet up with the wardrobe department at about midnight to be fitted for my costumes, including the pinafore dresses. At the same time, I was attempting to speed-read the script to figure out my character. I pulled an all-nighter trying to get ready.

The next morning I was on the set at sunrise with the rest of the cast and crew. The movie was filmed in a luxury home in Calabasas, California. Everyone else seemed ready to go. I was nervous.

A young page from NBC showed up with a sealed letter that he was to deliver to Sharon Gless. I knew it had to be important.

On the front of the envelope was printed, "To the beautiful blonde star of *The Stepford Wives* from a very important NBC executive."

It was obviously from Jay. It was formally written on NBC stationery, and read:

Dearest Angie,

Welcome back to NBC! We are so delighted that you're with us again. We were worried sick that we would have to get some silly twat Universal contract player to play the part. My best to Burt.

Jay Michelis

It was so funny and was exactly what I needed to soothe my nerves. I gave the part my all. It was no *Handmaid's Tale*, but I got to be the hero in 1980, when female hero characters were few in number. For the first time in my career, I was billed alone, over the title.

Six years later, the morning after I had won my first Emmy award for *Cagney & Lacey*, another NBC page delivered a small package to my home. NBC had produced and aired the Emmys that year. I thought I was getting a congratulatory gift. Inside was one lone anchovy in a small plastic container. The NBC engraved card read, "Ms. Gless, we were cleaning up the auditorium last night, and in all of the excitement found this left behind on your seat."

Jay's viewpoint was always, "Who needs a bouquet of congratulatory flowers delivered when a rude body substance joke would be so much more personal?"

Jay also never censored where or when was an appropriate time to talk about his exaggerations of my sexual predilections.

At the buffet reception following my father's funeral, I took my plate to sit at a table with Jay and some of my favorite male friends.

As I pulled out my chair, Jay said loudly, "Okay, anyone at this table who has *not* had Miss Gless, raise your hand!"

Jay's hand went up in the air.

Next to me sat Barney Rosenzweig, the executive producer of *Cagney & Lacey*. He also raised his hand. It was very classy of him, considering we had been having an affair for most of season six. He was the only one at the table with whom I was actually involved. And, Jay knew it, despite his insinuation that I would give it up to anyone at the slightest invitation.

$$= \cdot =$$

I'd won the Emmy for best actress for the fourth and fifth seasons of *Cagney & Lacey*. (Both of my winning episodes were directed by Sharron Miller.) Tyne Daly had garnered the prize for the first three seasons of the show. We were both, once again, nominated for season six. Lorne Michaels (of *Saturday Night Live*) was producing the Emmys that year and he asked me for a favor. Backstage during rehearsal, Lorne said, "Never before have we had a nominee present an award after their category. If they don't win, they feel awful."

I said, "No problem. I can do it. I'm used to it."

He handed me two speeches, one for if I had just won, and the other if I hadn't.

I hadn't. Tyne had. I still went on.

I walked to the podium. I fumbled with my glasses for a moment. Then I sighed and said, "Forgive me. As you know, I just lost. I had two speeches ready to present this next award. Being a positive thinker, I memorized the winning speech. Excuse me. I'll have to use my glasses to read this one."

The audience started cheering for me. The speech was a hysterical put-down of the Emmy committee, written by Lorne himself, where I refer to them as an "uneducated arbitrary group with no taste." It brought down the house.

Jay, who was sitting next to Judith Ann, turned to her and said, "She just won. No one is going to remember anything else about this show tonight."

A few weeks after my father's death, I was sitting on my couch in my Studio City home when my publicist, Pat Kingsley, called to tell me that Jay was dead. He had died in his sleep. I went to stand up and my legs gave out from under me. I fell to the floor.

NBC knew Jay Michelis was irreplaceable. Over time they hired three people to fill his one position. The week he passed away, NBC did a silent tribute to his memory. Instead of the NBC logo appearing in living color in the full-page ad in the *Hollywood Reporter* and *Daily Variety*, the famous peacock image was in shades of gray. A feather had fallen from the bird's plume and lay alone at its feet. There was one tear running down the peacock's face. The print read, "We will never be the same."

I thought it was wonderful. Jay would have crucified it.

⹀ • ⹀

Every ounce of comic timing I have is a result of the encouragement and humor of a handful of feisty female soul mates. Over the years, they have been my playmates, my confidants, my prankster pals, my sure things, and my early audience. They each have defined me in different ways.

The only gift in my having to join the snooty Hancock Park Bluebirds troupe as a seven-year-old was Susan Binney, another little blonde-haired blue-eyed girl, who accepted me without hesitation. I liked her right away. She would come over and spend the night almost every weekend. She thought I was a laugh riot, and I would push the limits of my mother's patience to keep Susan's joy at a peak.

Every Easter, Susan would always take me to her grandmother's home in Balboa, near Newport Beach. My mother would send me with a box of DeMet's Turtles as a house present. In the car, on the way there, I would open the box. Susan would eat one and I would consume row after row and hand it back to her, almost empty. Only Susan would find that hysterically funny.

Years later, when I was maid of honor at Susan's wedding, a part of me was afraid that I was losing her.

But I knew nothing of really losing her, until I actually did in 2018, when she died of brain cancer.

About a week before Susan passed, when she was no longer communicating and spent most of the day sleeping, I sent her a box of DeMet's Turtles. I removed all but two. I ate half of one, put it back in the box, and left the last one whole. I had it delivered to her door. Her husband called me, saying, "Sharon, I got the turtles you sent Sue. She hasn't spoken in a week. She won't know what this is. She's failing."

I said, "Please, Tom. Tell her it's from Sharon and open the box for her."

He agreed, hesitantly. Five minutes later he called me back, tears in his voice.

"She started laughing," Tom told me.

I knew my girl. Thank you, Sue, for your parting gift.

Julie Cheesewright was my friend from boarding school. The

evening that the school closed for the Christmas break, all of the girls would go caroling in the Monterey neighborhood. Then, Julie and I and three other LA-area girls would be put on the overnight train in sleeper cars from Monterey to Los Angeles. It was one of my favorite nights of the year. We would stay awake as long as we could and laugh and talk all the way home.

Julie was the most girly girl I had ever known. She was feminine in every way. We were debutantes together, and Julie found her husband-to-be, Bill, soon after. As a gift for her wedding night, I went to a sports store and bought her a men's white sweat suit and a white football helmet. I sewed pink gingham ribbons onto the sweat suit and glued ribbons along the helmet. Julie howled with laughter when she opened my gift; she later told me that on her wedding night, she emerged from the bathroom in the helmet and sweat suit before her waiting groom. Brava, Julie!

The day before I won my first Emmy award in 1986, I visited Julie's hospital room in San Francisco, where she was being treated for a brain tumor. I told her that I thought I might finally win. She was no longer speaking. She cooed her joy. Bill called me with congratulations the next night. He and Julie had watched the Emmys. She passed away two days later.

I had a lifelong bond with my cousin Elizabeth, who was born when I was three, the only child of my most-loved aunt Hoonie and uncle Jack. After Uncle Jack returned home from the war in Europe, all three of them lived with us in the Muirfield house while their new home was under construction.

For a bit, I was displaced and unhappy at losing my status as "the baby," but I couldn't stop myself from falling in love with Lizzie, my curly-haired brunette cousin. Aunt Hoonie and Uncle Jack would often take me on vacations with them, and Lizzie spent many overnights at my house. Even as adults, we spent many weekends together, and in our early twenties we rented an apartment together on the beach in Laguna, where we spent our summer months.

Her father, the casting director, also wanted his only child to stay as far away from show business as possible. She defied that wish and at age nineteen was one of 20th Century Fox's up-and-coming actresses in training, along with Jacqueline Bisset and James Brolin. At age twenty-one, beautiful, talented Elizabeth Baur beat out a hundred other hopeful young women to play alongside Raymond Burr in *Ironside* at Universal.

Lizzie and I were as close as it comes, until cancer took her life in the fall of 2017. Lizzie promised me that when it was my turn to go, she would be there, waiting with a luggage cart to welcome me. That will be heaven. For now, I miss her every day.

Finally, there was one girl who held the most sway in my young life, but not always for the good. Judith Ann. My mother and her mother were best friends and were happy when they both gave birth to girls one month apart.

Her family had a vacation house in Hermosa Beach, where my mother, brothers, and I would spend two weeks every summer. On summer days, I was always dressed in my brother's hand-me-down T-shirts and some type of cotton shorts. Judith Ann would be dolled up in a frilly sunsuit. She always envied my clothes and I coveted hers. As soon as we could get out of the sight of the adults, we would strip down and exchange outfits. Judith Ann was far more mischievous than I. When we were preteens attending cotillion, she figured out where the breaker switch was and cast the entire ballroom and the many attendees who were enjoying their punch into pitch darkness. Then we ran off to stand on the toilet seats in the bathroom stalls to hide from the patronesses who came looking for the culprits. There seemed to be infinite ways that Judith Ann could get us into trouble, but I followed her anywhere she went, happily enlisted to help pull off pranks for the first six decades of our lives.

The only thing Judith Ann couldn't pull off was surviving her ten-year struggle with breast cancer.

When she had to tell me that the fight was over, we were having lunch in a restaurant.

Judith Ann leaned over and said softly, "I'm so sorry I can't keep my promise that we'll grow old together."

I was devastated, but I wanted to make her feel better, so I whispered back, "I think sixty years is a fucking good run."

She smiled. "It is, isn't it?"

In my eulogy to Judith Ann, I said, "Sixty years ago, they put us in a crib together. I fell in love, and I never recovered."

No one really knows the rhyme or reason of why one person can thrive and another falls ill. I smoked and drank for decades of my life. I still eat crap. My compromise is to eat a full bowl of blueberries every day. I've dieted and fasted and overeaten and lived on peanut brittle, ice cream sandwiches, or See's lollypops for a day. I don't drink much water and I find most vegetables completely boring.

How did I luck out?

Every play has its characters. These smart, sassy, and supportive female friends were a few of mine. I've somehow made it into the third act, but the appeal of the full show has diminished with their passing. There is no sufficient dialogue to make sense of it, except two words.

Fuck cancer.

Twenty

But CBS Loves Her

There used to be a famous bar called Tail o' the Cock on Ventura Boulevard in LA's San Fernando Valley. I decided that would be the place to meet actor Wayne Rogers. His costar on the sitcom *House Calls*, the wonderful Lynn Redgrave, had recently been fired and CBS wanted me to replace her. They asked me, as a courtesy, to meet with Wayne. I was told to pick anyplace I wanted.

What did I know? He didn't smoke or drink. I had a scotch and a full pack of Marlboro Reds on the table. That was our beginning.

Shortly after hellos, Wayne said, very pointedly, "I could have saved her, you know."

I don't remember whatever else we talked about past his blunt opener. I only remember thinking, "What a passive-aggressive asshole! What a cruel thing to say."

Lynn Redgrave was hands-down wonderful in *House Calls* for its first two seasons. She was just as talented and hardworking as Wayne Rogers, and she was in just as many scenes as he was. But that doesn't matter if your costar wants to be the only star.

Wayne had left the hit show *M*A*S*H*, tired of being a sidekick to Alan Alda. His aim was to be a leading man rather than part of an ensemble.

He didn't like that Lynn Redgrave's name was billed over the title along with his. He also couldn't believe that she wanted to make as much money per episode as he did. But the request that

Wayne found completely outrageous was that Lynn wanted to bring her infant daughter to work with her to continue nursing for a few more months.

He seemed to feel strongly that Lynn's request to nurse her child for twenty minutes every three hours would topple the shooting schedule into chaos. He forced CBS to take action.

Lynn tried to challenge it, but they fucking fired her ass. Now, CBS wanted to hire mine.

Even though it was obvious that Wayne Rogers didn't want me, or anybody else for that matter, CBS had already decided that I was the one. So I said yes.

There was a cocktail gathering at the home of one of the producers, thrown by CBS, to welcome me to the show. Everyone—the entire cast, network executives, and all the writers and producers—was there. Monique was my date.

Wayne stood before the gathering to introduce me and welcome me to the show. The first thing that I remember coming out of his mouth was a complaint: "She was not my choice. But CBS loves her and says she's the new Carole Lombard."

I was stunned. How could he say that while I was standing right there next to him? It was the most unwelcoming introduction I had ever received.

I wish I had responded, "Too bad you're not the new Clark Gable. But for some reason unbeknownst to me, CBS likes you."

Two weeks after I arrived on the set, and while taping our second episode together, Wayne stood before the cast, staff, and crew of *House Calls* to announce that he was shutting down the show over a salary dispute: his. He never bothered to tell me first, which would have been appropriate, considering I was his costar. We all packed up, emptying our dressing rooms, not knowing when or if we would be back. The show went dark for two months, but CBS continued to write checks to hold everyone to their contracts. I assume Wayne finally got whatever money he was asking for, because eventually we all went back to work.

The week after we returned to film another episode, Wayne started to complain directly to me about my performance. He would take me to the side. "You're always angry. Can't you lighten it up? It's a comedy."

"First of all," I said, "I'm only angry at *you*. It's called comedic anger, where I toss my curls and slam the door."

He replied, "I don't want any more Carole Lombard. I want Grace Kelly."

I paused.

"I am giving you Sharon Gless playing your adversary, Jane Jeffries."

Wayne wanted some kind of elegant or sultry anger. I was doing the job. The director had no issues with my choices. Even so, Monique and I both wondered if I'd be fired from the show.

Even though the show was still rated in the top twenty-five, CBS pulled the plug. There would be no season four. I believe they read the writing on the wall. Wayne would probably only have more demands and less tolerance for anything that took the spotlight off of him.

At the wrap of season three, I threw a party for the cast at my little house in Studio City. I thought Wayne would bring the party down, so I didn't invite him. I decided to be a class act and invite Lynn Redgrave instead.

She was even classier. She accepted.

Before she hung up, she said, "Why don't we do something funny? Stage something?"

"Like what?"

"Let's have a fight, since you took my place on the show."

I loved the idea. "Fantastic! I have a long driveway. Pull your car in so I can see your lights when you arrive."

Everyone showed up and the party atmosphere was in high gear. Around 11 p.m., I saw Lynn's car pull in.

I announced, loud enough for all to hear, "Who's that?"

The happy group stopped talking to look.

I said, "Wait right here, everybody. I'm going to see what's going on." I went out my French doors, leaving them purposely wide open, and crossed the lawn to the driveway.

Lynn got out of the car. We had never met before. I whispered to her, "Hi, Lynn Redgrave."

She whispered, "Hello, Sharon Gless. Should we start?"

I loved her instantly.

She turned it up to a ten, shouting, "What did you just say to me???"

I yelled, "Why in the fuck would I invite you?"

She raised her voice louder. "I carried that show."

I responded, "Carried the show? You can't act for shit!" (Yes, ladies and gentlemen, I said that to a Redgrave.)

We went on and on, back and forth, until I shouted, "Get off my property! I'm calling the police!"

Lynn followed me across the lawn and onto the deck.

"Fuck you!" she screamed.

I yelled back, "Fuck me??? Fuck you!" I slammed the French doors in her face.

I turned to the astonished crowd, now completely silent in my living room, and said, "Jesus. What a cunt."

Lynn stormed off of the deck. I let it stand for a really uncomfortable and long fifteen seconds and then I started laughing, and said, "It's a joke, you guys."

I opened the door and shouted to Lynn, "Get in here! I'm sick of entertaining these people."

My guests all started laughing and clapping. Lynn was embraced back into the group, and it became an even better party. We got stoned on the pot that actor David Wayne, who played the grumpy older doctor, grew himself in Pacific Palisades. We drank cocktails, told stories, and laughed our collective asses off. All without Wayne Rogers.

Wayne had his own vision of the show. *House Calls* became a good lesson for me in not taking complaints too personally. There are some things that no amount of effort can change.

I can say this on his behalf: Wayne Rogers was a really good kisser.

I will say this on her behalf: I admired and respected Lynn Redgrave. She should have won the Oscar for *Georgy Girl*. Watch it. You won't forget her.

≡ Twenty-One ≡

The One with the Beard

I had a vision. I visit the set of a TV show. The face of the lead actress goes pale. She wants to see the upcoming script. She checks to see if her character has developed a bad cough, soon to be a fatal disease. My presence on her set means one thing. Replacement.

I didn't want the reputation of being the troubleshooter actress, pinch hitter, or Band-Aid for a bruised show or the last-ditch hope of baffled TV executives. I was beginning to feel that way.

First I was asked to step in for Angie Dickinson at the last minute when she dropped out of the TV movie *Revenge of the Stepford Wives*. I did it.

I also got a call that the lead actress in the TV movie *Hardhat and Legs* was being "let go" and that the male costar, Kevin Dobson, had requested that I take over the role. I did it.

Then CBS decided that I would be the one to replace Lynn Redgrave on *House Calls* for its final season. I did that, too.

And now I was the one requested by TV executive producer Barney Rosenzweig to step in to replace actress Meg Foster on *Cagney & Lacey*. I did not want to do it.

This was the third time I had been offered the role of Christine Cagney. I thought it was going to be the final time Barney Rosenzweig would be turned down by me.

Seven years prior, Barney had had an idea for an ever-popular buddy-style motion picture, the kind that typically featured two male actors, such as *The Sting*, which starred Robert Redford and Paul Newman. However, his idea was to break with tradition and have the two leads be female. He entrusted the woman he was then dating, Barbara Corday, and her writing partner, Barbara Avedon, to come up with a script for the concept. *Cagney & Lacey*, a two-hour screenplay, was the result. After it made the rounds, a deal was struck with CBS for a TV movie.

I knew both of the Barbaras from *Turnabout*, my earlier TV series, on which they had been story editors.

Barbara Corday was the first to suggest that I'd be a great choice to play Christine Cagney. Barney, who didn't care for *Turnabout*, disagreed, until months later when the two of them were screening *Moviola: The Scarlett O'Hara War*, in which I played the movie headliner Carole Lombard.

Barney pointed at the screen. "Now *that's* Cagney."

Barbara said, "That's Sharon Gless!"

A call was made to offer me the role in the upcoming TV movie. Unfortunate timing.

I had recently starred in a TV pilot, *Palms Precinct*, for NBC, as a female cop. The network executives decided they didn't like my costars. They wanted to keep me as the lead and reshoot the entire script with new actors. I said no. It seemed like a large heap of bad karma to me. The idea of packing a rod again, as yet another police detective, held zero appeal. So I turned down the *Cagney & Lacey* TV movie. Besides, Universal Studios still had exclusive rights to me. Loretta Swit was then cast as Cagney, opposite Tyne Daly's Lacey.

After the popularity of the TV movie, CBS offered Barney a series deal. Loretta Swit went back to *M*A*S*H*, under contract, and Barney again offered the role of Cagney to me for the series. I was still under contract to Universal and unavailable. No deal.

The contract system was being phased out, but my deal with the studio remained in place. They had retained me to costar in *House Calls*. Monique marched from her bungalow office to "the

Tower" at Universal Studios. She persuaded them to put me under a series contract instead of an exclusive deal. If *House Calls* should be canceled, my contract would end as well. I would be free. And that's what happened.

With no contract players left to shepherd, there was little reason for Monique James to stay with Universal. She chose to leave and walked away with a profitable pile of MCA/Universal shares and me as her only client.

Monique now became my personal manager. She had already bet her reputation on me. Now she was betting her future as well. It gave me a sense of security and the belief that with Monique I had a future in this business, too.

I was finally in a position where I could call my own shots, make significant income, and take on interesting roles, which, with Monique's help, is exactly what I hoped to do. I wanted to be in the movies.

Barney Rosenzweig wanted me to be in his TV series. After airing four episodes of the first season of *Cagney & Lacey*, CBS programming chief Harvey Shepherd told Barney that the show wasn't working, citing a lack of contrast between the two leads. Meg Foster would have to be replaced before they would consider giving the show another try.

Barney went to New York, where the networks were gathering to announce their fall seasons. As soon as the executives left the CBS planning meeting, Barney found out that *House Calls* had been canceled and that I was now free of obligations to Universal Studios. I was out of work for the first time in my career. Even before the West Coast had heard the news of the cancellation, Barney was on the phone with my agent, Ron Meyer, to make an offer.

Both Ronnie and Monique wanted me to meet with Barney to discuss the role of Cagney.

I admit that I was hard to convince. I really wanted a role that was mine to originally create. I just wasn't interested in playing Cagney.

Monique assured me that I didn't have to take the job but convinced me that the polite thing to do would be to show up to lunch and hear Barney out.

Show up we did. Monique and I went to Musso & Frank, Hollywood's oldest restaurant and my personal favorite hangout. (Starting at age five, I would go with Uncle Jack and sit at the counter for Musso's famous flannel cakes.)

Many entertainment deals have been brokered in the dark red leather booths at Musso's. When courting an actor or actress for a project, the network executives or producers usually trip all over themselves to make the actress feel fabulous. Then the actress, in turn, can demur modestly.

That's what I was expecting to happen when, for the first time, I met Barney Rosenzweig and Dick Rosenbloom, who was then the head of television production at Orion Pictures. Barbara Corday, by now Barney's wife, sat between the two men.

I took my place at the table, not wanting to be there, but thinking that the motivated Mr. Rosenzweig would kiss my ass big-time. I was ready to pretend that I was uncomfortably flattered and leave feeling terrific and not having to replace yet another actress in a shipwrecked show.

That is not how it went. He never kissed my ass. At all. Instead, he attempted to educate me on how hard this acting job would be for me. He wanted me to understand that the hours would be long and the schedule grueling. It could "get rough," he warned me. He wanted me to come on board with my "eyes wide open."

I was offended that he assumed I had no work ethic and was not familiar with long hours. I proceeded to explain that I had already been on four series, the lead on two, and that long hours and hard work were not strangers to me. Still, he persisted in explaining the sacrifices that would have to be made by me to play Christine Cagney.

It took great restraint for me not to shout, "Who do you think you're talking to?"

I stopped listening.

He stopped talking. He crossed his arms.

"What a jerk," I thought. I leaned back. I looked at my watch that I wasn't wearing. Was this over yet?

Dick Rosenbloom had been silent through this entire exchange. Seeing that it was now a standoff between two "children," he jumped in. He very nicely told me the things I expected to hear. He listed all the reasons I had been invited to the lunch and why I was the most desirable choice for the role and always had been. He cheered me up. I turned all of my attention to him and didn't make eye contact with Barney Rosenzweig again for the rest of the lunch.

It ended cordially, with the understanding that I would seriously consider the kind offer. We said our goodbyes.

Once we were in the parking lot, Monique once again "suggested" that I should consider the part.

My frustration grew. "You said all I had to do was have lunch with these people. I don't want to do another series! I want to be in the movies!"

Monique paused, then wisely attempted to defuse my anger.

"Well, of course. That's what we all want for you, Sweet Pea." (She was lying and I knew it.) "But in the interim, I think this might be an interesting role for you."

Not in the mood to give an inch, I stood resolute. "I don't want to do it. I don't like the guy with the beard."

"His name is Barney Rosenzweig."

"Whatever."

≡ • ≡

The film fairy godmother must have been hovering over that parking lot behind Musso & Frank, because, days later, I was invited to meet with the director of a new movie, a crime thriller called *The Star Chamber*, starring Michael Douglas. They were looking for an actress to play his wife, Emily.

I thought, "Here it is! My chance to break into the movies!"

I wanted to give it my best shot in every way possible.

I arrived at director Peter Hyams's office wearing a pale yellow silk dress with yards of material belted at the waist. I borrowed it from my wardrobe rack at Universal. I had given the designers my personal color chart—the results of a session I'd had with Suzanne Caygill, author of the 1980s phenomenon *Color: The Essence of You*—and they would buy my wardrobe items based on it.

The creamy yellow dress was working well, almost like a hypnotic suggestion. After two hours, he said, "Do you want the part?"

I responded, "Yes! But, don't you want me to read for you?"

He said, "No. I just want you to wear that dress in the film."

My God, I got a role in a movie! And with Michael Douglas, no less! I was the only woman in an all-male cast.

My longest scene in the movie was with Michael and me in bed together, postcoital. Both of us were to be bare-chested, me lying on top of him. The direction in the script read that the camera shot was to slowly pan up my naked back from the top of my buttocks to the back of my head and then, finally, to my face. Not even the wardrobe department could help me out with flattering colors when it was bare skin.

I worked out at the Y for three hours every day. If my complete back was going to have a close-up, I wanted to make sure it looked great!

It was the high heat of summer and the air-conditioning in the studio had to be turned off so the microphones didn't pick up the sound of it blowing. I had to lift my considerably large breasts onto Michael's bare chest before the director called, "Action!" I had a long monologue about how I was concerned that something bad was going to happen to him. The camera panned up my bare back and around to my face as I spoke. We had to do the scene many times for each of the camera angles.

Between takes, there would be an audible suction sound as I peeled my breasts off of Michael's chest, leaving behind a small pool of sweat on his skin. It was humiliating for me, but never because of Michael. He always averted his eyes until I was in place for the next take. He was a true gentleman. There was no spark of sexual energy between us at all. Nothing. I didn't know if I felt relief or disappointment.

Before it was over, Michael and I had one lunch together. I took the opportunity to ask his opinion about *Cagney & Lacey*. The first episode was supposed to start shooting right after we finished filming *The Star Chamber*.

"Michael, is it wise for me to do this TV show? I now have this feature with you. Is it a mistake to do another TV series?"

He asked me, "Do you remember a TV show called *The Streets of San Francisco?*"

I laughed. "Yes."

"Don't give up the TV show. I'll leave it at that."

Michael had given me good advice. *The Star Chamber* was no career changer. *Cagney & Lacey* would forever be my signature role.

⇒ Twenty-Two ⇐

Champagne and Chagrin

Tyne Daly is the most generous actress I've ever worked with, and I've shared the screen with many actors and actresses since 1972. I'm proud of the fact that we costarred in the first television drama that had two women as the lead characters. It came pretty close to not happening.

Tyne did not want to lose Meg Foster, who played Cagney for the first six episodes. They ate lunch together every day. She went to bat for Meg at CBS, even dangling the possibility of leaving herself. It was an honorable thing to do for a costar. But CBS wasn't in the business of giving out merit badges for loyalty; they wanted ratings. The numbers were showing that *Cagney & Lacey* was not working in its current form.

When I was considering joining the show, my agent, Ron Meyer, had the first six episodes sent to my house for me to watch. I wanted to see for myself what wasn't working for the viewers and for CBS. I put a bottle of J&B and a bucket of ice in the TV room and sat down to watch. It was clear after two episodes. The leads were too similar. Meg was playing Cagney too close to the way Tyne Daly was playing Lacey. There had to be more pronounced differences between them, other than the fact that one was a single career woman and the other was married with children.

I had already starred in four series, two in which my name had been billed above the title. The viewing audience was familiar with my face and name after having seen me week after week on *Switch* and *House Calls*. Tyne was a respected working actress with a number of movie roles and had been a notable guest star in dozens of TV series but had yet to star in one of her own.

Where an actor's name appears in the opening titles matters. It shows the importance of your place on the show and your status in the television industry. Even though our roles on the show were equal, I had already established my name in television.

Tyne saw it as her right to have top billing, and I couldn't blame her for it. She had already played the part in the successful TV movie, and for the first six episodes of the series her name appeared before Meg Foster's.

It all came down to Barney Rosenzweig. He was the executive producer, and the decision on the billing order was his, according to his contract with CBS. Wisely, he preferred to not play that card, even though he had been the one who decided that Tyne Daly would have top billing for those first six episodes with Meg. He didn't want to lose either Tyne or me. And he didn't want to resume filming the series with one of us being completely pissed. He was also trying to judiciously acknowledge and balance the requests and even the ultimatums of CBS executives, agents, managers, creative staff, and business partners. Not a task for the fainthearted.

He asked Tyne to give me a call from San Francisco, where the cast had assembled for the CBS presentation of the upcoming season to TV station owners from across the country. Everyone was there except for her costar. I had not yet agreed to play the part and didn't realize that there was a problem. I answered the phone, but I didn't recognize Tyne's voice.

In the six episodes I had watched, Tyne had used a strong grew-up-in-Boston-now-lives-in-Queens accent. She did it so believably, I expected actress Tyne Daly also spoke that way. When the phone rang, I wasn't sure if it was really Tyne or if it was a prank call. That didn't go over well with her. She told me that she had only made the call at Barney's request, which didn't go over well with me. Tyne called Barney and said that I had "frosted" her on the phone. I called Barney and reported that Tyne couldn't have been more "cold" to me. It seemed to be the end of the road.

But there was growing pressure from Barney, my agent, Tyne's agent, and the supporting cast, so Tyne was pressed to reconsider her position of not caring about the blonde actress of whom she "had never heard."

The day before my birthday, Memorial Day weekend 1982, I was at the Department of Motor Vehicles trying to renew my driver's license that would expire the next day. I decided to call Tyne. I wasn't sure what I would say. I only knew I had to call her. I went to the pay phone.

Luckily for me, she answered.

"Tyne, I'm standing at a pay phone in the middle of the DMV. I'm sorry for the noise, but my license is about to expire because tomorrow is my birthday. I'd like for us to talk, the two of us, with no one else around. Would you like to come to my house tomorrow?"

Kindly, she said sure.

She arrived with a bouquet of birthday balloons and a couple of bottles of champagne. I got out two glasses and we sat on my living room floor and proceeded to get smashed together. I liked her. Very much.

I told Tyne that I completely understood all the reasons she wanted to be billed first. She had already played the role twice. I said that unfortunately it would be a bad career move for me. To be billed in second position would be a step down.

She was very gracious, and we were both sad that it probably wouldn't work out. I wished her well. I truly meant it. We both thought that would be our first and only get-together.

Barney Rosenzweig wasn't about to allow his dream to be over. He came up with a billing idea. The compromise was that both of our names would appear on the screen at the same time, side by side. Each week the opening credits would alternate. One name would be on the left side of the screen, but slightly lower than the name on the right side of the screen. The next week we would flip. Our agents and Barney all agreed that it worked. Tyne and I put our feelings about billing into remission. It was on. I was to be the new Christine Cagney.

Before I had even read one word of a script or set foot on the set, I was shipped out by CBS to do a press junket for *Cagney & Lacey.*

Tyne and I were to do the Chicago–Atlanta tour. In both cities, the stars do every local TV show—morning, noon, and night—every newscast, radio show, and print interview that you can squeeze into a couple of days to promote the show and, in our case, introduce me as the new Cagney.

As it turns out, actress Betty White was on my flight from LA, heading to Chicago to promote a show, as well. While walking to our gate, we passed two nuns wearing full habits. One of them wore large gold hoop earrings, which protruded from the front of her wimple.

I pointed it out to Betty. Nuns never wore earrings! At least not during my Catholic-upbringing years.

"Can you believe that, Betty? Gold hoops!"

"You're right," Betty acknowledged. "Pearls would have been better."

Flawless timing. Eight decades of it.

I arrived at the downtown high-rise hotel in Chicago the same time as Tyne, who was traveling with her then husband, Georg Stanford Brown. As we checked in, I was given a room on the sixth floor. Tyne was given a room on the twenty-second floor with a good view. On the Universal Studios lot, it was always well known that the higher the floor, the higher the rank! I shared that information with Tyne and Georg. I told them, "I'm trying to not take it personally."

As I got off of the elevator on floor six, I said, "You'll be sorry when the fire breaks out."

They both laughed.

Later, Tyne and Georg met me at my room, on my lower floor, to all go out to dinner together.

My mother, Marjorie McCarthy, and my father, Dennis Gless, on their wedding day, June 26, 1937, under the arbor leading up to the pool at my grandparents' home in Hancock Park in Los Angeles. It all looked so promising. *Gless family archives*

My mother, my brother Michael, and my grandmother Marguerite McCarthy (Grimmy) holding me. (Already there was attitude.) It would be many years before my brother Aric was born. *Gless family archives*

My brother Michael (8) and me (5) racing the length of the Muirfield Road front porch, two years after we moved in. I was airborne, but Michael won. Damn.

Gless family archives

My grandfather, Hollywood's top entertainment attorney, Neil S. McCarthy *(left)*, with his best friend and client, the world-famous film director Cecil B. DeMille.

Gless family archives

My cousin Liz, my uncle Jack, and my most beloved aunt Hoonie would take me along on their family vacations to the Ojai Valley Inn every year. Lizzie and I thought we were quite fabulous in our cowgirl neck scarves.

Jack Baur personal collection

Life lost its luster, and I gained a tremendous amount of weight during my four years of boarding school at Santa Catalina School for Girls. My parents' divorce and being far away from home led to depression and obesity.

Sharon Gless personal collection

1961. I was the only debutante at the Las Madrinas Ball not presented by her father. My brother Michael did the honors. I was happy that night. I was forty pounds thinner. Here she is, folks! With my grandfather McCarthy and my cousin Rosemary.

Sharon Gless personal collection

1972. The missed cue that made my career. My fellow actors couldn't hold it together.

Courtesy of Candy Carstensen

On location in Colorado for the miniseries *Centennial* in 1978 with the very funny and fabulous Andy Griffith, aka "Dink Taylor," the good ole president of his own Sharon Gless Fan Club.

Sharon Gless personal collection

I fell hard for actor Jack Colvin. My father said he looked like a Kennedy, which wasn't a compliment from my very Republican dad.

Sharon Gless personal collection

Playing my favorite screen star, Carole Lombard, in *The Scarlett O'Hara War* (1980), with Edward Winter as Clark Gable. I read for the part three times. She was in my soul. *Sharon Gless personal collection*

Almost better than an Emmy award, this was the larger-than-life-size photo of me that hung in the Universal Studios executive commissary. It took me ten years to get up on that wall.

Sharon Gless personal collection

This is my favorite photo of Monique James, vice president of MCA and head of talent for Universal Studios, with her ever-present lit cigarette, a cup of coffee, and the *New York Times* spread out on the bed of her Manhattan hotel room. I owe most of my career to her. She was a force, never to be forgotten.

Sharon Gless personal collection

My best friend from birth, Judith Ann, and me. We were always in trouble. Always. I wouldn't have changed a moment. I miss her. *Sharon Gless personal collection*

If you want someone to make life seem picture-perfect, date your cinematographer. Hector Figueroa made me look beautiful on-screen as Christine Cagney and feel beautiful off-screen as his girl. He was a most amazing man. *Sharon Gless personal collection*

There were many expressions that would land on my face when I was drunk. This was one of my personal favorites. *Sharon Gless personal collection*

Making Tyne Daly laugh every day on the set of *Cagney & Lacey* was something I looked forward to for six years in a row. She is my all-time favorite acting partner.

Sharon Gless personal collection

On the streets of New York City, following a 3 a.m. outdoor scene being shot for *Cagney & Lacey*. Dancing with my dog. Only Nathan's would do.

Barney Rosenzweig personal collection

This is what happens when a TV police drama goes renegade. We look laughably nonthreatening. *(from bottom to top)* Sidney Clute, me, Tyne Daly, Marty Kove, Al Waxman, John Karlen, and Carl Lumbly. Missing is our desk sergeant, Harvey Atkin, and Dick O'Neill, Cagney's dad. What a cast! *Costumes, props, and photo courtesy of Marty Kove*

Between scenes with John Ritter for the TV movie *Letting Go* (with child actor Michael Fantini). You'd never guess that we were filming a drama. The man kept me laughing for six weeks. And, he introduced me to caviar. *Ken Faught*

This is my child. I didn't raise her. We raised one another. She is my niece, Bridget Kathleen Gless. I educated her with old motion pictures and metaphysics. She gave me the gift of her laughter. I am also her godmother. I'm sure her parents have forgiven me by now. This is my favorite photo of us. It is Bridget's twenty-first birthday party at Chasen's in Los Angeles. She is so happy (see empty champagne glass). My favorite parts of this photo are the pearls down her back and the fact that she hasn't a clue that the long-stemmed rose she is so proudly holding has broken off. Bridget is now a stunning, philanthropic woman who still puts that silly smile on my face.

Bridget Gless Keller personal collection

Celebrating my birthday in 1985 at L.A.'s then world-famous Chasen's restaurant, frequented by the most renowned actors and politicians of its era. Undaunted by this are: *(left to right)* Nancy Morgan (John Ritter's first wife), Robert Wagner, me, John Ritter, Barbara Corday (Barney's wife), talent agent Robert Walker with Monique James. Standing above: Barney Rosenzweig, Jill St. John, and Hector Figueroa. Hanging on the wall above us are photos of two of the world's greatest comics, Carol Burnett and Groucho Marx, Chasen regulars. *Barney Rosenzweig personal collection*

Robert Wagner gave my introduction speech in 1986 when I was presented with the Genii Award. In the world of leading men, he tops the list for me. I love him dearly, and he ain't hard to look at, either. *Sharon Gless personal collection*

May 1, 1991. My first wedding. Ever. It was a secret.

Sharon Gless personal collection

May 4, 1991. It was my second wedding of the week. This one was formal and in front of a crowd. Carole Smith, Barney's longtime assistant and my good friend, imparting a message from the groom. It was a disaster.

Sharon Gless personal collection

1992. I had just arrived in London to star in *Misery* in the West End, and was invited to do a presentation for the royals. I told Princess Diana how loved she was in America. The next day, the prime minister announced that she and Charles were separating. Also in line is my pal Barry Manilow.

Barney Rosenzweig personal collection

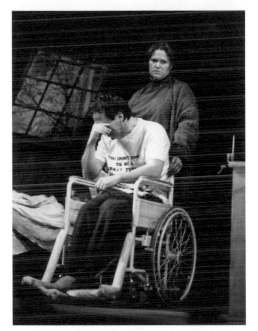

Costarring with the brilliant Bill Paterson in the original stage version of *Misery*. We performed at the Criterion Theater in the West End of London. I was not wearing any padding. At all.

Neil Libbert

The West End. The Aldwych Theatre 2011. What a high!

Peter Mackertich

Getting my star on the famous Hollywood Walk of Fame in March 1995.

Sharon Gless personal collection

Playing Debbie Novotny on *Queer as Folk* for five seasons. She was the sassy, saucy, and fully accepting mom that young gay people around the world wished they had.

L. Pief Weyman Queer As Folk © Showtime Networks Inc.

The wonderful cast of *Burn Notice*. Taken in a church after my "youngest son's funeral service." We were sad, having to say goodbye to him and assembled for a final photo. Then, Bruce Campbell (true to form) made some highly inappropriate comment and the moment was killed (you'll forgive the expression). *(left to right, front)* me, Jeffrey Donovan, Seth Peterson, and Gabrielle Anwar. *(back)* Bruce Campbell and Coby Bell.

Sharon Gless personal collection

Since costarring in *Queer as Folk*, I stand behind gay rights. This is my very best friend, Dawn Lafreeda, with me on the red carpet for a Human Rights Campaign benefit featuring Hillary Clinton. This is Dawn's favorite photo of us. Probably because my hand is in front of my face. *Courtesy of Lupita Corbeil*

I had been losing close friends. Barney suggested that I get younger ones. So I did. In my booth at my favorite hangout, Musso and Frank Grill, on Hollywood Blvd. are *(left to right)* Dawn Lafreeda (brilliant businesswoman), me (you know), Sandi Lifson (hotshot record promoter), and Vivienne Radkoff (wonderful screenwriter). A stellar cast. Musso's is recognized as making the finest martinis in Los Angeles. I can personally testify to that, as you can see by the two sitting in front of me. Those were the days, my friends! *Courtesy of Dawn Lafreeda*

When I got married, I inherited a fabulous family. I didn't raise these daughters, so we adore each other. Then, they gave me grandchildren. I did none of the work, but I get all of the rewards! Here we are in our favorite New York haunt, Serendipity. *(clockwise from left)* Alex Rosenzweig, Erika Handman, Hailey Laws, Barney Rosenzweig, Greer Glassman, Allyn Rosenzweig, Torrie Rosenzweig, and me. I'm having the best thing on the menu, a Sand Tart Sundae. Barney had flown all of us in to see *Hamilton*. *Barney Rosenzweig personal collection*

Tyne, Barney, and me, in a Manhattan restaurant. This is Barney's favorite photo of the three of us. Still holding on. *Sharon Gless personal collection*

When our elevator doors opened at the lobby level, I couldn't believe what was happening. As if I had conjured them, fire trucks with their lights flashing were parked in front of the hotel. Long, thick hoses lay across the lobby floor. There was a fire in the kitchen!

I looked at Tyne and said, "Don't fuck with me."

She burst out laughing. I knew we would get along.

When we returned to LA, it was time to start shooting the new season. I would be, once again, the new kid on the block. I was used to the feeling, but this time it came with the tremendous pressure of being the person who was coming on board to supposedly "fix" what had not worked with Tyne and Meg. CBS had made it quite clear that this would be the last chance for *Cagney & Lacey.*

The first script was sent to my house, and I read it through, hoping to get a handle on this character of Christine Cagney. Tyne called me at home. She suggested that the two of us read the script out loud together before anyone heard us at the table read the next morning. It was a great idea and a big relief for me.

Tyne arrived at my house with another chilled bottle of champagne, and we read the script five times, until we could feel the relationship between our characters start to solidify and we both felt comfortable.

The full cast and the writers were all present the next morning. I didn't know a soul. No one knew that Tyne and I had rehearsed it the night before.

When we finished, everyone in the room applauded, and executive producer Barney Rosenzweig stood up and said, "And that, ladies and gentlemen, is how it's done."

It took three seasons on the show for me to grasp how *Cagney & Lacey* was changing the national conversation about what was possible for a woman in the 1980s. Christine Cagney appeared before America's TV viewers with her own Manhattan loft apartment, a career as a police detective with a female work partner, dating men on her terms, with no intention of becoming someone's wife. *Cagney & Lacey* introduced mainstream America to issues that were important to women: financial independence, professional ambition, modern motherhood, women's health care, equality in marriage and the workplace, and mutual respect and justice for all, regardless of gender. The brilliance of the show was that Christine and Mary Beth were not activists, feminists, or even very politically vocal. They were not best friends. They were two women whose lives depended on one another.

What was true about the close relationship between Christine and Mary Beth would eventually become the case for Sharon Gless and Tyne Daly. Even though the press always seemed determined to paint the two of us as adversaries, that picture couldn't have been further from the truth.

If any reporters had stopped by the set at two in the morning, after any given fourteen- to seventeen-hour day of filming, they would have seen a production lot that was totally dark except for my trailer. If they knocked on my door, they would have found Tyne and me rehearsing our scenes for the next day, just like we'd done together before our very first table read.

We picked my trailer to rehearse because I kept the open bar. Long after the crew, writers, and supporting cast had gone home, we would rehearse until the lines felt natural and crucial, and often humorous. I was always looking for the laughs, especially in a drama. We were two actresses carrying the lead roles in a show that would live or die on our chemistry together.

I don't think actors alone can take credit for chemistry. It's either there, or it isn't. Barney Rosenzweig held the bigger vision of what the show could become. He brought on the best writers he could find, he gave us a brilliant supporting cast, he hired a variety of directors who kept it fresh on-screen, and he let Tyne and me build a relationship that viewers cared about through six years of *Cagney & Lacey*.

Twenty-Three

Best Intentions

You can count on New Yorkers. As a Californian, I had always heard that New Yorkers didn't give a shit about anybody but themselves. I was wrong. Stories of great heroism rise to be told from the streets of Manhattan. 9/11 eradicated any remaining stereotype that they're only out for number one.

Tyne and I had our own experience with the quick heroic response of New Yorkers in 1983. We were trying to film an addition to the main titles of *Cagney & Lacey* on the busy streets of Manhattan. The idea was to have a guy act as a purse snatcher, grab the handbag of an unsuspecting woman walking down a city sidewalk, coincidentally near Christine and Mary Beth. Of course, the two of us fly into action, chasing down the perp.

The actress playing the victim agreed to use her own purse. The young stuntman playing the purse snatcher was set and ready to go. The camera was placed down the block, on a production van, to capture Tyne and me in pursuit. It was meant to happen all in five to ten seconds at the most.

On the first take, the stuntman grabbed the purse and started to run. Two or three New Yorkers, unaware that we were filming, took off after him, grabbed back the purse, and knocked the stunt guy to the sidewalk. Ow! The would-be heroes were completely baffled when Tyne and I ran up behind them, shouting, "No, no, no! We're filming a scene." We tried a few more takes, but every time at least one "real" New Yorker would witness the purse snatching and tackle the beleaguered stuntman. The poor "thief" was exhausted from trying to escape the valiant New Yorkers, and the actress's purse was a tattered mess by the time she got it back. We never got the shot.

We ended up having to stage a chase through a subway car, with paid "extras" in all the seats. Then, Mary Beth and Christine emerge from the subway stairs with a perpetrator in handcuffs. A staged flasher standing at the top of the stairs opens his raincoat in front of us. Cagney gives him a once-over like, "What were you hoping to do with *that*?" No real New Yorkers jumped in to save us from a "flasher." I guess that's just par for the course in a Manhattan workday.

Nothing to see here, folks. Keep it moving.

Twenty-Four

Are You Irish?

My very first episode on *Cagney & Lacey* revolved around a police colleague being killed in the line of duty. Mary Beth ushers Christine into the women's restroom in the precinct, the only place they can speak privately, to break the news.

I had decided that Chris Cagney, being of Irish descent and the daughter of a former cop, would be outraged by the tragedy. That's how I played it, full-out emotion. I tore up the bathroom. I kicked in the side of the trash can, threw some props, and slammed my hand against the stall door. My nose ran.

Jane Fonda had a runny nose in *They Shoot Horses, Don't They?* She won an Oscar for that movie. I was out to prove that I was much more than a comedic blonde and could hold my own in an hour-long drama. I was an actress with acting chops, even if it meant crushing my foot by kicking the trash can. My "Ow, ow, ow," was not in the script. Tyne stood motionless, watching my reaction until I was finished.

Later that day, I said to Tyne, "You know, I think that was a bit much. Too over the top." Then I confessed my true motivation for my titanic performance. "I wanted you to think I was a good dramatic actress."

Tyne, without a moment of vacillation, said, "I thought you were great. I just stood there and let you do it."

She sure did. It was a brilliant choice, a powerful performance on her part, without moving a muscle.

Any embarrassment I felt wasn't compounded by Tyne. It was a relatively painless (notwithstanding my throbbing toes) but permanent lesson: character before ego. Always. Well, almost always.

I really liked Chris Cagney. She was selfish, which made her fun to play. She had a big dream: to be the first female police commissioner. She had a loft in SoHo. She loved the city, playing cards with the guys, and sleeping around. She planned to stay single. It worked for her. Chris Cagney wasn't beyond taking credit, cheating a bit, or turning the tables to climb the ladder. She was insistent and petulant, sarcastic and unapologetic. She was volatile and unexpectedly vulnerable. She was flawed. She loved to drink. A lot. She did everything full-out.

There wasn't another female character on national TV that was anything like Christine Cagney. I started to feel at home in her skin.

What I didn't feel comfortable with was the perception of Cagney by the two most influential women on the show: Barbara Corday and April Smith.

Barbara Corday and her writing partner Barbara Avedon had written the pilot TV movie for *Cagney & Lacey*. Barbara Corday was also Barney Rosenzweig's wife. They were a Hollywood power couple.

April Smith was the head writer for the series. Both women were talented. But talent doesn't equate with being correct in all circumstances. I've always been willing to listen to those in authority. I don't always agree.

I had accommodated their choice of hairstyle for Cagney, long in length with flipped-out layers, a popular look that year. The look was too Farrah Fawcett knockoff for my taste, but what the fuck, I can collaborate. Even the mid-calf petticoat skirts and formfitting tops could be tolerated, though it all seemed so wrong for this ambitious woman who wanted to be taken seriously by the guys in the precinct.

One evening, as filming wrapped for the day, Barbara Corday

and April Smith invited me to join them at Ruth's Chris Steak House in Beverly Hills for drinks. Tyne always went directly home to be with her two teenage daughters, Alisabeth and Kathryne, if we weren't rehearsing, so I didn't think anything about being asked to join them without her. We sat in a private booth.

After the obligatory niceties, the two of them teamed up and spilled the real reason for our happy-hour conclave. They were both in agreement that I was not playing Christine the "right way"—that is, not to their specific expectations. They explained that it was their third opportunity to get it right, after Loretta Swit and Meg Foster had played Cagney.

I set my drink down. "Am I being fired?"

Barbara continued on, not addressing my question, explaining how she had envisioned Cagney to be a very "cool" character, a woman who "kept a lid on it." April nodded in agreement.

"You're playing her with such anger, Sharon," Barbara concluded. She thought that Cagney should keep all emotion close to her bulletproof vest.

Whatever the outcome, I decided to speak up for myself.

"Excuse me, Barbara, are you Irish?"

With a quizzical look she shook her head.

"And you, April. Irish?"

Another no.

"Well, I am. I'm playing an Irish cop who is the daughter of an Irish cop. I don't know any Irish people who are cool and calm. We get pissed. We show it. But thanks for telling me."

I'm pretty sure we didn't stay for dinner after that.

I wasn't certain what my future on the show would be. I thought I was being fired. I called Monique James from a nearby pay phone and told her of the complaint.

She assured me that she would get to the bottom of it.

Monique placed a phone call to Barney, who was caught off guard that Barbara and April thought they could give one of his leading ladies their personal negative feedback on the side. He told Monique that I was doing great and to completely ignore their "helpful" insights. He very much appreciated that I had taken the character to a new place, one that completely contrasted with what Meg or Loretta had done before. He said he liked that I could siphon out a laugh through a look or an inflection on the written line.

This was not the first time I had heard complaints about my performance, nor the first time I'd been close to being fired. There was a lot riding on my being able to deliver this character. If I couldn't create a fresh and interesting contrast and chemistry between Cagney and Lacey, the show would be finished. I knew that as long as Barney liked what he saw on the screen, I was safe.

But the first television drama starring two women was ripe for criticism. An article in *TV Guide* referred to Tyne and Meg as "dykes." After I joined the show, one male critic wrote, "The blonde is from the Copacabana School of Acting." I was devastated.

One day, I asked Tyne, "Who's the enemy here?"

She told me, "Fear."

I understood that she meant fear of two strong women in leading roles. Our show was cracking the glass ceiling of TV dramas in the early '80s.

Weeks later, an actor from *House Calls*, Mark L. Taylor, came to the set to visit me. He handed me a rolled-up piece of paper, tied with a ribbon. I opened it. It was a graduation certificate with my name on it from the "Copacabana School of Acting." I framed it and it hung in my trailer for six years.

= • =

I began to assert myself in other ways. I defied my female producers. Cagney was not a woman who was going to risk having her three-inch boot heel get caught in a ruffled hemline while chasing a perp down a stairwell. I talked to the wardrobe department. I wanted jeans or trousers, sneakers or flat-heeled boots, and oversize sweaters and men's sport coats. I wore a better bra to subdue my breasts. I didn't want people to tune in to the show to see the blonde cop with the leotard top and a huge rack bouncing down an alley in a Laura Ashley skirt.

I had my long hair cut off. My hairdresser, Carolyn Elias, put it in pin curls, and I sat under a dryer every single morning. It ended up looking like naturally curly hair—soft, but with an attitude.

Cagney came to life. She talked tough and wore pink.

Tyne was also very open to me playing Christine Cagney in a whole new way. I think it gave her some fun new energy to play off of as Mary Beth.

It took a lot of guts on my part, but one day, early on, I asked Tyne for a favor. Would she mind if Cagney could burst through the door first, guns drawn? Cagney wasn't a careful person. She would jump in, even if doing so was risky.

Tyne was reluctant and confided to me that she didn't like it for obvious reasons. But she generously agreed, saying, "If you feel that is right for your character, then fine." I loved her so deeply at that moment. She knew that I wasn't trying to take attention from Lacey. I was trying to establish Cagney. I appreciated that she could see it that way. It made sense to me. Mary Beth had a husband and two sons at home to think about. She was a wonderful cop but had more to lose because she was a wife and a mother. She wasn't willing to take risks without consideration. Cagney wouldn't take the time to assess the risk. Often she was wrong. Okay by me!

We began to work out the details and eccentricities of our characters. Mary Beth drank her coffee from a ceramic mug. Christine always chose a Styrofoam cup. She didn't want the permanence. She wanted to be able to pick up and go at a moment's notice. Before we went out, Mary Beth would wash and dry her cup. Cagney would toss hers in the trash.

A ceramic cup made by a fan with "Cagney" inscribed on it was sent to the show for me. Christine would never use it for coffee; however, it sat on her desk, holding pencils. It now sits on my desk at home, holding my pens.

At one point in the first season, Barney told Tyne and me, "You are now the custodians of your characters. You must keep track of their experiences, and if something feels untrue, speak up."

We did speak up. Often. Barney began to call it the "cuckoo-clock syndrome." I would go to his office to say that a line or an idea didn't work for Cagney. He would call in a writer and have it fixed. As soon as I would leave, Tyne would appear with a grievance about what business in the script was not right for Mary Beth.

As actresses, we knew that we were nothing without great dialogue from our writers. But as the custodians of our characters, we felt obligated to make them as real as possible.

After Barney would watch the footage of what had been filmed that day, I would stop him on his way back to his office.

"How were the dailies?"

If he said, "Fine," I'd be infuriated.

"Fine?! Fine isn't good enough!"

Barney had a smart litmus test for creating a really special show.

He would say to Tyne and me, "Give me one good minute a day—one minute where you make me laugh or cry or surprise me. Do that, and we will have seven good minutes per picture, more than enough to make a terrific episode."

He liked to be taken off guard or delighted by an extra layer of something.

If it took seven days to shoot an episode, that would mean that seven minutes of each hour-long show (actually forty-six minutes, due to commercials) would stand out in a powerful way.

I had my own litmus test for a good performance—my nipples. My favorite scenes were always the ones of Christine and Mary Beth talking through issues in the jane—the women's bathroom at the precinct—where the two could let down and be themselves. The scenes were often raw and were loaded with energy, humor, and rage.

I always knew when we hit it. My nipples would get hard.

"That was good! Feel this!" Putting her hands on my breasts, I told Tyne, "If we're really clicking, I get chills and my nipples go up."

After that, whenever she and I would do one of those scenes together, she'd jokingly ask, "How'd we do?" and touch the front of my shirt to find out.

The hours at the studio and on set were grueling, and exhaustion was predictable. However, the reviews were very favorable. We felt good about what we had done.

Close to the end of season one, Barney sent Tyne and me to Washington, DC, to make an appearance at an event for NOW (the National Organization for Women). Tyne and I would appear in person, and the audience would get a sneak preview of the latest episode of *Cagney & Lacey.* That was the plan. Unfortunately, the episode was delayed in editing and couldn't be shown. As a replacement, Barney put together a collection of our best scenes from the twenty-two episodes, in chronological order.

Tyne and I sat in the back of the dark room watching Barney's presentation. By the end of the film we both had our hands over our eyes and were sharing the same thought: "Holy shit! What happened to us?"

The succession of clips was like observing two fresh flowers open up and blossom fully and then begin to curl up at the edges, wilt, and die. We had both aged at least twenty-two years in our first season together on *Cagney & Lacey.* Even if we didn't feel the exhaustion of the high-pressure shooting schedule, it definitely showed on our faces on film. What Barney had warned me about at Musso & Frank was reality.

We wrapped up our first season, expecting to see each other in three months for the next one. It was the summer of 1983. Tyne went home to her daughters and husband, and I went off to shoot a TV movie, *Hobson's Choice*, with Richard Thomas in New Orleans. I asked Monique to keep me busy with work, because I would feel restless after even one week off.

When I got back to my hotel room one evening after shooting on location in the French Quarter, there was a message from

Barney. A short time later he called again. I could tell by the sound of his hello that this wouldn't be a happy phone call.

Cagney & Lacey had been canceled. Over the phone, we got drunk together, he in a Manhattan bar phone booth at Frankie & Johnnie's, and me in the Big Easy. Nothing about this news was easy.

⟩ Twenty-Five ⟨

Raised from the Dead

More than two decades before Twitter was born, before the Internet was available to all, social media brought back *Cagney & Lacey*. It wasn't viral. It was a nationwide campaign through snail mail, thought up by Barney Rosenzweig.

After CBS had canceled our show, a messenger showed up at Barney's front door with three huge boxes full of thousands of letters from viewers. They were letters of protest from fans who were outraged that their new favorite show had been canceled. Barney called both Tyne and me to see if we had also received similar letters. We had. Lots of them. He sent a driver to each of our houses to get our mail.

Barney decided to send a letter to each viewer who had taken the time to write. But, in a moment of genius, he added a last paragraph.

It is my perspective that no one in power at CBS will even read your letter. My suggestion, should you still be agitated about this matter, is to write to your local newspaper as well as the *Los Angeles Times* and the *New York Times*, on the theory that network executives may not read their mail, but they do read their newspapers.

With the help of an assistant, thousands of envelopes were hand addressed and the letter was sent out. It was impossible to guess what, if anything, would be the result, but within weeks, both the *Los Angeles Times* and the *New York Times* published articles about the unprecedented volumes of mail they had received regarding the cancellation of *Cagney & Lacey.* Huge bags of letters were shipped to CBS from newspapers around the country. The viewers had come through for us. They loved the show as much as we loved making it. Barney's grassroots idea was growing.

A month later the Academy of Television Arts & Sciences announced four Emmy nominations for CBS's canceled show, *Cagney & Lacey.* Tyne and I were both nominated for best actress in a drama; there was one for best dramatic series and one more for sound mixing.

USA Today came out with a large photo of Tyne and me as Cagney and Lacey and the headline "CBS Canceled Cops Number One." *Good Morning America* flew us to New York for a segment on their show about our Emmy nominations, despite the cancellation. Other media outlets taunted CBS executives for prematurely canceling what was apparently a hit show. We were the only CBS show to feature two female leads; the summertime ratings had been great, rocketing to number one; and we had Emmy nominations and millions of dedicated viewers who were pissed off.

CBS's programming chief, Harvey Shepherd, the very man who had decided on the cancellation six months prior, was now receiving an avalanche of mail. He called a meeting with Barney. The end result was history making.

Raised from the dead by viewer demand, *Cagney & Lacey* was granted another season. Thanks to the inconvenience of the cancellation, Tyne and I became the highest-paid actresses on TV at that time. We never thought to ask what the men made.

The fans got it done by typewriter or pen and paper and a twenty-cent postage stamp.

Power to the people! And a very personal thanks to all the fans of the show who wrote in, from me.

Twenty-Six

"Frank-ly" the Best

Nathan's Famous hot dogs, Coney Island. They've been around for 105 years. They are New York history. They are part of my history as an actress.

Every year I would work out with great discipline during our hiatus from *Cagney & Lacey*. I would return for the beginning of the shooting schedule thinner and toned. Even my face would look different. I had a special trainer come to the house for an hour every day to help me do something called "face pumps," a ridiculous-looking set of exercises to keep your face firm and a bit more youthful.

In the world of television drama, very few scenes are shot in sequence. It takes hours for the cameras, sound system, and lights to be set up in a location and for the cast and crew to rehearse their shots. To be cost- and time-effective, all the scenes that happen in the precinct would be filmed in one group. All of Mary Beth and Harvey's scenes at home would be shot together. Every indoor shot may look like a New York police station or a brownstone apartment in Queens, but it actually all took place in the Lacy Street Studios in downtown Los Angeles.

We'd start each new season by flying to New York City to film exterior scenes that would be peppered throughout the year's episodes. This was cost-effective for production but held some challenges for Tyne and me. Many of the scripts weren't written in full yet. Tyne and I had to depend on the writers to tell us exactly why we were dodging between cars on Broadway. Expediency? Chasing a perp? What?

It would be midsummer when we shot all of these outdoor scenes in New York, often hot and humid, even at night. I would ask wardrobe for lightweight clothing. The problem was, months later, in Los Angeles, when we had to match the New York scenes, I could not fit into my already established costume. By the next season, the wardrobe department had figured out a way to camouflage my predictable weight gain. From then on, when filming our New York scenes, they put us in coats, hats, scarves, and boots. Let me repeat, it was August. In New York. In the heat. In 93 percent humidity.

One muggy Manhattan evening, I was on location for our very first shot of the season. It took place on a street corner, with me dressed in a winter coat and knee-high leather boots. The scene called for me to chomp on a hot dog as I walked down the street.

I asked the prop master, "Where did this hot dog come from?"

He pointed down the block. "The cart on the corner."

It obviously wasn't a Nathan's hot dog. I had heard stories about what gets packed in hot dog skins of the cheaper variety. Chicken trimmings and ground-up kidneys weren't going in my stomach if I could help it. At least Nathan's dogs were all beef. I decided to complain.

I said, "I can't eat this. I need a healthier hot dog."

Jesus. I had some nerve. I went so far as to tell the director that I wouldn't be filming the scene until I had a Nathan's-quality hot dog.

The executive producer was summoned to the set. Looking at his watch, Barney asked me, "What seems to be the problem?"

I said, "I have no clue what's in this hot dog. I want a Nathan's."

He nodded and then said, "There is no Nathan's nearby. It's late at night and we need to shoot the scene. Eat the hot dog."

This wasn't like him. He always made everything happen for us, whatever Tyne or I wanted.

In TV production, time is money. Barney wasn't going to hold up shooting for an hour while someone ran to Coney Island for a frankfurter. So, risking my very health for "the cause," I swallowed my pride and the "spare parts" dog from the corner cart. It wasn't that bad, and there were no subsequent side effects.

To make amends and get me to smile again, Barney somehow got the Nathan's mascot, a giant frank in a bun, to stop by the set hours later. In the middle of the night, in front of the cameras, I danced with a big stuffed wiener in Midtown.

By the way, in 1983 there were no "healthy" hot dogs. Not even Nathan's ever made *that* claim.

⇒ • ⇐

One exceptional late-summer afternoon in New York, I decided to take my hair and makeup people and their spouses out to lunch before we started shooting more scenes that evening. We went to the famous River Café, which is at the base of the Brooklyn Bridge, overlooking the East River with stunning views of the Manhattan skyline.

I looked across the restaurant and there, sitting alone at a corner table, was Barney Rosenzweig. I smiled at him. He lifted his glass to me.

"Will you excuse me for a moment?" I asked my guests.

I walked over to Barney's corner table. "Why are you alone? Please come and join us."

He turned down my invite. "No, thank you. I'm enjoying the view from here."

He said it in a professional manner. But I could tell from his smile that I was the view to which he referred, not the Brooklyn Bridge.

He was drinking a martini from a small stemmed cocktail glass and offered me a sip.

I could see when I handed back the glass that my one "sip" drained half of his drink. I knew he would only have one cocktail, as we were all still working that day.

I went back to my guests, called the waiter over, and said, "Would you please send Mr. Rosenzweig another martini."

My love affair with martinis began that day and ended decades later with my final drink made with perfect Hendrick's gin.

I've never had to swear off Nathan's hot dogs, though. No one ever complained to me the next day about my unsuitable behavior and memory loss after having a Nathan's.

There's a Nathan's hot dog stand in the American Airlines terminal in Miami. I will leave for the airport forty-five minutes early to be certain I have time to get one. However, it will never be as delicious as a very dry Hendrick's martini.

Twenty-Seven

Blondes Never Win

One of our guest actresses on *Cagney & Lacey* played a woman whose husband goes missing. Christine and Mary Beth go to her home to interview her about the disappearance. Every take, this actress sobbed, with tears running down her face. Take after take.

"God, you're good," I said to her after the fifth take from yet another angle.

Tyne agreed. "Very impressive."

The guest actress turned to Tyne and said, "All I have to do is look into your big, soft brown eyes and I go to pieces. I lose it."

There I stood, with my metaphoric finger up my nose.

The guest actress noticed and suddenly blurted out to me, "Oh! And I love your little tiny laughing blue eyes!"

I looked over at Tyne. Her "big, soft brown eyes" were brimming with suppressed laughter.

For the next six seasons, anytime there was occasion for it, Tyne would tell me, "Did I tell you today that I love your little tiny laughing blue eyes?"

Okay, I have deep-set eyes. The *Cagney & Lacey* cinematographer, Hector Figueroa, was well aware of it. He was a sensitive man who would have never called them "tiny." He arranged to have a special light put above the lens of the camera to better bring out my diminutive peepers. He named it "the Glessy."

Hector always made Tyne and me look better than we actually

did. That's what really good cinematographers do. And he was really good. He took care of me on the set. Then he took care of me off the set.

Hector was a gorgeous Latino man. When he would step close to me to meter the light near my face, I could feel my stomach do a little flip-flop. His dark eyes would be looking at the meter and mine would be looking at him.

One late evening we were filming at a downtown Los Angeles location, near some railroad tracks. I asked Hector if we could speak.

He followed me to a patch of dry grass between two rail cars, where we could talk without being overheard.

"I have a crush on you," I told him, with no lead-in.

"I have a crush on you, too," he replied, with no wrap-up. He smiled.

"Okay. Well, I just wanted you to know that."

We both turned around and walked back to join the others.

The next week, he started to visit me in the makeup trailer in the mornings. Cinematographers don't usually hang out in makeup trailers. The rest of the cast and crew didn't even have to speculate about what was going on. It was pretty obvious.

Hector was the sweetest, most thoughtful man I had ever known. And because he was single, we could actually be seen in restaurants together and he would accompany me to various events.

He would rub my feet at the end of a long day of shooting. I would drop off to sleep within minutes. The next morning, I would wake up to find that all my makeup from the previous day of filming had been wiped off with cold cream. Hector wasn't about to let my skin go to shit by my sleeping in full makeup for six hours. He had to film that face. When I finished showering in the morning, he would be standing there with a fresh hot towel that he would have warmed in the clothes dryer.

During every hiatus, Hector and I would take a trip to the South Pacific. He would carefully pack my suitcase, making sure I had everything I would need. During our vacation, Hector would find out what I was wearing to dinner and would have a lei made to match my dress. Come on! Who does that?

He was charming and funny and adapted to every situation. He would even be with me through the weekends with my best pals, Jay Michelis and Judith Ann. Hector would be the only sober attendee. They dubbed him "the Saint."

He *was* a saint. I felt so secure and loved with Hector. We were never apart.

By my second season on the show, I also felt more secure in my role as Cagney. I started to get more opinionated about the *Cagney & Lacey* scripts, especially when Tyne and I would rehearse in my trailer at the end of the day.

One night, after we attempted to read through an awkward scene twice, I said, "This is crap."

Tyne said, "It *is* crap. You go in and tell Barney tomorrow morning. It's your turn. I did it last time."

The next day, I knocked on our executive producer's door, walked in, and threw the script down on his desk. "This is crap."

Barney responded, "Crap? This is the best material that *you've* ever had in your entire career!"

I was so offended. "Fuck you."

He countered, "Fuck *me*? Fuck you!"

I think it went better for Tyne.

The last thing he heard was his door slamming as I walked out.

Carole Smith, Barney's longtime assistant, would just look up from her desk with a bored expression that simply read, "They're at it again." She knew it would all blow over.

Barney knew the scripts were sometimes overwritten, but he would let it stand until after the table reads. Tyne's and my chemistry was such that once we fully understood the intention of the written line, the words might no longer be needed. It could be done through physical or facial expressions alone. Barney counted on that. He would often say that the best writing on *Cagney & Lacey* was done with an eraser.

Barney was the one who stayed in the edit bay all night, deciding which take to use, which of us would have the close-up, what footage best told the story. He knew our every nuance. He felt a great responsibility for the way females were represented in the show. Neither of us had been asked to show cleavage, wear a teddy, or act girly. (Well, once in a while, Cagney would shamelessly use her femininity to get something she wanted. I thought those scenes were funny.) We were two professional women.

Our days on the set continued to be really long. A short day of filming would be fourteen hours, but we were often there for sixteen or seventeen.

Maybe because I was dating one of their own, one Friday night I took it upon myself to be the crew's advocate and defender. We were shooting in downtown Los Angeles. It was a warm September night at 11 p.m., and we were filming a scene on top of an office building for our holiday episode. It had already been a twelve-hour day and we were supposed to move back to the studio to shoot the inside scenes at the precinct until two in the morning. We were all exhausted.

I thought I'd be a hero for our hardworking crew. I decided that we should wrap for the day and do the precinct scenes on Monday morning. How's that for a blazing ego?

We had all gathered in Tyne's trailer. Someone had phoned Barney, who was attending a black-tie event, to let him know that I had suggested we change the schedule.

Tyne told me, "I've got your back. I'm right here." Marty Kove and the other actors gave their full support as well.

About fifteen minutes later, Barney arrived. He was wearing a tux and dress shoes. He stepped up inside Tyne's trailer. The crew lingered outside the door, waiting to hear whether they were done for the day.

As was Barney's pattern when production came to a standstill, he looked at his watch and then asked, "What seems to be the problem?"

I boldly stepped forward. "The crew is exhausted. We have all worked a long day. I think we should do the precinct scenes on Monday morning."

Very calmly Barney replied, "Well, that's not going to happen."

I was tired and furious and, without thinking, responded by calling Barney a fucking shit.

I can't even tell you how fast that trailer emptied out.

Then Barney said, "We are now going to move production back to the studio and continue working. You're not going home. We have three more hours of work to finish."

I huffed, "Fine!"

I grabbed my script and belongings, got into the car, and headed back to Lacy Street Studios.

Once back at the precinct, we did a rehearsal for the scene we were about to shoot. Barney came to the set too, but I was still angry. I wouldn't look at or talk to him.

After the rehearsal, I walked back to my trailer for a wardrobe change, still pissed.

A minute later, I heard the sound of Barney's patent leather dress shoes approaching my trailer. I wasn't about to talk to him, so I went into my tiny bathroom at the back of the trailer and slammed the door shut. I heard him enter the trailer and close the door behind him. I stayed in the bathroom for five long minutes, but I could tell Barney wasn't going to leave. I felt like such a fool, trapped in the can. I threw open the bathroom door and stormed right past him.

With my nose in the air and in my haughtiest voice, I said, "This is ridiculous!"

I slammed the trailer door behind me and went back to the set. Barney didn't try to talk to me again that evening. Tyne and I finished the night's work.

On Monday, Barney called me into his office before we started filming.

He said, "Sit down. I want to talk to you."

I was still carrying around a pile of indignation, but I flopped into a chair. "What?"

He said, "The next time you want something, you come to me, privately, and ask. I will probably grant your request. But if you call me out in front of a crew, you will never win. Ever. The crew wants to know who is the boss, and they don't want it to be you."

He wasn't speaking with anger. He was telling me how it was going to be.

He was right, of course.

I said, "Okay. Got it. I'm sorry."

His reaction to the incident only increased my respect for him.

$$= \cdot =$$

Every year of the series, Tyne and I were both nominated for the Emmy for lead actress in a drama series. Tyne Daly won three Emmys in a row, in 1983, 1984, and 1985. Despite the personal sting, I was always gracious. I love Tyne Daly. And if I couldn't be the winner, I was happy for it to be my costar.

Every year, the day before the Emmys, Barney would stop by my trailer, hoping to spare me upcoming disappointment.

"You're not going to win, you know. The blonde never wins."

I told him, "Oh, I'll win. You'll see."

He would then say, "Blondes never win in the dramatic category. Blondes only win in comedy."

His theory proved true for the first three seasons. In our fourth year, I felt like I had a strong chance. I had already won the Golden Globe award for lead actress in a drama that year. I had a feeling that the Emmy might be mine that season, too.

Michael J. Fox was presenting for my category, along with Ali MacGraw. Someone told me that during the earlier rehearsal, Michael had ad-libbed, announcing me as the winner. That night, when he opened the actual envelope, he said, "Oh, this is so great. Sharon Gless!"

I was stunned but thrilled when he called my name.

The first thing I said when I reached the podium to accept my Emmy was, "I'd like to thank my partner, Tyne Daly, who I am sure is the most relieved woman sitting in this room tonight."

Later that night, Hector and I went to the post-Emmys party at Barney's home in Hancock Park. He and Barbara held a big catered event each year we were nominated. It was a great party. As we were getting ready to leave, I called out to Barney from across the room.

"See, Barney? I told you a blonde *can* win an Emmy for drama."

He walked toward me as I held my first Emmy award aloft.

"No, they can't," he sweetly said. "Not unless they are you."

If there were an exact moment to pinpoint when my feelings for Barney shifted, it would be in those silent seconds that followed. I didn't know it that evening, but I'd never really see Barney in the same way again.

I knew he was married. I knew he was my boss. It had been well established from the beginning that Barney, Tyne, and I were a team, equal parts of a strong triangle.

I clasped my Emmy award tighter, hoping to quell my skipping heartbeat, and walked out his front door.

Before I got in the car, I decided on a course of action. I would pretend my feelings for him didn't exist. I was an actress, after all . . . and, at last, an Emmy award–winning one at that!

Twenty-Eight

Buckle Up!

The New York State Police had a complaint about *Cagney & Lacey*. They called the studio to file a request. It was 1985 and wearing seat belts in cars had become a mandatory law. The officers reported that when they stopped someone for speeding and noticed they were not wearing a seat belt, the driver would often say, "Cagney and Lacey don't wear seat belts!"

It was true. We always jumped in our unmarked squad car and drove off. The real-life police officers wanted us to buckle up on TV.

It wasn't an unreasonable request from the police, and it wasn't one that CBS would refuse. However, I thought Christine Cagney would. She would feel that she should be exempt from this oppressive requirement. She wouldn't want the extra hassle of unbuckling a seat belt. What if she had to jump out of the car quickly?

Mary Beth would get behind the driver's wheel and say, "Seat belt, Christine."

I wouldn't comply, until she said, "I'm not moving until you buckle up."

I wasn't fully aware of the momentum and the impact that our show was beginning to have on a national scale, that millions of people were tuning in and felt moved, inspired, or intrigued by the lives of Chris Cagney and Mary Beth Lacey.

I didn't track the growing numbers of viewers or our overnight ratings, or read the bags of fan letters that arrived at the studio. I didn't have time. I accepted that things were going well as long as we were given a go-ahead to shoot the next episode. I was happy.

Monique was pleased when Pat Kingsley, the famous publicist who represented Sally Field, Doris Day, Natalie Wood, Jack Nicholson, and Robert Redford, noticed the increasing popularity of *Cagney & Lacey* and asked to take me on as a client. Pat usually only handled movie stars.

Pat traveled with me for a big weeklong publicity tour. Tyne took one half of the country, and I took the other. Early on in the week, Pat and I were in Washington, DC. We spent the day going from show to show, doing interviews on every local TV and radio station, riding between venues in a stretch limo.

Upon returning late in the day to the high-rise hotel in which we were staying, I opened my car door and was getting out when I heard Pat yell to me, "Run!"

I had no idea what was happening. I ran full speed alongside her up some concrete steps, across a slate-floored courtyard, into the glass-fronted hotel and through the lobby. She guided me into an open elevator and pushed the "close doors" button. Looking out from the elevator, I saw about fifty people chasing after me, shouting my name, trying to catch the elevator. I was petrified. My mouth dropped open. I pressed against the back of the elevator as the doors closed just in time.

Pat was instantly cool and collected, straightening her jacket, like it was just another workday for her.

We were reaching our floor when I finally broke the silence.

"Am I famous?"

Pat started to laugh as we exited the elevator.

She said, "Oh, please God. May you never change."

Soon after, I was invited to be on a popular BBC talk show hosted by Terry Wogan in London. When I was introduced and appeared from the side of the stage, the place erupted in screams. I flew off the ground! I'd had no idea the studio audience in this large theater-style space was packed with avid *Cagney & Lacey* fans.

As soon as I got offstage, I decided to get some fresh air. I went out the large wooden service door into the alley. The door closed behind me and, too late, I realized it automatically locked.

I wasn't concerned until I turned to see hundreds of fans sealing off the end of the alley, people who had been unable to get seats at the show. They now noticed me, and more fans were joining them until they filled in all the empty space. I turned around and pounded my fist on the barn door.

"Let me in! I'm locked out! It's Sharon Gless."

I heard a crewmember say, "Sure you are," from the other side of the door, some scoffing laughter, and the sound of feet moving away.

I tried hammering on the door. "Please! Let me in. It's Sharon. I'm locked out."

Even backstage security ignored my desperation. "Yeah, right!"

The only way back into the theater was through the alley and to the front door, which was blocked by countless fans. I was afraid they might start to rush toward me at any moment, but for now they stood in stunned silence, wondering, as was I, what to do.

I cleared my throat and tried to steady my shaky voice.

"Please, everyone. I'm very uncomfortable. I'm trapped back here. I was locked out. I need to get to the front door and back inside."

The fans kindly parted, clearing a path for me to walk through. No one grabbed at me. Halfway through the crowd I was praying, "Please God, keep me safe."

It's no wonder my mother would often tell me, "Sharon, stop being so dramatic!" I don't know what I thought would really happen, but the *Cagney & Lacey* fans in England were both gracious and sympathetic to my situation. They have continued to cheer me on for decades and still hold a place in my grateful heart.

A couple of months later I was invited to a private party at Chasen's restaurant in Beverly Hills. Many of the big-name executives and producers from the television industry were there. Monique had encouraged me to go to the party and mingle, but my natural shyness had me standing inside of the door, by myself, hesitating to go in.

Suddenly, Steven Bochco, the *Hill Street Blues* creator, appeared beside me at the entrance. I had not seen him in years, since we were both under contract at Universal, I as a young actress and he as a fledgling writer. We'd been promising kids together. He had since gone on to major success and Emmy wins for creating and writing *Hill Street Blues*, and I had gone on to *Cagney & Lacey*.

He gave me a quick hug.

"What brings you here tonight?"

I couldn't answer, "My manager told me to come." So I said, "Oh, I just came to hang out with all the swells."

Steven turned me toward the crowded room. "Do you recognize anyone here?"

I was a bit embarrassed, but I answered truthfully, "No."

He leaned in to whisper to me, "Me either. I think that means that you and I are the swells now. Come on. Let's go enjoy it."

I left twenty minutes later.

Twenty-Nine

"Blow"-ing My Cover

I would never drink or do drugs on the job. God knows I did some damage on my own time, but never on the set. For me, timing is everything. Acting is like music; the note that is put on a specific word affects the emotion of an entire line of dialogue. I had to be completely sober to perform. Booze and drugs did only one thing: throw my timing off.

We worked with a large variety of directors on *Cagney & Lacey*. It kept the show fresh. I was closest to Ray Danton. Ray had been an actor. He was philosophical and intellectual but appreciated everything done well artistically. On the set, between lighting setups, we sang show tunes together. The musical *Sweeney Todd* was a Broadway smash at that time. I taught Ray the words to one of Sondheim's best. ("Nothing's gonna harm you, not while I'm around. Demons are prowling everywhere, nowadays. I'll send them howling. I don't care. I've got ways.") The night I won my first Emmy, I arrived home late to a telegram left on my front door. It was from Ray Danton. "Demons are prowling everywhere," he wrote. "But not tonight. Love, Ray."

He had the highest expectations while directing, which got him invited back often, to the dismay of the crew. They had T-shirts printed up with the words "I Survived Midnight Danton."

He wouldn't let actors get away with anything less than truly authentic performances, and he was direct when he thought any of us were sliding into a "bag of tricks" or our "typical" routines.

Once, he took me to the side and whispered, "I think we've seen that before. Don't you?"

I burst out laughing. I knew he was right.

With Ray, there was always a second chance to make a performance better. I loved him for it.

= • =

I was fortunate enough to be given a couple of second chances on *Cagney & Lacey*. One of those, I didn't deserve.

Tyne and I always put the show first. We would come in early and stay late. She would show up every morning looking fabulous, dressed in a sexy outfit and heels, and then transform herself into Mary Beth Lacey, with her skirts and practical blouses. Tyne would say that she felt that Mary Beth was a person who never had time to look at the back of her head in a mirror. She thought she should have electric-roller dents in her hair.

I was the complete opposite. I'd roll out of bed, take a shower, and wash my hair. I'd head into work with wet hair, wearing nothing but a terry-cloth robe and penny loafers. Because of our long hours, the show supplied both Tyne and me with cars and drivers to take us to and from the studio each day.

The hair and makeup people would be waiting to turn my tired and perhaps hungover face into that of Chris Cagney.

One morning, my makeup man said, "Who was that in here yesterday? Your younger sister?"

No matter how rough I looked, my team could piece my face back together. I hope they liked a good challenge, because I often gave them one. By the time they finished, I'd look in the mirror and think, "Wow. I look pretty." My dresser would have my wardrobe laid out for me, from foundation to footwear. I didn't have to think about any of it.

After we were done for the day, and Tyne and I had rehearsed in my trailer, I would strip back down to only my robe and penny loafers, often go out for sushi, have a scotch or two, spill a little soy sauce on my script, go home, and fall into bed at about one in the morning. I'd always make it back for the next day of work, starting at 5 a.m.

Work never impeded me from indulging in a couple of drinks at the end of the day or enjoying a little cocaine on my days off. It was the '80s. Cocaine was rampant in the entertainment industry.

John Belushi died of an overdose, Richard Pryor set himself on fire, automaker John DeLorean was arrested for smuggling, and Boston Celtics top draft pick Len Bias collapsed and died, all connected to cocaine in the 1980s. But that's the problem with the drug. It makes you believe that you are the most indestructible and fascinating superhuman to ever tread the earth. You have no clue what a crashing bore you really are.

Barney was intolerant of any drugs and fired a whole camera crew when he found out that they were using cocaine on the set. Ironically and unbeknownst to Barney, I would buy my cocaine from one of those crewmen.

One evening, Tyne and I met up for our regular nightly read-through in my trailer. While we were rehearsing, we had a couple of drinks. Everyone had left, except for our two drivers, who were waiting to take us home.

We should have gone home this particular night, but I decided to break out the cocaine. I take complete responsibility for my being so . . . well . . . irresponsible. We both partook. I knew better, but I've never been one for self-denial. We became undefeatable, indefatigable, and impressively insightful about our interpretations of the lines. Then it all wore off at 4 a.m. I had lost track of time. I was due back for my call time in one hour. I panicked. I knew I couldn't be on camera anytime soon.

"Tyne, I can't go to work. I'm in really bad shape."

Tyne seemed almost fine. She would have probably pushed through and done her work for the day, but I couldn't.

I devised a plan.

I called Monique James. I needed her help. I could tell her just about anything, but using cocaine was not going to be cool with her at all, especially not at the studio.

"Miss James . . . I've been up all night with Tyne. We were running lines in my trailer. We had drinks. I'm loaded. I can't work today."

Monique said, "Okay. Thank you for calling me. I'll call Barney now and tell him you got the flu during the night."

I knew by my calling in "sick" that Barney would rearrange the schedule to not lose time. Tyne would be expected to film her scenes with Harvey and the two kids. She didn't seem happy about that.

Tyne said, "I don't want to work if you aren't."

I came up with part B to my plan, so that Tyne could go home, too.

I looked at the call sheet for the coming day of filming.

"You're in luck," I said. "John Karlen is on a 'hold' and not a 'will notify.'"

The difference is that a "will notify" actor may be called in to work, so he must stay near his home phone. With a "hold," the actor isn't obligated to stay home at all.

"Call Johnny," I told Tyne. "Tell him to go to the racetrack for the day."

There were no cell phones in those days, so John Karlen would be unreachable. If he wasn't available, then Tyne would be free as well.

It was a pretty foolproof plan. And it worked.

I went home and to bed. Shutting down production for a day cost roughly seventy to eighty thousand dollars in the mid-'80s. To recover the costs through insurance, the studio had to send an insurance doctor to the ill actor's home to confirm that she or he was really too sick to work. It was almost a joke in Hollywood.

They phoned the industry physician that actors referred to as Dr. FeelGood, because he was so predictable about reporting "the flu" for celebrities with hangovers or drug withdrawals. He came in, gently poked my stomach twice, and filed the report that I was suffering influenza. Thank God he didn't look up my nose. He probably knew better.

Even though this "cover my ass" plan had worked in total, I was choking on my own guilt. I had cost the studio and Barney a lot of money and angst.

The next day, my shame was so consuming that I went into Barney's office before we started filming for the day. I told him the whole story, except I didn't mention that it was cocaine. (If he had fired a whole camera crew over cocaine, I thought he might look up Loretta Swit to play Cagney again, since *M*A*S*H* had recently gone off the air.) I stuck with the story I'd told Monique about being drunk. I confessed that I'd thought up the whole scheme for getting the day off.

Barney listened, leaned back in his chair, and said, "Thank you for telling me."

I felt so chagrined. "I will pay you back," I said. "I will write you a check for all of it."

"I may have you do that." Barney nodded. "I'll get back to you."

He was not smiling.

I hadn't expected him to say that. If I wrote a check to cover it, then the insurance company and studio would also know the truth about my "sick day." I didn't know how I would live that down.

Barney let me sweat it out all day long. I couldn't believe that I might have to pay five figures and live through the humiliation of being the one who was too drunk to work. I suffered in silence. Tyne had no idea I had told Barney anything at all. I was alone in my panic.

At the very end of the day, Barney called me into his office and closed the door.

"You're off the hook. It's all been handled . . . this time. But if you ever do something like that again, you will be writing me a check."

Check.

Big check.

Got it.

≡ Thirty ≡

We've Got Issues

Mary Beth Lacey has a lumpectomy and the stress of a breast cancer scare.

Christine Cagney grapples with her moral conviction regarding abortion when she has a possible unplanned pregnancy.

The detectives have to decide if a little girl is the victim of sexual abuse.

Cagney conceals a heroic illegal immigrant from the FBI to keep him from being deported without his wife and children.

Lacey provides her high school–age son with a condom for his prom night.

The show covered it all: date rape, female abduction, teenage sex, women's health issues, alcoholism, and domestic violence.

For the first time on national TV, topics that were of concern to women were the subject matter of a prime-time television drama with two female leads. They were detectives. They took action on issues. The language was definitive and strong.

Mary Beth could go to work and her husband could cook dinner for the kids. Christine could date, sleep around, and never consider marriage. They could aspire to job titles only held by men in the past. This was a dramatic departure from TV dramas of the time, in which women were most often relegated to playing supportive wives, nurses, receptionists, waitresses, or victims of crime themselves.

Cagney & Lacey also had numerous female writers and directors, many more than any other one-hour drama show in the 1980s. And the fans loved it. Twenty to thirty million viewers watched *Cagney & Lacey* every week.

At one point, on a hiatus between seasons, I was in Toronto doing a made-for-TV movie, *Letting Go*, with the wonderful comic actor John Ritter. In the movie, his wife had died in a plane crash. He was raising his young son alone and trying to overcome depression.

I played his new love interest, a teacher who was struggling to be free of a bad relationship. We met in group therapy. Though the circumstances were serious and sad, there were plenty of comic moments between John and me.

John was the most thoughtful and funny man, both on and off the set. He could make me laugh all day long. His dad was the famous cowboy actor-singer Tex Ritter, his mother the Western actress Dorothy Fay. He was a verifiable Hollywood kid, but had none of the entitlement or snobby quality of being from a famous family.

His mother told me that when John was five, they lived on a ranch in the San Fernando Valley. John's favorite animal was the rooster that would crow at sunrise every morning. One day, the rooster suddenly died. Dorothy sat John down and explained to her young son that the rooster had become very sick and had to go to rooster heaven. John took in the news and then sadly asked, "But Mama, who will bring the dawn?"

John died unexpectedly at age fifty-four. A few days before he passed away, he asked if I would play opposite him in a stage play he wanted to do. I would have loved working with him again.

Once you knew John, you couldn't imagine not knowing him. I still can't believe he's gone. Who will bring the dawn, indeed?

During my second week of the five-week shooting schedule for *Letting Go*, I got a phone call from Barney with the news that Tyne Daly was pregnant. I was asked to return to LA immediately. They needed to start production on a number of scripts before Tyne's belly would begin to show. It was going to cost no less than a cool million dollars to bring back the cast and crew and have production up and running six weeks before scheduled.

I understood the dilemma, but I wouldn't abandon John Ritter and our movie before it was done.

I called Monique to tell her the news.

I was contractually supposed to be given three full months off from *Cagney & Lacey.* That would have been plenty of time to film a TV movie and then take a two-week break before returning to work on *Cagney & Lacey.* Not this time.

I came back to LA the day after filming wrapped and went immediately into costume fittings and script readings. We had to shoot six months' worth of my scenes with Tyne in about six weeks. Eventually, it was written into the season that Mary Beth was pregnant. It was emotionally loaded and realistic. Tyne had two teenage daughters; her oldest was already seventeen. Mary Beth had two teenage sons. Art would reflect real life.

Tyne had asked to not film the scene in which Mary Beth Lacey delivers her "show" baby until after she had given birth to her real-life infant. After a short maternity leave, Tyne returned to the show with her new baby girl, Alyxandra, in tow. She was given a pregnancy belly to wear, constructed from foam rubber. Tyne had them make a different one, insisting that a pregnant woman's belly moves and is heavy. They redesigned it at her suggestion, using birdseed in place of foam.

One of my favorite scenes to shoot was Mary Beth calling on Christine to get her to the hospital when she had gone into early labor. Chris, in her yellow Corvette convertible, frantically drives Mary Beth across New York's Fifty-Ninth Street Bridge until traffic gridlock brings them to a standstill. Then her car breaks down. Production had actually rented half of the bridge for the day.

Considering it was a full-day shoot, the nanny would bring baby Alyxandra to Tyne to be nursed in the convertible, in the middle of the Fifty-Ninth Street Bridge, and production would pause for twenty minutes.

Unlike on *House Calls*, where Lynn Redgrave was fired for wanting to nurse her baby at work, our producer and crew made accommodations for our newest "family" member, building a nursery for "Xanny" next to the precinct set. And the show went on.

≡ • ≡

I won my first Emmy for an episode ("The Gimp") about crimes targeting disabled people in wheelchairs. Actor James Stacy, who had lost an arm and one leg in an actual motorcycle accident, plays a disability advocate who is assisting Cagney in the investigation. Though the connection is initially combative, Cagney finds herself attracted to him. In one scene, it becomes obvious that they are about to become sexually involved, as he unbuttons the top of her blouse. He did it with great skill. I guess if you practice, only one hand is needed. His physical disabilities become only a background to his magnetic charm. Cagney is smitten. It shook the foundation of traditional romance. It was compelling storytelling. And, I thought, very sexy.

I never wanted Cagney to be a victim of an outside force that she couldn't handle. I wanted any pain she faced to come from her own choices. Addressing any negative truth about herself was not her greatest skill.

Right before we broke for hiatus, the writers met to discuss the direction of the lead characters for the upcoming season. What would be the "arc" of the story line for *Cagney & Lacey*, for the women together, and each alone? Christine and Mary Beth were now each fully ensconced in midlife. How had four years as partners on the NYPD changed them? Would they be more defined and refined by their successes or bothered by a haunting "what if" scenario? Would there be a shift in their personal relationships, a misfortune, a boost or a blow to their self-esteem?

Earlier in the month, an interviewer had said to me, "It's so obvious that Christine is the adult child of an alcoholic. Everything she does, from her lack of commitment to anyone, to her impulsivity, to stuffing her feelings down, is a trait. Anger is her root emotion, not to mention the fact that she is an alcoholic herself."

I took the observation to Barney. Though neither of us had ever thought of Cagney as an alcoholic, there was no doubt that she was a drinker.

It was never written into the script, but some mornings, for the sake of humor, I would ask Tyne to have two aspirin ready for me in her open palm when I walked by her desk. Lacey would know that Cagney was often suffering the aftereffects of drinking the night before. I would play the hangover headache by dropping into my desk chair and pressing my thumb into the corner of one eye.

Barney asked me if I'd be willing to explore the idea fully.

I was.

He reminded me that I had never wanted Cagney to be portrayed or played as a victim.

I said I knew I hadn't. But this was different and I was willing to look at it.

Soon after, Barney went before the show's writers.

"Let me give you the last line of dialogue from the last scene of the last episode of the forthcoming season," he began.

He set the scene for the listening staff.

"We are in a tight two-shot of our stars, and they are seated. We don't know where they are. Finally, Cagney stands and says, 'My name is Christine, and I'm an alcoholic.'"

The writers stopped taking notes and looked up at Barney.

He continued, "A wide shot then reveals they're at an AA meeting. The end."

The staff applauded. This was fresh stuff. No lead on a TV drama had ever dealt with this disease.

"Now," he said, "your job is to backtrack over the twenty-one episodes that precede this and figure out a way to get us to that moment."

Cagney, the heroine, was about to have her own day of reckoning and would fall from her professional pedestal because of her personal life.

Sharon, the actress, would fall in love with her married executive producer and keep it on the down-low for professional reasons.

It seems we both had issues. Art imitates life, bliss and mess and all. How's that for a cliffhanger?

Thirty-One

We Had Issues

London was calling. It was the fiftieth anniversary of the BBC. *Cagney & Lacey* was one of the hottest TV shows on the air in England. The Brits were besotted with the New York female cops. Tyne and I received invitations to appear at the Theatre Royal Drury Lane for their anniversary celebration performance. We were the only Americans invited to appear onstage that evening.

The biggest British celebrities would be there. The press would most certainly be there in huge numbers. Paul McCartney was on the bill to perform.

Her Majesty, the queen mother, would be attending. She would be greeting each performer individually after the show.

I tried to focus on the honor of it all, but I was in a head-spinning trance from the passionate and unrestrained affair I was having with my executive producer, Barney Rosenzweig. Love really must be blind, because before the show, Paul McCartney asked me for my autograph, and I didn't recognize him. Unimaginable, yet true. I didn't even ask him for his autograph in return. Jesus.

Our affair didn't start in London.

Months earlier, I had been chosen for the Genii Award from the American Women in Radio & Television in 1986. It was a great honor. Robert Wagner and the executive producer of *Turnabout*, Sam Denoff, both spoke for me. They also asked Barney to give some introductory remarks about my work before I was presented with the award. He chose to not speak. Instead, he edited together a compilation film of the highlights of scenes from my career. The flow of countless images of me across the screen was musically supported by the Joe Cocker recording of "You Are So Beautiful." In the dark room, Barney reached over and held my hand under the table and then whispered, "I wish the lights would never come up."

My heart went into free fall.

Our intense mutual attraction surged higher with each passing day after that, until one night Barney and I had spontaneous sex in my trailer on the studio lot. It was a completely reckless thing to do.

The next morning, before we started work for the day, Barney stopped by my trailer. I was still on an emotional high from the previous night.

"Any regrets?" I asked, confident his answer would be the same as mine. I was smiling.

The grin left my face when he answered, "Yes."

"This was a mistake," he said. "I'm married. I'll never be with you for any important occasions, your birthday, or any holidays."

He continued on with a litany of reasons why this affair would never work.

"I can't even call you whenever I want," he said.

The stakes were monumentally high in both his personal and professional life. Everything he had worked so hard to build could be destroyed if anyone found out about us.

We both decided that our trailer tryst would be a onetime lapse in judgment. It was a bad idea to ever let anything happen between us again. For a while, we held to our word.

Then London called. Tyne's then husband, Georg Stanford Brown, would be traveling with her. Barney's wife, Barbara, was by this time president of TV production for Columbia Studios and was too busy to make the trip. And so it was the four of us. We had first-class seats and a long transatlantic flight from LA to London. Barney and I sat one row ahead of Tyne and Georg. They slept. We did not.

I was given a beautiful suite at the Ritz hotel, with tall French windows and billowy, diaphanous curtains. A canopy of silk hung over the bed. The trip had been planned so that we had a full day to rest up before appearing in a professional capacity at any event. Twenty-four unscheduled hours broke our will, and soon Barney came up the back stairwell of the hotel to my suite. A winter thunderstorm blew into the city, and as the rain pelted the windows, Barney and I made love. When we rested, we would find a reason to have an argument. We had many issues with no resolution. It was infuriating. The makeup sex was great.

I don't think we ate or slept at all before it was time to be presented to the queen mother. I was worried that Tyne might sense that something had gone on between Barney and me, but she didn't. I felt like a stranger to myself. I would never have intentionally hurt her. Luckily, she was with Georg, and the excitement of the royal event provided plenty of distraction.

The night before we flew back to the US, the four of us decided to see a new musical that had opened only days earlier in London's West End. It was *The Phantom of the Opera*. Barney and I had spent our final day of the trip, still in the hotel room, making love and then arguing, making love and arguing again. He isn't one to pad any of his opinions, and at some point he said something that cut me to the quick. He left to get ready for the theater, and I spent the next hour in tears. In our shared limo, on the way to the theater, we chatted with Tyne and Georg but didn't engage with each other at all, not even making eye contact.

Four tickets had been set aside for us, but not together. Tyne and Georg took the pair of seats toward the back of the theater, leaving Barney and me in the very front row. I stayed silent. I was still so hurt. Fifteen minutes into the first act, I found myself crying again. I couldn't believe how much the story line of the musical reflected my current reality. The heroine, ironically named Christine, must choose between this otherworldly and compelling figure of mystery or return to the safe arms of her loyal beau. The parallel aspects of *Phantom* seemed to be affecting Barney as well. We were in a dream that could so easily become a nightmare, but neither of us was willing to wake up to reality yet.

During the intermission, I went to the ladies' room. I had dressed for the show in a red suede suit with a gorgeous long skirt and knee-high boots. My eyes were shiny from crying.

When I came out of the restroom, Barney was there with a cocktail for me. He whispered in the sexiest, saddest voice, "I want to fuck you right here. Right now."

Other people may not understand this, but in that moment, it was the perfect thing to say to me.

Once we landed in Los Angeles, Hector and I had plans to immediately catch a flight to Monterey to spend Thanksgiving with my mother in Carmel.

Barney got into his waiting limo. Barbara had come to pick him up. She had run into the terminal to get something Barney had left behind on the plane. The darkened window in the rear passenger seat was rolled up. I knocked on the glass to say goodbye. Barney opened the window, and I could see that there were tears on his face.

That's the moment I knew it was more than a weeklong affair that would only become a secretive memory. He was in love with me.

⇒ • ⇐

I continued dating Hector, but my thoughts were always on Barney. Hector and I had been together for five years. I loved him very much, but I knew it would never be the same.

"You have to love him enough to let him go," my therapist advised me.

She was right. Hector deserved a lot better than a woman who was in love with someone else, even though I knew my relationship with the very-married Barney couldn't go anywhere.

One morning, as Hector left to go to work, I told him that I had met someone else. I didn't say who it was. I was crying.

As he walked out the door, he turned to me and said, "I'm a good man."

That weekend, I decided to drive to Carmel. I was devastated by what I had done to Hector. I needed the comfort of my mom, and to get out of LA.

My doorbell rang. It was Barney. He had heard that I had broken it off with Hector and had come by to check on me. He wanted to see if I needed anything before I left on my trip.

"I'm not okay." I began to sob. "I miss Hector, and I can't pack my fucking suitcase."

Barney looked at my various piles of clothes, hats, and shoes, and said, "Would you like me to show you how to pack?"

I thought it was such a loving offer.

I choked out a tearful, "Yes, please."

I sat on the couch, wiping the tears from my eyes.

Barney packed the suitcase beautifully, smoothing out all the clothes and fitting my shoes perfectly into the sides.

Then he asked gently, "There. Did you see how I did that?"

I nodded, now smiling, and said, "Yes. Thank you."

He said, "Good."

Then, with one swift move, he picked up the suitcase, flipped it over at waist level, and dumped everything out onto the floor.

I sat in complete shock.

He said to me, "Cute and helpless isn't sexy anymore, Sharon."

I had no argument. Could I defend my being an insipid little crybaby? I was embarrassed to the core. But my face wasn't red with humiliation; it was flushed with attraction.

Barney wasn't going to enable my childishness. He expected more of me. He was very strong. He sat on the couch and watched as I picked up each piece of clothing and put it back in the suitcase. It was sexy as hell. I knew I would be treading into dangerous territory with this married man. I was familiar with the trail, but had no idea of the destination.

Thirty-Two

Any Room You're In

We were obsessed. We were oblivious. We drank more than the occasional martini. We made love in obscure hotel rooms set up by Barney's assistant, Carole Smith. At his request, she would bring us each a key so we didn't have to stop in the hotel lobby to check in. She was the only other person walking the earth who knew what was going on. I'm sure she would have preferred it to be otherwise.

At least once a week, reality would crash in. One or the other of us would become engulfed with regret, fear, or guilt. One of us would break it off, Barney most often. He had more reasons to be concerned about the total lack of rationality in having a secret affair with one of his leading actresses.

As Barney would explain, "I created a show that is focused on women's rights, feminism, and gender equality in the workplace. Now, here I am, fucking the blonde!"

He continued to lament, "I've become the biggest cliché in show business."

There were only three major networks to watch during prime-time hours and a total of forty-eight scripted shows in 1986. *Cagney & Lacey* had earned its place as one of them. We had millions of viewers. I was a recognizable celebrity wherever I went. Barney had a current wife, an ex-wife, and three grown daughters. Our secret affair could become a public and personal mess at any moment. It was already an emotional mess for me.

I was shocked by how long I was able to keep my affair with Barney a secret from Tyne. When we were working, my complete attention went to her and to our scenes together. She and I were fully occupied with one another. Off the set, our lives went in separate directions. We were like the characters we played—not really friends, but partners. Still, leaving Tyne in the dark about the affair with Barney was a source of great sorrow and regret for me.

Monique and I always spoke on the phone multiple times each day. I rarely made any decisions without her, from the style of my next haircut to picking out a new car, and now even that was changing. Barney was occupying more of my time and many of my thoughts, but I couldn't tell her about it.

Monique and Barney had a rocky relationship from the start. He wasn't accustomed to heeding the requests of a manager, especially one who insisted that a copy of the dailies be sent to her home at the end of every workday so she could view them and give me—and occasionally Barney—notes.

One afternoon, Monique and I were having lunch. Finishing her lobster bisque, she set down her spoon, dabbed her mouth with her napkin, and asked me bluntly, "Are you having an affair with Barney Rosenzweig?"

I feigned being appalled. "No! Why would you ask me that? God, no!"

Monique's response was silence. She lit a cigarette and adjusted her glasses. She stopped looking at me.

Five seconds later, I caved. "Okay, I just lied to you. I am having an affair."

I didn't know what she would say. I was hoping for some motherly advice.

Instead she blew out a stream of smoke and said, "Well, I'll say this. You have finally met your match."

She was right. Barney was my match. I was in love with him. When Barney would ask me where I wanted to go, I would answer, "Any room you're in."

⇒ • ⇐

One workday at Lacy Street Studios, Barney called me into his office. He handed me a script for a two-part episode called "Turn, Turn, Turn" that would deal directly with Christine Cagney's drinking problem. For four seasons, she had always been characterized as the free and single social drinker type.

Now, the heroine was about to fall from grace.

I took it home and read it. I knocked on Barney's office door the next morning.

"It's brilliant," I said. "Who are you going to get to play it?"

I had deep reservations that I could pull off this devastating material. Alcoholics were always only used for laughs on TV series, like Otis on *The Andy Griffith Show*, and in the 1980s we had Norm in *Cheers*. But there had never been a lead character, the hero, in a TV series so flawed with an addiction. Would it work? I didn't want the viewers to hate Cagney. But the story had to be told.

Barney and the writers decided that there would have to be a dramatic impetus that pushed Cagney's drinking off the rails. Her father, Charlie, played by Dick O'Neill, was everything to her. He was a retired Irish cop who was tough. He was also an alcoholic. Cagney finds him dead on the floor of his apartment. He had gotten drunk, fallen, hit his head, and bled to death.

In "Turn, Turn, Turn, Part Two," Cagney arrives home already very drunk after being out in the bars with her gay neighbor. Her boyfriend shows up for a late dinner, which she has totally forgotten. To add insult to injury, she has missed Mary Beth's promotion party for making detective second grade. Cagney is on a forty-eight-hour bender.

Cagney had to become progressively more and more wasted from scene to scene in this episode. She goes from drinking from a glass to drinking straight from the bottle to eating frozen cheesecake from the box to sitting on the floor with her head on the couch, because lying down would give her the "whirlies." I requested that the writers put that piece of blocking in the script. From personal experience I knew that lying down flat while drunk produces a feeling that the room is spinning

Cagney was deep in grief over her dad, lost in the loneliness of having no family nearby, and she had shattered her own professional image after showing up drunk at the precinct earlier. She was in crushing pain. Alcohol was her medication.

Shooting in sequence was important to me, and Barney agreed to do that, despite the extra time it took. I knew what I had done in the previous scene and where I still had to go.

≡ • ≡

In the parallel universe of my real life and my affair with Barney, I had no idea where to go or what to do about my feelings. I found myself on the verge of tears all the time. Barney was not in a good mental state about it all either.

At last he decided to permanently break it off with me and remain with Barbara. He had successful shows, Golden Globes and Emmy awards. He drove luxury cars, lived in a beautiful home with a pool and a tennis court. Barbara had always rallied him emotionally and cheered on his career. Why would he blow that up?

I understood. I didn't even cry.

At that time in my life, I wore a quartz crystal necklace of gem quality that had an emerald attached to it. Emerald is my birthstone. It was on a long gold chain and the crystal lay right at heart level. I slept nude, but would never take that necklace off. I woke up the morning after Barney's decision to end it with me, and my crystal had cracked from the inside. The outside remained flawless.

That evening was the screening of the two-part episode of "Turn, Turn, Turn" at the Fine Arts Theatre in Beverly Hills for press, CBS executives, and any invited friends. Not only was I reluctant to see Barney, I've never been an actress who wants to watch herself on-screen. I become too self-critical. I feel that once I have finished the work, and the producer signs off on it, then it is done. Now I would be watching myself with 799 people sitting around me.

For the screening, Barney sat to my left and my best friend Judith Ann to my right, on an aisle near the back. Every seat was filled. The two-part episode played like a ninety-minute film. By the time it got to the scenes with Cagney, alone in her loft, shattered and wasted, the whole audience would applaud after every scene. I have to admit, I lost my own self-conscious critical view and was swept into the story. The place erupted into applause at the end, with the audience rising in a standing ovation.

Barney moved me to the aisle, whispering, "Stand here. Let people come to congratulate you."

I wasn't prepared for the lineup of press waiting to shake my hand and speak to me. I was overwhelmed.

═ • ═

I won my second Emmy award for the episode "Turn, Turn, Turn, Part Two."

The mail that arrived at the studio after the episode had aired proved the impact the subject matter had on the audience. Daughters asked their fathers to watch the show as a way to have a conversation about how much their parents drank. Parents watched with their teenagers before having frank discussions about the consequences of drinking. Wives wrote about their husbands; husbands wrote about their wives—the letters poured in to the show.

It was good to know that we were touching so many people. However, my own life was still somewhat of a mess; my personal life was one big "whirlie" spinning out of control.

Though we were no longer together, Barney decided that he was going to confess the affair to his wife, move out of his house, and then tell Tyne about the two of us. There was plenty of evidence that it was all about to break in the news anyway. One of the tabloids had tracked down my father, who was in palliative care, dying of kidney failure at age seventy-four. They pretended to be a friend of mine and had the nurse put the phone up to my father's ear.

"Did you know that your daughter is having an affair with a married man?"

My father didn't respond, but the tabloids had enough second-hand information to run stories, especially after the *Hollywood Reporter* gossip column printed, "What blonde star is having an affair with her married executive producer?"

After that, it was all over the place. The gossip columnists and the tabloids let me have it big-time, surmising that I had single-handedly destroyed the great marriage of a very popular and powerful television industry couple. My publicist, Pat Kingsley, was called in to do damage control.

As the press lambasted me, I tucked my chin down against the storm. I couldn't and wouldn't defend myself.

I was a fractured mess. And I was alone. Barney had decided that he loved producing more than he loved me. I couldn't blame him.

I only wanted one thing: to escape.

Thirty-Three

Five of Twelve

I walked in shitfaced. The front desk receptionist did a huge double take.

"I know. I know," I said. "I bought my own act."

Other people had shown up drunk for rehab, I'm sure. That wasn't the reason for her reaction. She recognized Christine Cagney. *Cagney & Lacey* had just wrapped. And now here I was, checking into Hazelden Addiction Treatment Center. But I wasn't doing so in character as Chris Cagney.

Sharon Gless was checking in to go through the real deal. I was here in Center City, Minnesota, for what I thought would be one month to "get sober." It wasn't my idea.

My agent, Ronnie Meyer, gave me an ultimatum when he took me out to dinner one evening. I didn't see it coming.

"I know why you asked me to dinner," I said, hanging my head a bit. "It's because I'm getting fat. I'll work on it."

Ronnie shook his head. "That is not the reason. I asked you to dinner because I think you're an alcoholic."

I was sitting at a table with four empty martini glasses in front of me. Ronnie probably told the waiter to not clear any empty glasses from the table so he could have physical evidence to back up his claim. Still, I was stunned.

Looking around to see if anyone had heard, I whispered, "How can you say that to me? Don't do this! Everyone is staring at me!"

He said, "Let them stare. I may lose you as a client. I may even lose you as a friend. But I don't want to lose you!"

I sat there, embarrassed and unsure of how to respond.

He didn't wait for a response.

He asked, "When do you wrap up the season on *Cagney & Lacey*?"

"April eleventh."

"If you're not in Betty Ford on April twelfth, I'm doing an intervention on you."

Now I had something to say. I no longer tried to keep my voice quiet.

"What in the fuck is wrong with you? Stop this!"

We hadn't ordered dinner yet. I wasn't about to sit through another hour with my extremely rude friend. I had him drive me back home. He walked me to my front door. I did not invite him inside.

"I don't want to talk to you ever again!" Those were my exact words.

He didn't need to talk to me. He had already talked to Monique. And to Barney, the man who I thought was dramatically tilting the rotation of my happy world. We were shooting the final two episodes of the show. It was not convenient, but Ronnie asked Barney to rearrange the work schedule so I could go to an appointment with Elizabeth Taylor's doctor at St. John's Hospital in Santa Monica. Reluctantly, I kept the appointment he had made.

I thought, "Oh, what the hell. It's Elizabeth fucking Taylor's doctor! He will certainly see that I'm not an alcoholic!"

"I know your work well," the doctor said. "I thought you were a recovering alcoholic when I watched the episode where Christine is completely wasted in her apartment. You are really good. Extraordinary work."

"I was sober for every single shot of that episode," I said, to prove to him that I was in control and didn't need intervention.

I expected him to say something like, "I don't know why you're even here."

I couldn't wait to get back to Ronnie and say, "See? I don't have an issue with alcohol!"

Instead, the doctor continued with, "I don't know if you're drinking because you're depressed, or you're depressed because you drink. They are different."

Unexpectedly, I began sobbing in his office. I couldn't stop.

He said: "I'm going to send you somewhere in the Midwest."

"What's in the Midwest? I want to go to Betty Ford in Rancho Mirage, like Elizabeth Taylor!"

Since my dinner with Ronnie, I had started thinking that maybe it wasn't such a big deal—I could handle the Betty Ford Center if it would make Ronnie happy. I wanted to get out of town, anyway. I'll use the month there to have a good rest.

That's what was going on in my head. I swear to God.

The doctor said, "No, I want you to be away from this business you're in. I don't want you around showbiz people, or anyone that has anything to do with it."

It suddenly became shockingly clear to me that this doctor was defining me as an alcoholic. What were the guidelines on how to judge whether a person is an alcoholic? Could he tell just by looking at me?

I had never considered myself anything more than a social drinker. I never got smashed at home alone, like Christine Cagney had. Everyone I knew had a drink or two at the end of the workday. No one thought twice about it. Growing up in my family, the cocktail hour was revered. All day long.

I waited until the end of every workday to have a drink. It never interfered with my job. As soon as the assistant director would call the day a wrap, my personal dresser on the show would put scotch on the rocks in a Styrofoam cup and hand it to me. She called it my "apple juice."

CBS executives would often ask that I represent the show at all extracurricular events. I always agreed. I'd go to cocktail parties with sponsors or station program directors from across the country.

Before going to a party or event, I would have one drink at home while I put on my makeup. It made me feel less critical of myself. It loosened me up. I could look in the mirror and think, "I look good." With one drink I could remember names and faces. I felt articulate and charming. One drink before a social event made me a fun person. Two drinks were nice, too.

I didn't see any of my behavior as alcoholic, even when I experienced what I later learned were defined as "blackouts." Every once in a while I would wake up and have no idea how I'd gotten home. My car would be in the driveway. I had driven myself home. But I'd have no memory of having done so.

Even with this doctor's professional diagnosis, I was not convinced I needed rehab. I was worn out from six seasons of *Cagney & Lacey* and the emotional turmoil of having an affair with my married boss. I only needed a couple of weeks to rest and heal my broken heart.

Still, I agreed to go.

First, I knew I would have to tell my mother.

I called my brother Michael and asked him to come with me to Carmel to help break the news.

He agreed. We flew into Monterey for the day to take my mother out to lunch. I could tell by the way my mother was acting that she thought I was going to tell her that I was getting married. I kept the small talk going for a while.

Finally, Michael said, "Sharon, if you're not going to tell her, I will."

I took a long breath in.

"Mom, I'm going away for a while, to a place in the Midwest, because people think I am drinking too much."

She said, "Darling, I think a farm in the Midwest sounds wonderful. You need to rest. You've been working so hard."

She didn't acknowledge the part where I said that I had been drinking too much.

I tried one more time.

"They think I'm drinking too much, Mom. That's why I'm being sent away."

She smiled and took a sip of her cocktail.

"I think it's wonderful that you can rest," she said.

We didn't talk about alcoholism in my family. Ever. My mother sipped all day long. Alone.

She would have a glass of vodka (without ice, so it appeared to be a glass of water) and a handful of vitamins for breakfast. She never acted anything other than proper and poised. She never blacked out.

It wasn't until the early '90s that I fully understood that my mother was a functioning alcoholic who couldn't do without booze. She was in her late seventies and was in the hospital recovering from surgery on collapsed veins in her legs. I could see my mother's hands shaking. She would never have asked for a drink in a hospital. Ever. So I did it for her.

I approached her doctor. "May I bring my mother a cocktail in the evenings?"

He said, "Absolutely."

That evening I brought in a bottle, an ice bucket, and glassware. I told her the doctor had allowed me to bring her a libation. She was so thrilled. I made her a bourbon on the rocks, her drink of choice in the evenings. Her hands stopped shaking. I may have given her a second one. I took the bottle home with me and brought it back the next evening with a fresh glass and ice. I'm sure she knew she was having withdrawal symptoms, but it wasn't discussed.

Judith Ann flew with me to Minneapolis when I went to be admitted to rehab. My initial plan was to go alone and get a car service to take me from the airport to Hazelden.

Judith Ann had laughed at me. "You are so naïve. The tabloids will have the story before you get out of that limo. I'll fly with you, rent a car in my name at the airport, and take you to Hazelden."

She and I spent the first night in a hotel in Minneapolis, as I wasn't expected to check in at Hazelden until the next day. We had a drink or two, maybe three, at the hotel bar. I decided that I should enjoy my last day as a drinker. That "last day" carried over into the next morning, when I ordered the two of us Bloody Marys with our breakfast.

About a half mile from the front door of Hazelden was a roadside bar. I looked over at Judith Ann. "Let's go in and have our final drink together. Want to?"

She was game.

It was midafternoon, so the bar was almost empty. I ordered a martini from the bartender, who luckily didn't seem to recognize me. It was the best one I had ever had.

I said to him, "May I have a roadie, please?"

He mixed us each a second martini and set them before us. "This one is on the house."

What I didn't realize at the time was that the hundreds of coins lining the top of the bar behind him were sobriety tokens. Later, I was to find out that this bar owner prided himself on getting recovering alcoholics to drink. He would trade their first AA token for their first free drink.

Judith Ann and I probably hadn't made it out of the parking lot before the bartender was on the phone with *People* magazine, giving them the goods and enough quotes to fill an article. Asshole! And I'm a great tipper! But I guess *People* was his Christmas bonus.

The receptionist at Hazelden led Judith Ann and me into a private conference room to await my counselor. I was toasted. And I was scared.

My counselor entered the room and opened her arms to me. Without hesitation, I went into her arms and started crying, a reaction I didn't anticipate at all.

She assured Judith Ann that I would be okay. I didn't want Judy to leave and could tell she didn't want to leave me there either. Months later, she told me that on the way back to the airport, she had to pull off the road because she was crying so much.

The first couple of nights at Hazelden, they put me in the infirmary and gave me some type of pill to spare me a severe withdrawal from my earlier consumption of gin. The medication's effect on me was the opposite of alcohol. Instead of becoming relaxed, I became extremely paranoid. It seems, from what I was told later, I made quite a fuss.

The press and paparazzi soon started sending me telegrams and flowers to see if they would be accepted. To protect my privacy, the Hazelden staff would stamp everything with "addressee unknown" and send it back. Unless I recognized the name, everything that came through the door went back out. Keeping it would be proof enough for the press to report that I was a patient.

One arrangement of flowers I kept. They were from my dear funny friend Jay Michelis. Only six words were on the card: "These flowers are *not* in water." I actually dipped my finger in to see if it was gin. No such luck. If anyone could get it done, it would have been Jay, but he loved me too much to sabotage me.

My roommate was a fiery British girl. My introduction to her was when she flew into our room after private therapy, whipped her red cardigan sweater from her shoulders, threw it across the room, and yelled, while crying, "They say I haven't surrendered yet! Surrender?! I've done everything they told me to do! Fucking surrender? Who do they think I am, the bloody Japanese?"

I spent my evenings writing letters to family and friends using crayons, which I brought from home, making a joke about how I was "locked away and they wouldn't let me have any sharp objects."

I wasn't taking the whole rehab experience seriously. Why would I? I didn't believe that the people who knew me best actually thought I was an alcoholic. Monique was adamant that it had been blown out of proportion. (But then, Monique rarely went a day without a drink or two, so there's that!) Neither of my brothers nor my mother or father thought I needed treatment. My cousin Lizzie thought the idea of rehab was "absolutely ridiculous." Barney was also unconvinced. He thought my addiction was to him, which was partly true.

I was sure I didn't belong there, though I found my fellow residents to be absolutely fascinating. They told stories in our unit meetings of their countless ingenious ways to get loaded. One woman confessed to hiding her vodka in her steam iron. Another described storing her booze in the garden hose. Brilliant!

The more they talked, the more convinced I became that I had no real issues with alcohol. I contributed and responded during the meetings, but when I introduced myself, I would only say, "Hi. My name is Sharon. I'm sorry, I cannot apply the word *alcoholic* to myself because I don't believe it."

I went to Hazelden's large all-campus AA meetings twice a day to listen to phenomenal speakers. The entire program was centered on the Twelve Steps.

Outside of the meetings and speeches, we filled our days with chores. No one was exempt. I suppose it was to equalize the group, keep us humble. Even Elizabeth Taylor probably had to push a mop or two at the Betty Ford Center. The unit I lived in had a den. I was assigned to dust and vacuum the den every day.

I would put my earphones on and play love songs, fantasizing that Barney really missed me and that he had realized in my absence that he couldn't live without me.

After two weeks, they allowed Barney to fly in to visit on a Sunday when all the other patients could have guests. He was on his way out of the country for a solo spa vacation. We went for a walk around the beautiful grounds to avoid being seen by the other guests.

I said to Barney, "I have to try something out on you that I've never been able to say before."

He stopped walking and looked at me.

"Okay. What?"

I stepped away from him, saying, "You stay over there. I want to do this on my own. You don't have to say or do anything."

I paused, still not knowing if the actual words would come out of my mouth. I was embarrassed, but also knew that it had to be said. I wanted to say it first to him.

"My name is Sharon. And I'm an alcoholic."

He answered, "I know. Thank you for telling me."

In the last hour of visitors' day, Barney and I ended up sneaking into the infirmary and making love on the hospital gurney. Unless you count a car, I had never before made love on a bed on wheels.

I asked him, "Do you think I'm the only patient who has ever had sex in the infirmary?"

His two-syllable answer: "Today."

Every week, my agent, Ronnie, would call me to check in. There were no individual telephones, just one communal pay phone down the hall.

I told him, "I hate it here. All they want to do is talk about God."

"All right. I'll send you a ticket to come home."

"Fuck you, Ronnie!"

He said, "What did I say? I'll come and pack your bags."

I replied, "You know I've never quit on anything in my life! I'm not quitting on this either."

"Okay. What do you do there for fun? Do you watch movies?" he asked me, trying to calm me down.

"No," I said. "We don't have a VCR."

The next day a brand-new VCR was delivered to our unit along with five movies that had not yet been released. All of the women on my unit were so excited about the new addition. We voted on which movie to watch and picked *Dirty Dancing*.

The next morning everything was gone. I had a message to see my counselor. She was not smiling.

"You know better!" she admonished me.

I had no idea what I had done wrong.

"You're here to concentrate on your treatment. You, particularly, Sharon, are not to have any outside influences. There's a reason we don't have a VCR on the unit."

From then on, every single delivery was sent to her office first.

The next week, my counselor called me in again for a special meeting. I wasn't sure what I'd done wrong this time either.

"We'd like to offer you a room in Jellinek," she said. When I didn't answer, she explained that Jellinek was the long-term facility Hazelden uses for patients sentenced by the court.

I was completely floored. I'd thought I'd be leaving the next week.

I said, "What the fuck are you taking about? You just had to take the woman down the hall to have her stomach pumped for drinking the goddamn hair spray! There are people here on heroin! So what, I've had a few martinis in my life and a little cocaine!"

She responded, "Sharon, we are offering you a gift. You were so emotionally battered when you first came in here that we didn't push you."

I didn't move to the long-term facility, but I did stay a full seven weeks. It took me that long to get through the first five steps of the Twelve Steps of Alcoholics Anonymous.

At the end of six weeks, I wanted out of Hazelden, ready or not. I was determined to go home and get back to my life.

I had tried to do everything perfectly at Hazelden, to prove I was "a good girl," like I was still in parochial school. Every night, I was to write out my feelings on paper and put it under my counselor's office door for her to read in the morning. I had my assistant send me yellow Liquid Paper so that I could correct any mistakes I wrote by hand on my pristine legal pads. In forty-two days, my counselor never once seemed satisfied with my thoughts. She was tough. She knew what she was doing. Beautiful cursive and perfect grammar didn't impress her.

In my seventh week there, I gave up. I wasn't going to try anymore. I did my homework, but I didn't stay within the lines.

I scribbled across the paper: "I'm so sick of this fucking place. I just want to get the fuck out of here. I don't give a fucking shit anymore."

I filled the page with anger and venom. Every other word was *fuck* or *shit*.

The next day I expected my counselor to tell me that I should reconsider moving to Jellinek for a longer-term stay. Instead, she surprised me. She put my journal paper down on her desk, looked up, and said, "You're ready to leave."

I guess I had finally stopped trying to control everything. Was that surrendering?

In my last week at Hazelden, I learned from a contraband *New York Times*—newspapers weren't allowed at Hazelden, but people sometimes managed to sneak them in—that *Cagney & Lacey* had been canceled. That's how I found out it was over. I had no work to go back to once I was released. I didn't know what the future held.

Before I was scheduled to fly home, my counselor made me promise that I would return to Hazelden, when I was ready, to do "Family," a required weeklong commitment to meet with other patients' family members and help them understand addiction. I hardly considered myself an authority, but I agreed.

She then put me on a Hazelden bus that would be taking me to my first outside AA meeting.

I didn't know anyone there. I raised my hand to speak. I stood up and said, "My name is Sharon, and I'm an alcoholic."

I almost choked on the words. I explained: "I'll say it here, because I know I'm supposed to say it. But it's not coming out right. It doesn't feel right."

No one said a word back to me. I continued speaking.

"I have never been in a real AA meeting where they weren't lighting me and adjusting the camera. I did one of these scenes for *Cagney & Lacey*, every episode, every week, for a full year. I would have to stand and say: "My name is Christine, and I'm an alcoholic."

I confessed to the group that I was having a hard time saying my real name in this real meeting. Then I sat down.

At the end of the meeting, a man approached me as I was gathering my things and said, "You're never gonna make it."

Then he turned and walked away.

I was so horrified and enraged by his cruelty. For seven weeks, I had been learning how to be brave at Hazelden. Now I was shattered. And angry.

The next day I told my Hazelden counselor what had happened.

She said, "Sharon, it's not the people. It's the program. Everybody has his or her own thing, which doesn't apply to you. He was wrong to say that. But it doesn't matter. You need to work the program."

This was our last session together, so she stepped out into the long hallway to say goodbye. I walked the length of the hallway to the front door, knowing she was standing there, watching me leave.

At the door, I remembered the question I wanted her to answer. I turned around. "Did I ever surrender?"

She shook her head. "No."

Then, with a smile, she added, "Not yet."

She had been tough and caring, relentless and remarkable. I had received her best. And she *was* the best. I knew no one else could have done better with me.

Knowing I would never be a big fan of Alcoholics Anonymous, my counselor made me promise that I would do therapy at least once a week in Los Angeles. I kept that promise, going twice, sometimes three times per week, two hours at a time.

≡ • ≡

Judith Ann picked me up from the airport in Los Angeles. When I saw her, I started to feel light-headed and my vision went dark. I had never fainted in my life. I think I was overwhelmed by being out in the world again. She took me home to Malibu. I didn't step outside for two weeks.

Nothing about my life seemed real. Christine Cagney was gone. I had no character to play or any crew or director who would be waiting for me at the studio.

As part of my contract with *Cagney & Lacey*, I was to inherit the entire wardrobe that Christine Cagney wore on the show once the series ended. In an ironic twist, someone had backed a truck up to the wardrobe department and had stolen every single Cagney item from all six seasons, from her jogging headband down to her leather knee-high boots to her pink Reeboks. However, not a single strand of pearls or high-necked polyester blouse worn by Mary Beth was taken. It was funny later. Much later.

At this point, though, nothing was funny. I was now home, by myself, facing an unknown future as me, Sharon, though I didn't know who in the hell that was.

I found an envelope in my mailbox that had not gone through the postal system. It only had my name on it. My neighbor, actor Jack Lemmon, had handwritten me a four-page letter about his own struggles with alcohol. He wrote that he was proud of me, listed his private phone numbers, and invited me to call him personally if I needed advice, encouragement, or a friendly ear. I was very moved and more than a little awestruck that this brilliant actor would care enough to reach out to me.

When Monique came to visit me at the beach, I told her that I didn't want to work for the next two years. I was so battered by last year's exposure in the press. I was sure the paparazzi couldn't wait to see me fall off the wagon and onto my ass.

After my first week back, Barney came over to see me. We were both nervous. Neither one of us knew where our relationship stood. We needed to talk about it, but ended up getting in an argument.

Barney sat on my bed with his arms crossed over his chest.

Suddenly, looking over at his petulant posture, I hit a breaking point. I no longer cared what the fuck would happen between us. I was completely over it all. I was done trying to please him . . . or anyone. I wasn't emotional. I was just done.

I modulated my voice to be sure Barney would listen closely. I needed to be heard.

"Uncross your arms, or don't, Barney. I don't need this crap."

Barney was astonished at the surety in my voice. I didn't give him time to respond. I continued, speaking slowly.

"I just spent almost two months in a nuthouse. And I stayed, even though I didn't want to go in the first place. I've lived through months of the tabloids calling me a whore. I've survived the press labeling me a homewrecker and now a drunk. As of this month, I've got no job. I have to do goddamn therapy three times a week. My father is ill. And I could really use a drink right now, but I'm not going to have one, at least not at this very moment. If you're not happy here, Barney, there's the fucking door. Right there. I've got enough on my plate. I'm done. So you can uncross your arms and talk to me with respect, or you can get the fuck out. Does that work for you?"

Barney uncrossed his arms. His face softened.

"I'm sorry," he said. "I hear you."

The atmosphere changed drastically. The storm clouds moved out. I didn't have a drink.

A week or so later, Barney called to say he wanted to have a goodbye *Cagney & Lacey* dinner with Tyne Daly and John Karlen, who played her husband, and me. He wanted to celebrate us. It was decided that we would meet at Wolfgang Puck's Spago, the original restaurant overlooking Sunset Boulevard.

I was driving up the hill to the parking lot when I saw a man walking down the street to the restaurant. It was my agent, Ronnie Meyer. I stopped my little red woody wagon right in the middle of the road and got out.

Ronnie walked over to me and said, "God, you look beautiful. Are you boring?"

He always knew how to make me laugh.

"I don't know," I said. "I'm about to find out."

Tyne and Johnny had already toasted with a couple of shooters by the time I walked in.

I had nothing to talk about. I was sober and felt so uninteresting.

Tyne wrapped her arm around my shoulder. "You look like you're lit from within."

"Really?"

She said, "You do."

I sat there sucking on 7 Up, so sure I was a bore.

A bottle of champagne arrived at our table. The waiter told us that it was compliments of another customer. The note with it said, "Thanks for all those great years of TV."

It was from Sue Mengers. Sue topped the list as one of the most powerful agents in Hollywood. Her clients included Barbra Streisand, Candice Bergen, Joan Collins, Cher, Gene Hackman, Steve McQueen, and Farrah Fawcett. Without a drink to bolster my social abilities, I felt too shy and insecure to go over to Ms. Mengers's table and meet her. That's one hand I still regret not shaking.

When we left the restaurant, a horde of press and paparazzi followed me to my car. I smiled wordlessly in the glare of the flashing bulbs, ignoring their questions about my newfound sobriety. When I got home, Barney phoned.

"I just called to say that you were the most interesting person at the table tonight. You need to know that."

I loved him for that, although I didn't believe him.

Barney was the reason the countless paparazzi had surrounded the restaurant, the reason why they even cared about what was going on for me. He had taken me, an actress with a high TVQ, and turned me into a household name. And at the end of six groundbreaking television seasons, I couldn't even raise a glass and toast him for that, because "My name is Sharon, and I'm an alcoholic."

What the fuck!

Thirty-Four

His Best Doll

My father would always dress to the nines whenever he would visit me on the set of *Cagney & Lacey*. His charisma and allure never diminished. The cast and crew found him charming. They'd bring him a director's chair, and he would watch the action from the sidelines. I knew he was proud of my success. That meant a lot to me.

In the three decades since their divorce, my mother had not spoken to my father. They had both attended Michael's and Aric's weddings, but my mother never acknowledged my father's presence.

I decided to host Thanksgiving for the entire family at my Malibu beach house. My father was in full-time care by this time. I wanted him to see the beach house I had bought with my TV money from *Cagney & Lacey*. I was so proud of it. I hired a private ambulance and two nurses to bring Daddy to Malibu, even though he wouldn't be able to sit at the table or eat the Thanksgiving meal with us. When they arrived, I had them roll his gurney onto the back deck so he could get some sun and see my beach and the ocean.

My mother had spent the previous night with me at the house. When my father arrived, she stayed inside, sitting on the couch, with her drink in hand.

I pleaded with her, "Mom, he knows you're here. Won't you go out and at the very least say hello? It's been thirty years."

For my sake, she rose from the sofa, walked outside, and stood stiffly next to my father's gurney.

He looked up at her. He smiled.

"Hello, Marjorie."

She did not look at him. She was not smiling.

"Hello, Dennis."

There was an awkward pause.

My father broke the silence.

"So, I understand you met the pope."

"Yes," my mother said, staring straight out at the sand dunes.

My father tried again.

"Well. That must have been exciting."

He was making a valiant effort.

My brother Michael and I were watching through the screen door, appalled at how awful the interaction was but trying not to laugh at the same time.

My mother adjusted her cardigan sweater.

"It was," she finally answered.

At this point, my mother excused herself and walked back into the house.

About an hour later, after Daddy had talked to more arriving family members, I had the nurses move him upstairs and into my bed so he could be more comfortable and have the ocean view from my bedroom windows.

Downstairs, the rest of us all had dinner together, making small talk around the huge elephant in my bed in the room above us.

My mother had a few more libations.

I guess it was somehow fitting that the last conversation my two very Catholic parents ever had was regarding the pope. They were as far removed from one another as the pope is from most of the church's one billion members.

The only consistent lifelong relationship my father had was with the USC Trojans football team. His loyalty to that college team could not be broken. He followed their every play and attended every game, sitting in his fifty-yard-line seats. The year the Trojans had a terrible season was also the year my father decided to end his life. I guess he felt there was no reason to stay. His team was failing and so was his health.

He was seventy-four and sick with type 2 diabetes and kidney failure. He had been confined to bed for most of the previous two years and required dialysis several times a week. His final year he lived at the St. John of God nursing home in LA, run by an order of Catholic brothers.

I had hired the best set decorator from *Cagney & Lacey* to decorate his room, to make it fabulous for him. It was thirty-five thousand dollars' worth of fabulous. Even the privacy curtain that could be pulled around his bed was of designer fabric. The decorator put in a secretary desk with a leather blotter pad and a daily diary for the licensed vocational nurse I hired to be with him. There were overstuffed armchairs for visitors and tinted venetian blinds. She used the small photos he had of Michael, Aric, and me and enlarged them into huge framed pictures for his walls, as his eyesight was failing.

I would go to visit him almost every evening after work on the final season of *Cagney & Lacey.*

One day he turned to me and in a raspy voice said, "I never thought you'd be here for me at this time in my life."

I said, "But Daddy, you were always my best beau."

He took my hand and he said, "Well, you were always my best doll."

Even though I was a grown woman, on the inside I was feeling just like the little girl I used to be—the girl who always craved his attention.

One late August day in 1988, I tracked down the doctor at the nursing home. I was going out of town for five days and wanted to make sure my father would be okay.

The doctor assured me that my father had a very strong heart and would be around for at least two more years.

I returned to Hazelden to attend "Family," keeping the promise I had made to my counselor.

When I flew back to LA, I decided to go straight to the nursing home from the airport. I called my brother Michael from the airport to ask how our father was doing.

"He has about two weeks left," Michael said.

I had no idea what he was talking about.

Michael then explained that our father had decided to refuse further kidney dialysis. Daddy had already told both Michael and Aric about his plan. He had not told me. I felt I had been sent off to boarding school once again, the only child who had no idea that she wouldn't see her father anymore.

I drove to the nursing home and went into his room. He was lying on his side, which he never did. He didn't look at me. He seemed to be staring at something else in the room.

"Hi, Daddy."

"Sharon!" he said. Then he closed his eyes.

I asked the LVN, "Is that it? Is he in a coma?"

"No, no. He's just taking a nap."

I watched his face for about five minutes, and finally I turned to the nurse.

I said, "He's never going to talk to me again, is he?"

She tipped her head down, unable to answer or face me.

I ran out of the room and down the hall to the little chapel. It was the only empty room, and I wanted to rage in private. Believe me, I did not go there to pray.

The priest who was the director of the nursing home came looking for me. I guess the LVN must have told him I was upset.

"Sharon, he couldn't tell you. He couldn't go through with it if he had to look you in the eyes. He wants to go. He needs to go."

I couldn't speak.

The priest continued, "If you want to help him die in peace, he needs to know that you children forgive him for the father he never was."

Michael arrived and found us in the little chapel. For the first time, I didn't care to hear what my brother had to say. I was so angry.

"Stay away from me. You could have called me," I said as I walked around him and out the door. I felt completely alone.

Later that day, I sat on the couch in my therapist's office, devastated about how in the past no one had told me my father was leaving our family home when I was fourteen, and now no one had bothered to tell me that he was leaving my life forever.

My therapist said, "You've been through enough. After this session, I want you to go directly to his room and tell him everything you feel."

I followed her advice and got back in my car and drove to the nursing home. His eyes were closed and his breathing was shallow.

I talked to the LVN. "Can he hear me?"

She said, "Every word."

I asked her to give us some privacy.

I began pacing back and forth near the end of his bed. Then, everything that I'd held in for decades came out in one rapid-fire monologue.

"I know you can't talk, Daddy, but you can hear me. You did this to me once before. You walked out of our lives. I know you didn't want to go, but nobody told me. I found out months later. And now you're doing it again."

I stayed on my feet, walking back and forth.

"The funny thing is, Daddy, that I am the child who would have supported your decision to end your treatment. But it's too late now. You're never going to talk to me again. You never gave me closure."

Once the anger was drained out, I sat next to his bed and held his hand.

"The priest said that you wanted to know that Michael, Aric, and I have forgiven you for not being a good father."

I felt his body sigh in sadness. My heart ached.

"We forgave you a long time ago, Daddy. We love you. You can go. Honest, we will be fine."

I thanked him for the laughter and music he'd brought into my life. I sang to him "I Wonder What's Become of Sally," a song he taught me as a small child.

I put my hand under his and said, "If you can hear me, Daddy, squeeze my hand twice."

It had to be twice. One squeeze might be only a muscle twitch, I thought. He squeezed it twice.

"The doctor told me that you have a couple of weeks left. I'll be here every day for you, Daddy. I'll be back in a couple of hours."

When I went back later that night, my father had his eyes open and was looking at someone or something I couldn't see.

The LVN ran to get the on-duty head nurse, who put her stethoscope on his chest and said, "Sharon, he's dying tonight. Call your brothers."

I was sure Daddy could still hear everything, so I ran down the hallway to the lounge area to call Michael. Aric lived too far away to make it in time.

Then the nurse yelled from the door of my father's room, "Miss Gless, come now!"

Michael heard her over the phone. He didn't make it in time.

I didn't know what to do with myself after my father took his final breath, so I brushed his hair so he'd look nice. I believe he had stayed for me. He had allowed me closure.

Michael, Aric, and I picked out our father's casket and prayer cards. I hired a full choir to sing all of the beautiful mass songs at Daddy's funeral. The flowers that covered his casket were the Trojans football team colors. The top was a blanket of cardinal-red roses. In the center were three golden-yellow roses, one for each of his children. Four Trojans football friends were pallbearers. I wore a white dress and walked between my brothers, dressed in their black suits, behind the casket.

As we left the church, the choir sang "An Irish Lullaby." There wasn't a dry eye in the house.

His room at St. John's, still decorated for my father, was next given to a Catholic archbishop. Daddy would have liked that.

Thirty-Five

Fan-atic

I know what it feels like to be a rabid fan. It can be overwhelming to meet someone you have watched on-screen or onstage for years. For me, that someone was Dame Maggie Smith.

The first time I had the pleasure of watching Dame Maggie was in the movie *The Prime of Miss Jean Brodie*. There wasn't a false note to that performance, or any of them since. She knocks me out every time.

In 1999, I was in London, so I got a ticket to see Maggie Smith performing the stage version of *The Lady in the Van*. I had met her once before, briefly, when I was starring in *Misery* in London's West End. She was welcoming and kind, but I didn't say much—I was too starstruck.

After her standing ovation at the end of *The Lady in the Van*, I gathered up my courage and walked up to the doorman and asked if I might be able to say a quick hello.

I could tell that he recognized me. "You wait right here."

He returned moments later, smiling. "Maggie is ready to see you."

The door to her dressing room was open. I stood in the doorframe. "Dame Maggie, I don't know if you remember me. . . ."

She burst out laughing, pulled me into the room, and said, "Oh, will you stop! Please!"

She gave me a big hug and gestured for me to sit down. She said, "Are you still not drinking?"

I said, "Yes. I still don't drink. I can't believe you remember that!"

"I remember everything about you," she replied.

I was speechless.

"You know, that drunk acting you did on *Cagney & Lacey* was the finest I've ever seen on television," Maggie said, catching me off guard.

"I wasn't drunk when I did those scenes, Maggie. Honest." I wanted her to know.

She swiveled her head to look at me with her laser-blue eyes. "Honey, you can't be drunk and do that kind of work."

I'll dine out on her words of praise for the rest of my life. I was so surprised to find that she actually watched all seasons of *Cagney & Lacey.* What an honor!

⇒ • ⇐

The *Cagney & Lacey* fans had always been respectful and kind to me. In my years on the show, it had never occurred to me that any fan would be out to do me harm.

One afternoon, during the final season of the show, we were shooting a street scene in downtown Los Angeles. Production couldn't shut down city sidewalks for the purpose of filming, so anyone could watch us working from the sidelines.

While on a crew break, my friend and assistant-on-set, Beverley Faverty, brought a young woman to meet me. She had long hair, no makeup, and was wearing a flower-child peasant dress. She seemed desperately shy.

"This is the girl who has written you so many letters," Beverley told me.

During those years, it was Beverley who kept track of all of the fan mail for Tyne and me.

I chatted with the young woman for about five minutes before I was called back to the set. Before I left, she asked, "Can I have a hug?"

"Of course."

She shook like a little bird in my arms.

I went back to work, not thinking about it again, until a couple of weeks later. Barney was contacted on the *Cagney & Lacey* set by the Los Angeles Police Department. The psychiatrist of a young woman had called to alert them that her client could be of danger to Sharon Gless. It was the same young woman. Earlier that day, she'd shown up at the studio with a bouquet of roses for me. She had apparently told her therapist that she was planning on shooting herself in front of me, but she had left her gun in the trunk of her car.

After getting the warning call from the police department, the studio hired a bodyguard for me.

I was emptying out my trailer at the end of the season when Beverley brought me a large bag full of mail from the young woman the police had warned the studio about.

Beverley said, "Hang on to these. You may need them one day."

I put them in storage, thinking the whole situation was long over.

⇒ • ⇐

Months later, my publicist, Pat Kingsley, got a call from an employee of the Kodak film-developing kiosk in the parking lot of a Hollywood shopping center. The employee told her, "I have some photos your client might want to see."

The photos belonged to the same young woman. One was of her chopping off her long hair into a butchered short cut. Another was of her dressed in army fatigues, holding a press photo of me in one hand and a gun to her head in the other hand. The third photo was of a rifle lying across a bed on which many of my press photos had been spread out.

Soon after, while I was visiting my mother in Carmel, the young woman left her parents a suicide note. She had emptied her bank account, bought me a very expensive ring, and drove up from Irvine to present it to me. The note her parents found revealed that she planned to give me the ring and then go to Cagney's loft at the studio and kill herself. The parents called the police, frantic. The police went to my small house in Studio City and found the young woman sitting in her car. She had left the ring with my assistant. When she saw the marked police car, she peeled out of the cul-de-sac and managed to lose the pursuing police on the freeway. She checked herself into the psychiatric unit at a hospital in Irvine.

I went about my life, thinking the young woman was getting the psychiatric treatment she needed. I didn't know that the hospital could only hold her for seventy-two hours without a court order.

Weeks later, I returned from Malibu to my Studio City home to find a repairman replacing the glass in my French door.

My personal assistant, Brooke Plantenga, who was at the house, informed me that someone had broken through the pane and entered overnight. The alarm had not been set the previous evening. Not much was missing except my personal address book and some underwear from my dresser. It was obvious someone had lain across my bed, as there was an impression of a body in my down comforter.

Brooke made me promise I would not stay at the house that night, so I left to spend the night at Barney's. He was now living in a fabulous Art Deco apartment once owned by screen star Gloria Swanson. Barney's divorce was in process. Our relationship had resumed, and for the first time, we no longer had to hide it. We still had our issues.

The two of us argued late that night, so I decided to leave. Halfway to my Studio City house, I thought about the promise I had made to Barney to never leave angry. Reluctantly, I turned around and went back to his apartment. Keeping that promise most likely saved my life.

Around 3 a.m., Barney's phone rang. I heard him answer, "Yeah, she's here. Okay."

Then he hung up the phone and rolled over to go back to sleep.

"What was that about?" I asked him.

"It was Brooke, wanting to make sure you're here. There seems to be some hostage situation happening at your house," he mumbled. "Go back to sleep."

There was no way I was going back to sleep. I went into his den and turned on his TV. The local Los Angeles news was broadcasting live from my Studio City cul-de-sac. I knew it must be the young woman. She had come back for me.

She had climbed onto the hood of her truck to jump over the top of the new gate. Unable to break the new security glass on the French doors, she used a jackknife to painstakingly cut through the wood. This time the house alarm had been set, and when she finally opened the door, the alarm was triggered.

A security guard who worked for my alarm company arrived at the house. He was confronted by the intruder, who put a rifle to her head and shouted at the guard, "If you come one step closer, I'm going to kill myself."

The guard backed off and called the police.

The police arrived and emptied out all the occupants of nearby homes, and, not knowing exactly what would be needed, called in a SWAT team.

The SWAT team surrounded the house as a police negotiator rang my home phone to talk the young woman into surrendering peacefully.

She didn't want to talk to a man. She would only talk to a woman, and she requested to be able to see me. She informed them that she had a rifle and five hundred rounds of ammunition.

A female officer who had just finished her training as a negotiator was flown in by helicopter. This was her first case. However, after five unsuccessful hours, it occurred to the officer to say that I was outside in the cul-de-sac waiting to talk to her.

It was a lie, but it was the only way to end the situation without anyone getting hurt. I watched the live news coverage as they brought the woman out in handcuffs at 10 a.m. She had a shy grin on her face. She was looking around for me.

I drove over to my house after she had been taken away. The

policemen told me that she had planned to force me to have sex with her. She was then planning on killing me and then turning the gun on herself so "we could be in heaven together."

I had to show up in court to testify about the events leading up to the incident.

It was uncomfortable, to say the least. The worst part was that her parents were there. I felt so sorry for them. The young woman stared at me the entire time with a shy smile and a flushed face if I looked in her direction.

The judge sentenced her to six years in prison.

The year before, the young star of *My Sister Sam*, Rebecca Schaeffer, had been shot in the chest, close range, by an obsessed male fan in the doorway of her apartment building in West Hollywood. The man who killed her had obtained Rebecca's apartment address through the DMV.

A while later, the Screen Actors Guild called me to testify before the Superior Court of California in Sacramento about obsessed stalking. I did. The laws on releasing personal information through the DMV were permanently changed that day.

I escaped a violent death at the hands of a stalker. Rebecca Schaeffer was twenty-one years old when she was killed. Twenty-one.

⇒ Thirty-Six ⇐

Dick About Theater

Broadway legend Elaine Stritch called me.

"People say we're alike," she announced in her deep contralto voice. "I want you to come play my kid."

Elaine had been cast as the matriarch in Lillian Hellman's *Watch on the Rhine*. It was a big fund-raiser for StageWest in Springfield, Massachusetts. She wanted me to play the lead female, her daughter, Sara.

I was flattered, but I turned the offer down. "Thank you, Elaine. But I don't know dick about theater."

Elaine roared back, "I'll teach you theater!"

Cagney & Lacey was over. I was taking a break from TV and TV movies.

I told Barney about the opportunity.

"Elaine Stritch is offering to teach you stage acting?" Barney said. "How bad could that be?"

As it turned out, pretty damn bad.

I packed my trunk and headed off to Boston. I'd always thought that if I ever did theater, it would be a comedy like *Same Time Next Year*, not a drama about the rise of fascism before World War II. I was terrified that I was in way over my head. But I clung to the hope that Elaine Stritch would guide me through.

Then Elaine quit the show. She walked out after the first week of rehearsals. I couldn't believe it. I drove around Springfield to every listed AA meeting I could find looking for her. She was very open and public about being an alcoholic, and I knew she attended meetings daily. I found her at the last one on the list.

"We had dinner plans," I reminded her. "What is going on?"

"I'm leaving the show, kid," she told me. "The director doesn't know what he's doing."

It wasn't true. Eric Hill was a wonderful director who cared deeply about his theater. She wouldn't listen to him. She would decide that she could change the blocking, moving the child actors around on stage, all the while arguing why it should be her way. She disrupted the rehearsals.

I knew it was mostly nerves. She was tearing at the cuticles of her fingers until they bled. If Elaine Stritch was anything, she was intuitive. I think she sensed that she was about to be canned. The director told me, privately, that he was one day away from letting her go. I couldn't feel sorry for her, though. She'd gotten me into this play, and now she was ditching me.

I called Monique. She had no qualms about me packing my bags and catching the next flight to LA since the original agreement had changed. I didn't have to stay.

But the theater had sold out the run and had already raised almost a million dollars, based on our two names, to keep StageWest in business. I refused to abandon them with an expensive production. I stayed.

Kim Hunter took over the grande dame role. She had won the Academy Award and Golden Globe for playing Stella in *A Streetcar Named Desire* and had done all genres of acting: stage, big-screen, and some television. She didn't try to "teach" me theater, but I still learned a lot from her. She had her lines down within days and fit into the production as if she had been there from day one. Mostly, she was so kind to me in my virgin voyage across the boards.

It was never fun. There are no second takes in live theater. But I did it. The reviews were good. The audience was very respectful.

Elaine went back to her beloved Broadway, and I saw her in Edward Albee's *A Delicate Balance* six years later. I went backstage to see her costar Rosemary Harris, whom I knew well.

Elaine shouted out from her dressing room, "Hey, kid! Are you going to walk past and not say hi?"

No. I couldn't walk by. I couldn't even mention the past. That was the influence of Elaine Stritch. She had such a vulnerable presence. You couldn't stay mad at her. She was always contentious. She was difficult. Brilliant people can be, and most people who have worked with her would agree that she was a genius onstage. I respect that. I respected her.

In an odd way, she did give me a great lesson. I stepped out of my comfort zone and tried my talent at theater, and I was rewarded with standing ovations. I know *Watch on the Rhine* wasn't a tour de force for me, but I had been given some grace to take a risk, and I took it. And for once, the complaint wasn't about me.

Thirty-Seven

Starmaker

Near the end of the first season of *The Trials of Rosie O'Neill*, Monique James told me, "When you were young and starting out, I did you a great disservice. I wrapped you in cotton wool. I only told you about the people who liked you, the ones who thought you were a knockout. I never told you about the people who didn't like you and didn't want to cast you or work with you."

Clearly, she was trying to hurt me. And she was successful.

She was feeling unappreciated by me, even though I knew how much I needed her. I had never learned how to manage the business side of my career. Monique took care of everything for me. I could always leave any problem—professional but sometimes also personal—to her to handle so I could put my entire focus into my performances.

Now, nearly ten years after leaving Universal Studios, Monique's influence with producers and the television industry had waned. She could also tell that Barney's opinion of my work held sway for me. Throughout her entire career, everyone always listened to what Monique James had to say. Except Barney.

When *Cagney & Lacey* ended, I think Monique had hoped to be done dealing with Barney Rosenzweig and his influence over me. But that didn't happen.

In 1990, Jeff Sagansky, the CBS president at the time, had given Barney an open door and a financial guarantee to produce a one-hour drama with me as the lead. Barney created *The Trials of Rosie O'Neill*, in which I played a Beverly Hills attorney who gets dumped and taken to the cleaners by her ex-husband. She sets up her humble desk as a Los Angeles city court public defender. The show opened each week with Rosie in her psychiatrist's office talking about her life.

Carole King wrote the theme song, and Melissa Manchester recorded it. I won my second Golden Globe award and received my seventh and eighth Emmy nominations for this show.

Many talented actors and actresses appeared on the show with me: Tyne Daly, Ed Asner, Helen Hunt, Brenda Vaccaro, Meg Foster, and my dear friend Robert Wagner. R. J. agreed to a guest star appearance for three episodes as my new love interest. I was nervous kissing him after having played his young assistant on *Switch*. When it came time to shoot that scene, I was on the set alone. When I asked where R. J. was, the director told me that he had gone to his trailer to shave. It was late in the day and he said he didn't want to scratch my skin with his five-o'clock shadow. What a guy! And kissing R. J., with or without whiskers, was kind of wonderful. He always knew what he was doing on camera, including covering an actress's neck with his hand when he kissed her. He protected her from the close-up camera capturing the creases. You could love a guy like that! And I do. Very much.

Monique would come to the set of *Rosie O'Neill* and give Barney feedback about the show and my character. It wasn't well received. Barney and Monique would argue over something concerning me almost every day. Barney would want it to be one way; Monique would think it should be the complete opposite. They would have it out with one another and walk away, often angry. I would be the one who paid the emotional price, the pawn in the middle. I couldn't agree with one without hurting the other.

I was constantly torn between the two most influential people in my life. I was now in a serious relationship with Barney—who was once again my boss—but I had trusted and relied on Monique as my mentor for over twenty years.

One day, Monique asked me to come to her house. She was sitting in her bed with the open *New York Times* and a full ashtray. She looked exhausted and sad.

"I think I'd like to call it a day. This is clearly no longer working well. It's too difficult now."

She was breaking it off with me. I was in shock.

I had trusted her judgment implicitly, because she always told me the right thing to do. She couldn't possibly be serious, I thought, sitting in stunned silence next to her bed.

Monique had an ironclad will, cushioned by a great sense of humor. But there was no magical thinking when it came to the entertainment industry. She fearlessly faced the reality of the business—and to her, the reality was that our relationship had run its course. I didn't know how to move forward without her.

From the beginning, the day Monique signed me as a Universal contract player, her goal had always been to keep me working. She sure as hell did.

Over our time together, she would get word to me, no matter where I was, to make sure I knew about opportunities being offered, even having me paged at the packed Orange County Fair. This was before cell phones. She once got a call through to me on a cruise ship, which was no easy feat in the early 1980s. She had a made-for-TV movie offer for me and needed an answer before the ship would dock. The script was the story of three female astronauts-in-training, each vying to be the first US woman to travel to outer space. The script was pretty cheesy, but they were offering great money.

Monique gave me some sage advice: "There are times in our career when we do a project not because it's great, but because it puts us in a different income bracket. This is one of those times."

I couldn't argue with that. I took the large check.

Monique came through professionally for me, every time, without question. I thought about the day she invited me to lunch in the executive commissary at Universal Studios. There, on the wall, was an enormous backlit publicity photo of me in what she called "my signature look"—trousers and an open sweater, my hands in my pockets, and smiling with "that thing" I do with my mouth that she tried to discourage for years. She had it prominently placed among the photos of the biggest stars at Universal Studios, where every important entertainment executive would see it. Having my photo on the wall meant that I was a significant player in their wheelhouse of stars. It took me ten years to get up there. Monique wanted to surprise me with it. She did. For me, that photo was better than winning an award.

= • =

And now she was done with me. I couldn't imagine not having Monique as my manager, adviser, confidant, and closest friend. I was devastated.

I drove home to my Malibu beach house that Monique had helped me decide to buy. Everywhere I turned was a reminder of her influence in my life. To go from a relationship in which I told her everything to having her now merely be a part of my history was awful. It felt like a piece of my heart had shut down, never to be recovered. And I believe from the bottom of my heart that her pain was equal to mine.

Even though she was no longer representing me professionally, we couldn't stay away from one another. In the months that followed, Monique and I would get together for lunch or dinner every so often, but there was a delicate wedge between us that remained.

One day she called me to her home for a private conversation. She had cancer. It occurs to me now that she'd known she had cancer when she fired me.

I knew it was serious. She was in bed. I could see she was weak. She asked me to close the door and sit next to her. She told me she loved me.

The last thing she said to me was: "You be a good girl, Sweet Pea."

I was living in Toronto in 2001, shooting *Queer as Folk*, when

I got a phone call from Monique's grown daughter, Pammy, aka "Sweet Potato."

"Sweet Pea, Mommy died today."

I'm not sure if I spoke in response. For the first time in years, I shut down completely. I went numb.

When I told Barney over the phone that Monique had passed away from cancer, he tried to console me, but his words of comfort were pointless to me.

I yelled at him, "I never had the nerve to tell you both that the two of you always ruined it for me with your constant fighting. You were both awful, and the only person either of you hurt was me."

Barney felt terrible about it. He apologized. It didn't help. I missed my friend and mentor.

$$\Longrightarrow \bullet \Longleftarrow$$

I didn't grieve for Monique when she died. I had cried countless tears in the previous years.

Her obituary noted her place in entertainment history as one of the twentieth century's "best-known and most successful talent agents." They called her the "Starmaker."

Everything I am and have today traces back to her.

I'll say it. Forever.

Thank you. I love you, Miss James.

Thirty-Eight

I Do. We Did. Twice.

It was Pearl Harbor Day. Barney and I sat in a corner booth in Dan Tana's restaurant.

We had plans to vacation together in Hawaii for Christmas during our upcoming hiatus from *The Trials of Rosie O'Neill*. My relationship with Barney had been both controversial in the public eye and personally fragile for over two years.

Finally, the turmoil of our past seemed over. Things felt gentle. Sweet.

After his martini arrived, Barney leaned toward me. "I need to tell you something."

Oh my God. After all this. He's got cancer.

His eyes were teary. I was so frightened.

"I want to marry you," he said.

"What?"

"I want to marry you!"

"Oh my God, I thought you were going to tell me you were terminal. You just scared the shit out of me!"

Barney seemed unfazed. I was freaked out. I had secretly wanted him to ask me to marry him, but I had never actually thought about how I'd answer if he got around to it.

My mind was racing.

I finally replied, "Can I get back to you on that?"

He didn't even flinch. He calmly said, "Take all the time you need."

It was a serious contemplation. To be . . . or not to be . . . a wife. I needed time.

I called my mother the morning after Barney's marriage proposal. She now lived by herself in her Comstock cottage in Carmel and dedicated her time to doing bookkeeping for a priest. Although it was five in the morning, I knew she'd be up and getting ready for Mass at the Mission. She was always the first one there.

My driver had picked me up in Malibu and was heading to the studio. I was a mess. I was crying as she answered the phone.

"Bug, what's the matter?"

Her tone always soothed me.

"Barney asked me to marry him!" I sobbed.

My mother said, "Well, that's wonderful, Bug. Isn't that what you wanted?"

"No," I cried. "It will ruin everything!"

Without pause, she said, "I understand, darling. You certainly have had no role models of a happy marriage."

Even if I had witnessed happy marriages, I still wasn't sure marriage was for me.

I felt like I was always changing and growing. I worried about waking up one day and thinking, "Who is that next to me?"

In the makeup trailer they put ice on my face to take down the swelling from crying. I'm sure they thought I had suffered some personal tragedy and not a loving proposal.

A week later, Barney and I went for a walk on the beach in Malibu. We crossed paths with Gary David Goldberg, the writer and creator of *Family Ties*. He had been with the same woman, Diana, for decades. Even they had decided to finally get married.

A few minutes after we passed Gary and Diana, I said to Barney, "I don't want to wait as long as they did."

That's all I said. That's how I accepted his proposal.

He was so happy. I was so hopeful. And so full of trepidation.

A while later, Barney and I went to Carmel to spend a weekend with my mother. The guest room had two twin beds.

My mother, in her proper manner, informed Barney and me of the house rules.

"Barney may stay with you in the guest room, only if you leave the bedroom door open."

Premarital sex was not welcome in her home. When she went to bed, she left her door open, too.

Barney was amused and turned on by the challenge of making love to me without either of us emitting a sound, while my very Catholic mother slept across the hall.

"Sex without sin is like an egg without salt," he always told me.

I understood exactly what he meant, but it also gave me pause. Since we no longer needed to meet up secretively in hotel rooms in the middle of the day, would the intrigue be gone? I wasn't sure I could keep it interesting, week after week and twenty-four seven, without some kind of taboo restriction.

Barney knew he wasn't marrying a woman who was a homemaker kind of wife. There would be no French toast for breakfast unless he made it. I didn't own an apron, though I did collect cookbooks. I had hundreds of them. I spent hours reading delectable recipes. That's all I did. Read them. My pots and pans remain in mint condition.

Barney knew all this. He still wanted to marry me. I wanted to marry him, too. We made plans. Two sets of plans.

Barney and I were married at my Malibu beach house, out on the dunes. Twice. In one week.

Our legal wedding day was on May 1, although for a long time, only five people in the world knew it. I wanted it to be private. My wish was to say my personal vows to Barney. We needed witnesses, so we asked my brother Michael and my cousin Lizzie.

May 1 was a Wednesday. I chose high noon. Three p.m. might have been a better choice, because at 10 a.m., I was upstairs barefoot, wearing only a terry-cloth robe, and sitting at an old electric typewriter, pecking out my personal vows. That's where my cousin Lizzie found me, a cigarette dangling from my mouth and looking with bewilderment at a few typed pages covered in ashes, markings of crossed-out words, scratched-out quotes, and arrows drawn from the end of one sentence to the next readable one. Lizzie helped me cut and paste it all into something coherent.

I wore a finely pleated satin skirt, a cashmere sweater cut on the bias, and a sloping brimmed hat, all in ivory. I had commissioned the head designer at the Ice Capades to make my real wedding dress, my repeat wedding dress, and a fallaway satin honeymoon nightgown.

Michael walked me out onto the dunes for the intimate ceremony and then stood in as Barney's best man. Lizzie was my maid of honor. Naomi Caryl, a personal friend, was our minister. I read my prepared vows to Barney. He had prepared nothing. He winged it. Barney is good on his feet, and he knows it.

I had a post-ceremony surprise for Barney ready to go. We had planned to have a wedding luncheon for the five of us on one of the patios of Geoffrey's restaurant, overlooking the Pacific. I had prearranged a small-plane skywriter to spell out "I love you, Barney" across the clear blue afternoon sky.

I could hear the buzz of the plane engine doing its thing, so I told Barney, Michael, and Lizzie, "Come over to the railing with me. Look up."

I was so excited. Unfortunately, there was a hefty ocean breeze that day, so the skywriter had to settle for a heart instead of the word love and a "U" instead of "you." And the wind had blown most of the letters lopsided. By the time he had chased the letters to spell out *Barney*, the *e* and the *y* were over Burbank, about thirteen miles away, as the crow flies.

Still, I thought Barney would be so smitten, seeing his name across the sky over Los Angeles!

I could tell Barney loved it, but his sharp wit won out over any sense of romance. He shook his head at the sky and said, "Wow! That Barbara just doesn't give up!"

Our second wedding day was on May 4. A Saturday. We did a

dress rehearsal at my house the night before, followed by dinner at a restaurant. The wedding party arrived at my house in a celebratory mood and had a cocktail. And then another. And, again, one or two more. Before we could rehearse, everyone was smashed, except for Barney's brother, Joel, and me. Our wedding coordinator, who had been hired to organize and direct the rehearsal, was useless.

By the time we got to the restaurant, the group had sobered somewhat. On my chair, I found a baby-blue Tiffany box. Inside was a sterling silver frame with a photo of Michael and me as children.

I looked down the table at my older brother, who was sitting at the opposite end. He was smiling with a look that said, "No one would ever come between us."

When he toasted me at dinner, he lifted his glass and said, "To the first girl I ever loved."

May 4 had all the potential of being a perfect day. The weather was mild. Large canopies had been set up to hide the ceremony from the paparazzi flying overhead in helicopters, hoping for the first photo. Small white twinkle lights resembling stars lined the undersides of the large tents. The dunes had been raked and all of the chairs were in place for the attendees. The caterers were arriving with six pounds of Russian caviar and a spectacular menu.

About 3 p.m., after handling a lot of details, I went to take my bath. There was a gentle tap on the bathroom door, and I heard my mother ask if she could come in.

She stepped into the bathroom with a small stool and put it right next to the tub and sat down. She didn't say anything. She took the soap and washed my back. I was so touched by her gesture. I knew it was a small loving ritual for my mother, preparing her daughter for her wedding night. It was the calmest five minutes of the entire day.

My second wedding dress had been designed to be an exact replica of the dress that Katharine Hepburn wears on her wedding rehearsal night in *The Philadelphia Story*. The designer watched and paused the film dozens of times so he could match the look of the dress and the sparkle from the thousands of beads that made up the midriff of the gown.

I had three silk men's suits in pastel colors made for Barney's adult daughters: Erika, Allyn, and Torrie. His girls were his "best men" for this ceremony.

Allyn's then five-year-old daughter, Hailey, was our little flower girl. Her dress alone was the cost of a house payment. But I spared no expense to have it all be perfect.

Judith Ann was my maid of honor.

Starting with that decision, the day became a fiasco.

Judith Ann showed up, stormed up the stairs, and announced that the valet parkers had refused to take her car.

I threw on a bathrobe and went down the stairs, barefoot, and to the driveway to where the valet attendants waited. "Judith Ann is my maid of honor. Could you please take her fucking car!?"

Judith Ann was an emotional wreck. She had skipped my bachelorette party because she was in a bad mood, which seemed to be carrying over. It's a good thing that I loved her so much, because on the day she should have been helping me, she couldn't even manage to get her earrings through the holes in her earlobes. Her hands were shaking. I had to do that, too.

I had bought my mother a beautiful pink suit with silk heels dyed to match, and had her hair and nails done. She was very pleased with it all. Just before the ceremony, though, she asked my permission to wear her pink bedroom slippers with the outfit because her feet hurt.

I said, "Mom, couldn't you at least walk down the aisle in your heels? Aric will escort you. Then at the reception you can put your slippers on."

She said, "All right, Bug."

As she limped away from me, I caved in. "Okay, Mom. You can wear the slippers."

What else could I do? As always, she remained as poised and proper as ever, even though she had been "sipping" since lunch.

Barney, who arrived dressed and ready, had no private "groom" quarters at my home where he could be alone. Not by choice, he ended up having to play host to the arriving guests while I continued to get ready.

After an hour, Carole Smith appeared at my bedroom door.

"Barney said to tell you, 'Let's get this show on the road.'"

"Are you kidding?" I responded.

"No," she said.

Obviously, Barney was wearing his producer's cap and was anxious to get started.

I took one final look in the mirror and headed down the stairs.

Judith Ann had preceded me and was barking at the wedding coordinator for forgetting to send our little flower girl down the aisle. We saw all of this on our wedding video later. It included footage of the hapless wedding coordinator gesturing frantically to our guests to rise to their feet as I approached the center aisle.

The paparazzi helicopters that had hovered over my house lowered down to the opening of the tent. A photographer was dropped down on a wire. My hairdresser ran to the tent opening and stood, with his middle finger extended, to block the photographer's view.

I watched, thinking, "Okay. Well, that's going to be the wedding photo for the press."

My wedding cake had collapsed in a van with no air-conditioning while it was being driven up the Pacific Coast Highway from Redondo Beach. It looked like one of those grade-school volcano science projects.

As awful as the wedding band was, the female singer who performed "All I Ask of You" from *Phantom of the Opera* for our first dance as bride and groom was even worse. She could not remember the words to the song or stay on key. It was so unbelievable that Barney and I started laughing.

The next morning, at the wedding breakfast at the Bel Air Hotel, Judith Ann proclaimed loudly to Barney, "When you married Sharon, you married me!"

"My wildest fantasy realized," Barney answered dryly.

I'm sure he didn't envisage exactly to what degree Judith Ann would consider herself our extra spouse. Barney had planned our honeymoon to end in a palatial Palm Beach house right on the Atlantic Ocean. We both were ready to relax and have some alone time with the balmy sea breeze as our only company. As it turned out, Judith Ann blew into town for business meetings and thought it would be "just fine," since we had such a large rental house, to bunk with us to save herself hotel costs.

Again, I was too afraid to say no. I loved her. I didn't want to hurt her feelings. Instead, I got a three-day migraine.

I couldn't have guessed then that our wedding week was the template of our now thirty-year marriage: hope-filled and heated, charmed and very challenging, angry, unpredictable, lonely, exasperating, and enlightening. We've laughed a lot, sometimes out of desperation, and most often because we are both pretty damn hilarious when we want to be.

Thirty-Nine

How Would You Like to Be Me?

If I had taken photos, I could have published a coffee-table book of Dairy Queens across the United States in the early 1990s. Northeast to southeast, southeast to southwest, I've been a happy customer at most of them.

My newlywed spouse and I took a couple of long, long road trips together. The first one was an extended honeymoon, from New England down to Florida. The second road trip was from Florida to Los Angeles. Barney loves to drive. I prefer flying. I'd rather watch movies than the road.

But I do enjoy looking out the car window for Dairy Queens. We traveled countless back roads through small towns. Barney likes all things historical and quaint. I like all things cold and creamy. We put about 4,750 miles on the odometer and about thirteen pounds each on our bodies.

Barney has a fascination with early American cemeteries and headstones from hundreds of years ago. He would improvise an elaborate story based on a family grouping of headstones from the early 1800s. It was fun. Twice. After that, not so much.

⇒ • ⇐

Close to our one-year anniversary, while Barney and I were vacationing in Palm Beach, he got a call with the news that CBS was canceling *The Trials of Rosie O'Neill*. It wasn't totally unexpected.

The executives had changed our time slot six times in our two seasons. We would start to pick up viewers, and CBS would move it to a different night and time. Despite my earning two Emmy nominations and a Golden Globe award, if the viewers can't find the show, then eventually there will be no show to find.

Suddenly I was a nonworking actress married to an executive producer without a show, living in Los Angeles, where keeping a foot in the entertainment door is crucial to future success. Marriage is number seven on the Holmes and Rahe scale of stressful events. Losing a job is number eight. Retirement is number ten. Neither one of us was ready to get to number ten.

One afternoon, I walked into the den to find Barney with tears streaming down his face. He had been on the phone with his mother and learned that her breast cancer had metastasized into her brain, a fatal diagnosis.

I asked him how best I could support him.

He said, "Please stop smoking! Please. I went through so much to get you. I don't want to lose you."

Barney had quit his cigarette and cigar smoking cold turkey on his fiftieth birthday, during the final season of *Cagney & Lacey*.

I had already given up drinking. I couldn't give up smoking. It was my strongest addiction. I thought.

"You ask too much," I said. I walked out of the room.

I had been reading a book about the seven components of love. One of them was "making your loved one feel safe."

I thought, "Okay, got it. My smoking isn't allowing him to feel safe. If I really love him, I have to stop frightening him."

We decided we would both go to fat farms to lose some weight. He went to one in California, and I went to another in South Carolina. While I was there, I decided to quit smoking. My spouse had a complaint. I was going to fix it.

It's a big mistake to quit doing anything for someone else. It's a hefty plate of pressure, with a side order of resentment. It wasn't

Barney's fault, but he was on the receiving end of my withdrawal symptoms and the simultaneous onset of full-blown menopause.

He didn't know what had hit him. I was kidnapped by runaway hormones and felt isolated and confused. I didn't have an acting job to escape to. I didn't have my cigarettes. There was no martini at the end of the day. I would pace the floor all night long and be exhausted all day. I would feel like the walls of the room were shaking around me. I would lose my car keys, my house key, my wallet, and anything not surgically attached to me.

One day, in complete frustration over my misplacing something important, Barney yelled, "You are driving me crazy!"

Incredulous, I shouted, "How would you like to be *me*?"

Barney said, "You're right. That has to be worse."

When we were in public, I would make light of it, introducing him as "my first husband."

Barney would follow up with, "And this is my last wife. Please, God."

I was no longer his Cagney or Rosie O'Neill. When I was his actress, he would stop what he was doing to pay attention to my ideas or my complaints. I was queen.

The role of wife wasn't the same at all. If I went into his den, he would most likely respond, "Sharon, I'm working. I will talk to you at the end of the day."

Then a letter inviting me to star in a West End play in London showed up in the mail. The offer was to play Annie Wilkes in the stage production of *Misery*. There had already been the film adaptation of Stephen King's best-selling book in 1990 with Kathy Bates as Annie.

Stephen King said that he had always envisioned *Misery* as a two-hander onstage. London playwright Simon Moore decided to make it as close to the book as possible, which was much, much darker than the movie.

I thought, "Why not?" I was raging through menopause. Why not put it all into a character onstage?

I took the letter into Barney's den and announced, "I don't like the way you treat me. I just received an offer to star in a play in London. I'm going to accept."

Barney didn't put up an argument. He's a feminist. He wasn't about to tell me I couldn't go.

I accepted the role and was instantly terrified by the commitment. I was about to star in the West End. The West End!! London's Broadway on steroids, where I would be one of two people carrying the show!

Dame Maggie Smith, Sir Derek Jacobi, Sir Ian McKellen, Sir John Gielgud, and Dame Judi Dench were all stars on West End stages. Their names made me breathless. Had my erratic hormones distracted me from what was realistic?

As soon as I received the script, I had to start learning my lines. It was a two-person play, so I had a lot to memorize.

I wanted to have my lines down before I left for the London rehearsals, but menopause made concentration almost impossible.

Worse yet, days after the script arrived, there was a huge earthquake near Los Angeles. I kept feeling massive aftershocks, day after day. The floors and the walls were shaking and my heart would race. No one else seemed to be reacting to them. I couldn't understand it.

My therapist wanted to send me to a psychopharmacologist. Barney insisted on going with me, because he wanted the doctor to "know what was going on in our house."

As Barney was telling the doctor about my recent behavior changes, mood swings, trouble sleeping, and daily crying jags, the office walls started shaking violently. The chair I was sitting in was bouncing up and down.

Excited to prove my point, I said, "See? It's all shaking! I'm not crazy. It's all shaking!"

Barney and the doctor exchanged long, knowing glances.

"Well, lock me up then!" I shouted.

I started to cry. This violent shaking couldn't possibly be coming from within, but apparently it was.

The doctor said, "Sharon, you need some antidepressants."

I refused. "I don't want to take them. I'm going to London to do a play. I can't star in the West End and be on medication!"

The next day, I called the doctor in a panic. "I'm trying to memorize my dialogue for this play. I can't remember these lines."

"Sharon, you need to take the pills," was his calm reply. "Take the pills, and you will remember the lines."

He was right.

My going to London was probably the best way to save our floundering marriage. I had to throw myself into the part of Annie full-time, and Barney could be free from emotional turmoil for a while.

I packed my trunk and went off to live in a little house in Chelsea provided by the theater.

This play was going to be an intense experience. I knew Annie was not to be played as only a demented torturer. She actually believes she is having a relationship with her imprisoned writer, as sick as it is. She is aware that her mental illness is getting worse and worse, but she is incapable of regulating herself. She is in love with him.

Annie needs to be plump due to her obsession with consuming fast foods.

One of the producers, Andrew Welch, told me, "Of course, we will build you a fat suit."

I said, "You don't have to do that. I can get there myself."

I was in menopause and had already gained about seven pounds from not smoking. I was miserable without cigarettes, and I couldn't wait to just eat whatever I wanted. I denied myself nothing. I'd send my assistant, Sarah Chanin, out for pints of ice cream and popcorn with butter, all of which I would eat, every night, in bed. Needless to say, over the course of rehearsal, I gained a lot of weight.

While I was in early rehearsals, I went to see the stage production of *Kiss of the Spider Woman*. The week before I had presented an award to Chita Rivera, the star of the London production, at a large theater awards show in London.

I'm very shy, and I really almost chickened out on going backstage to say hello. But then I thought about it. She was an American actress, too. We were both far from home.

I said, "Chita, I'm sure you don't remember me. I'm Sharon Gless. I presented your award to you last week."

She said, "Of course I remember you. Do you know anybody here in London?"

I said, "No."

She said, "I don't either. Do you want to have dinner sometime?"

Chita rallied two famous English-born actresses, Rosemary Harris and Maureen Lipman, to join us. Rosemary is a phenomenal stage and film actress. (American viewers probably know her best as Aunt May in all three of the *Spider-Man* movies.) Maureen is a well-known face on British stage, television, and film, and an amazing comedienne. She has now been knighted a dame. She calls herself Dame Mo. For three months, we all had dinner together once a week. The three of them had a natural back-and-forth that was so fast and witty that whatever they said would make me howl with laughter. I was in heaven. Chita kept telling me to "cheer up."

Toward the end of the rehearsal period, I looked the part of Annie. My hair was dyed a medium brown for the role, and I had to go out to buy men's corduroy pants and oversize sweaters to wear, as nothing I had brought with me fit anymore with the weight gain. I was still enjoying my carefree indulging. Maybe too much.

One Sunday evening, producer Andrew Welch invited me to a homemade dinner with his wife, Emma, and their two young sons. When I arrived, there was a cheese and grape board sitting on top of the bar. As we chatted, I helped myself to the wonderful cheeses. No one else ate any. I didn't mind that. I enjoyed almost the whole plate.

At the end of dinner, and eating everything offered, I jokingly said, "Okay! What's for dessert?!"

The boys dropped their eyes down to their laps and Emma turned to look at Andrew with a desperate expression.

Andrew cleared his throat and said gently, "Well, you already ate it."

I had completely forgotten that the British often serve a cheese board at the end of a meal. Fortunately, they all thought it was funny. I could have died.

The extra pounds I was carrying didn't bother me. The only thing I noticed was the fact that no one gave me more than a passing glance. I walked around London completely unrecognizable.

One morning, when I arrived for rehearsal, I heard laughter from the back of the theater as I walked out onstage.

"Well, you did it! Unbelievable!" roared the playwright-director, Simon.

He was referring to my size.

I played the part for three months, which is what my costar, Bill Paterson, had agreed to when he signed on. Bill is Scottish and works nonstop in British film, television, and stage. He played the long-suffering dad on TV's multi-Emmy-winning *Fleabag*. He is a dream to work with and has become one of my dearest friends.

Onstage, *Misery* was undeniably violent, much rougher than the film. The play got good reviews and sold out every weekend, which was impressive considering it was not typical West End fare.

The audience would nervously laugh at first and then gasp at the violence and in anticipation of what Annie would do next to control and manipulate Paul. One woman fainted in her seat during the scene where Annie amputates her kidnapped writer's foot with an axe. Firemen took her out on a gurney. Believe it or not, her husband refused to leave. He wanted to see the rest of the play. During another performance, the prosthetic foot flew out into the audience. The audience always emitted muffled screams at this point in the play, but this night one scream was bloodcurdling. It came from the person who got the severed foot in her lap.

Audience members would wait at the stage door for Bill and me after the show. Bill would duck out. I basked in it all.

The only person who wasn't happy with my performance as Annie was Barney. He flew in the night we opened and went straight to the theater from the airport to catch the show. I think he was shell-shocked. His blonde bride had now turned into a drab-haired, fat-as-hell, insane nurse. He was more than a little upset.

I defended myself. "Robert De Niro gained sixty pounds for *Raging Bull*, and everyone applauded *him* doing that for *his* craft."

"Well, I don't know what *Mrs.* De Niro had to say," Barney replied, "but I'm not a happy camper."

Almost every journalist who interviewed me also focused on my weight. They seemed aghast that I would let myself go to such an extreme. I had by now put on forty pounds.

Concurrently, under the subject heading of ghastly extremes, my treasured Malibu beach house was being destroyed while I was five thousand miles away in London. I had leased the house for the months I would be doing *Misery* to Dodi Fayed, the firstborn son of an Egyptian billionaire and the owner of Harrods in London, later to become famous as Princess Diana's beau. He liked my property because there was a guesthouse for his maid. I was encouraged by that information. I thought a live-in maid would keep it spotless.

Dodi had a girlfriend he hooked up with in California who moved into my house with her large German shepherds, despite his having signed my contract stipulating that no pets were allowed in the house. The untrained hundred-pound dogs urinated all over the interior, shredded the retro fabrics on my furniture, and scratched the wooden floors. The Berber carpeting became flea-infested. My rose garden was trampled completely flat. There were food stains and spills that were never cleaned up.

Dodi's father sent me a check to repair the damages. But it still didn't cover the amount of time it took to make over the whole house.

In a bizarre twist of fate, upon my arrival in London, I was asked to do another presentation for the royal family. This time I met Prince Charles and Princess Diana. Charles was handsome, genuine, and very charming. He leaned in to whisper in my left ear, "I'm a great fan of yours."

That made *my* night.

Diana was very shy and reserved that evening, leaving a lot of distance between her and Charles, keeping her eyes lowered. I could see that her skin was broken out under her makeup.

She smiled and took my hand and said, "Thank you for making the trip here."

I said, "You are very loved in my country, Your Royal Highness. I hope you know that."

It was the last time Charles and Diana appeared together in public. The next morning the prime minister announced their separation.

Ironically, Diana's new controversial relationship would be with the man who had laid waste to my Malibu home.

Following Dodi's death, a reporter from the *Los Angeles Times* called me. It had leaked through the tabloids that Dodi had once rented my house. The reporter wanted to know if I had any comments about Dodi.

I answered, "Yes. He was an absolute pig."

The reporter was speechless. I guess she expected some charming story of princely chivalry.

"He did everything but roast a goat in my living room."

I was hoping they would print my quote, but they didn't.

When I returned to Los Angeles after *Misery* had closed, Barney had mellowed and was sympathetic as I slumped back into a dark mood that I couldn't stop. Now, I was both fat *and* depressed. I wanted to smoke and drink and have a TV show to do.

Barney sat across the table from me. He wanted me to feel good about myself once more.

"I understand," Barney said. "I'd like to send you to a spa in San Diego where they can help you lose weight. What do you say to that?"

I agreed. I threw myself on the mercy of the spa's weight-loss coaches and left a month later twenty pounds lighter.

Ready or not, CBS was throwing a black-tie gala for their super-executive, Jeff Sagansky, and we had received our engraved invitation. Never mind that it was on the same day as my birthday.

"What's the big fucking deal?" I shouted over my hair dryer when Barney notified me that we were running late. "It's not like we have a show on CBS's fall schedule."

A limo delivered us to Rex, a trendy downtown LA restaurant that CBS had taken over for the Sagansky event.

Outside the front door was an easel set up with a large photo of Jeff Sagansky, but the expected gaggle of paparazzi for an event of this magnitude was nowhere in sight. We walked inside.

Many beautiful tables had been set up with black-and-white place settings and engraved menus at each chair. Hundreds of black and white balloons bobbed around in the silent room, near the second-story catwalk. But there were no people. Barney and I were alone in the huge dining room.

Suddenly, the catwalk was filled with over a hundred people, all singing "Happy Birthday." To me! Barney had managed to pull off a phenomenal surprise fiftieth birthday party for me. Friends from every series I had ever done were there, along with old friends from my boarding school days and people connected to *Misery* who had flown in from London. The whole CBS celebration was a ruse, elaborately conceived by Barney, along with the ironic twist: Executive Jeff Sagansky was there to honor me, instead of the other way around.

I had done a made-for-TV movie called *Hardhat and Legs* about a decade before, and the famous musician and singer Bobby Short had been featured in it. He had flown in with his three-piece band at Barney's request and entertained all night.

Barney's daughter Torrie had filmed birthday hellos from so many people that I love and admire. Johnny Mathis had always been my teenage crush. There he was, on film, singing "Happy Birthday" to me, a cappella.

My good pal Barry Manilow appeared on the tape next, sitting at his piano, saying, "So, Sharon. I heard Mathis sang 'Happy Birthday' to you. Well, fuck him! Here you go." Then he sang his version. Perfect!

It was such a fun night. I was overwhelmed with love from all my friends and my family.

The next morning, we woke up at my newly refurbished Malibu beach house. On the flagpole outside of my glass balcony doors was a flag printed with "Happy Birthday, Sharon!"

Barney was already up. "You better get up and get dressed. Everyone is coming over for a barbecue today."

All the friends who had come in from out of town and my family and Barney's family came over for the day. A photographer from London, Judith Hull, had been flown in to photograph me at age fifty on the Malibu dunes I loved so much.

I look very content and poised in the photos. It must have been the leftover glow of the career success of my thirties and forties. The froth of the crashing ocean is the backdrop for many of the photos. It suited how washed-up my television career would become for the next decade.

Forty

Get Off My Ass

I wasn't ready to return. It had been seven years since the series had ended.

Now there was to be a movie: *Cagney & Lacey: The Return*. Barney had made an agreement with Jeff Sagansky to produce four made-for-TV movies for CBS with Tyne and me reprising the roles of Mary Beth Lacey and Christine Cagney.

I read the first script. Then I rebelled. Christine Cagney was now a lieutenant, but she was working at a supervisory desk job for the district attorney. She was living in an elegant brownstone and was married to a wealthy man. Desk job??? Married??????

All I could think was, "Jesus! Is this what sobriety did to Christine? Has she lost her mind? Is she hitting the bottle again?"

I had played the character for six seasons, 119 episodes. I knew her better than I knew myself. There was no way Cagney would settle for working a desk position, even on her way to her dream job of being the first female police commissioner. Especially unbelievable was that she would now be married and living this piss-elegant life. The script I read opened with Christine throwing a fancy party in her home. She's wearing a long string of pearls. Pearls?! I don't think so. I'm surprised she didn't hang herself with them.

I almost left Barney over this one. He stood by his writers. Barney tried to defend the idea of a now-married Cagney. I was not convinced. In fact, I was appalled.

"I didn't say she'd *stay* married," Barney told me. "And it's not like she's married to just anyone. I got James Naughton to play your husband."

Well, no offense to the mega-talented, Tony-winning James Naughton, with whom I had costarred twenty years earlier in my first TV series, *Faraday and Company*, but I was adamant that Christine Cagney would never tie the knot. At least not while she had career goals to pursue.

The fans agreed with me. By the second movie, Christine was divorced.

I filmed the first movie with the worst perm ever put on a human head. Combine that with the fact that I was still twenty pounds overweight. The camera was not my friend. Tyne had put on a few pounds over the previous five years, too. I don't know who nicknamed the quad of movies *Cagney & Lacey: The Menopause Years*, but I wouldn't want to tune in for that. I was living it.

But apparently the fans had a different view. They showed up for us in record numbers. The first reunion movie swept the ratings for the entire night and came in second as the highest-rated television movie that year. A huge, well-promoted boxing rematch between forty-five-year-old George Foreman and heavyweight boxer Michael Moorer was on the same night and at the same time, but we still prevailed. CBS sent lots of flowers. They were in love with us again.

The next day, Jay Leno's opening monologue for *The Tonight Show* contained the following joke, leading the audience to think he was talking about the aging, overweight Foreman and his out-of-shape opponent.

"So, everybody. How about those numbers? I guess it goes to show that it doesn't matter how old or fat you are, you can still land a hit. But enough about *Cagney & Lacey*. . . ."

Hopefully Jay's wife, Mavis, kicked *his* fat ass that night.

Journalists—most of them male—reviewing the movies went crazy writing about my size. One Pulitzer Prize–winning reviewer with the *Los Angeles Times* wrote that my backside looked like a sack of potatoes.

Years later, he apologized.

I asked Barney why the media was so focused on, and so cruel about, my weight.

He said, "Because you were the blonde. You broke their heart. They'll never forgive you."

Could it be that the public was that shallow in 1994, or was it more that Barney himself couldn't forgive me?

Even though our first movie scored the highest in the Nielsen ratings, it didn't seem to matter to the new president and head of programming for CBS, Les Moonves. I had known Leslie since we were both young acting students in class together. To me, he was just another kid hoping to be an actor.

In his position as CBS president, Les decided that he was going to shake it all up and attract an audience of younger viewers in the way that the Fox Network was doing at the time. And the way to attract younger viewers was to air shows starring beautiful younger actresses.

He wasn't at all interested in grown-up female-centered dramas and comedies, like Linda Bloodworth-Thomason's *Designing Women*, though it remained a hit show. He told me that he'd always hated *Cagney & Lacey* and labeled its major success "a fluke." He killed the franchise.

Ironically, his inappropriate treatment of actresses, as well as female writers, producers, and assistants, led to his eventual demise at CBS and in the industry.

Tyne, Barney, and I had to do most of our own promoting of the last two movies, which were shuffled into impossible time slots and intentionally buried by Moonves.

CBS might have forgotten about *Cagney & Lacey*, but women had not. In April 1995, Tyne and I were invited to join actresses Whoopi Goldberg, Lee Grant, Valerie Harper, and political activists like Bella Abzug, Betty Friedan, and Gloria Steinem onstage in a rally for women's equality sponsored by the National Organization for Women. Hundreds of thousands of women and a few men, including Barney, filled the National Mall in Washington, DC, under the shadow of the Washington Monument. Tyne and I received a lengthy ovation. Looking out at the huge crowd, it was the first time that I completely grasped how *Cagney & Lacey* had represented the pulse of the future, a marker on the timeline of feminist and women's history. That's the thing about history. You don't know you're making it when you're in progress. But if it's good, the ripple effect goes on and on.

⇒ • ⇐

Even though I was in my fifties, I was still trying to figure out who I was becoming as an actress. One morning, I received a phone call with an offer to play the lead role of Jennie in Neil Simon's *Chapter Two*, at the Gielgud Theatre in London's West End. I would play opposite the very sexy Scottish actor Tom Conti. As popular as Neil Simon's plays had been for decades in the United States, they were very rarely produced across the pond. It made me nervous, but I wanted to accept the challenge. After all, being the female lead in a Neil Simon play and working with Tom Conti? How good is that?

Barney had found an apartment we both loved on Fisher Island and, ready to escape the "show business" view of Los Angeles, he happily sold his Hancock Park property and produced a renovation and move for the two of us to the placid small island off Miami's shore. I kept my Studio City cottage. As long as I still had a home in Los Angeles, I was fine being a bicoastal citizen.

As he headed to sun and ocean views, I memorized my lines and reconnected with the narrow and foggy streets of London.

Early on during the *Chapter Two* rehearsals, the director had a complaint. It was during Jennie's famous monologue, and I was giving it all I had.

He stopped me in the middle of it.

"Keep your arms down. All you American actors flail your arms around too much," he said. "During your long monologue, just sit down on the chaise and tell me honestly how you feel."

I followed his direction. I sat down. It was more intimate, but it was far less emotional.

One night, after we had opened, unbeknownst to the cast, Neil Simon was in the audience. It wasn't one of my better shows. The audience didn't seem to be responding the way they usually did.

Neil came backstage after the show to say hello to the actors. He was very cordial and warm, shaking our hands and repeatedly saying, "Great job."

When he said it to me, I knew better. It was clear to me that he had things to say about the performance, but he wouldn't speak his opinion with others nearby. Neil was harboring a complaint. I wanted to know what it was.

Very conversationally, I asked, "So, Neil, where are you staying?"

The next morning, at 9 a.m. on the dot, I phoned him at his hotel.

When he answered, I dove right in.

"Neil, there's something I'm not doing right. I don't know what it is. Please tell me."

He plainly said, "Get off your ass! Get on your feet when you do that monologue. In the '70s, when *Chapter Two* premiered, that monologue would get an ovation. Every performance. It won't anymore, but get on your feet when you deliver that monologue."

I thanked him profusely.

That night Neil returned to see the show again. I did the monologue exactly as he had advised, and the audience responded with spontaneous applause. By the time I got off the stage and to my dressing room, Neil was there.

He was so happy that he lifted me off my feet and spun me around!

And that took some serious strength!!

Tom and I stay in touch, and recently he told me a story of our time onstage together that he swears is true.

Close to the end of the play, my character is drunk and in a big fight with her husband, George.

The line as written, my character feigning a Southern accent, says, "Ah'm jes a dumb ole country girl from Cleveland, George."

Tom recalls that one night, onstage, I said, "Ah'm jes a dumb ole cunt, George."

He said, "You're a what?"

I said, "I'm a cunt."

Backstage, following the curtain call, I asked Tom, "Did I just say the word *cunt* on a West End stage?"

He responded, "Twice."

That's how Tom Conti tells the story. I deny everything.

⇒ Forty-One ⇐

Every Nine Years

After nine years of marriage, my husband asked me for a divorce. Well, he didn't really ask . . . not directly.

I was starring onstage in Claudia Allen's *Cahoots*, a madcap comedy, at Chicago's Victory Gardens Theater. She had written the play with me in mind. I wasn't all that busy in May of 2000, so I gratefully said yes.

All of the buzz and crazy predictions about Y2K, the arrival of a new century, had been nothing more than a dull fizzle. At the moment, it resembled my career.

I had no TV show, no TV movie, and no manager. Then Ron Meyer, by now my agent for two decades, decided to leave Creative Artists Agency for an executive career at Universal Studios. He was the only agent I knew, so I left CAA when he did.

It seemed I was soon to be a candidate for one of those mawkish "Where Are They Now?" cable shows. They would find me in a ninety-nine-seat theater on the north side of Chicago with my thirty extra pounds of menopausal weight. I had no idea how to define myself anymore. And I couldn't visualize my future.

At the same time, Barney could no longer see *his* future with me in it.

One night, following the show, sitting in the little apartment provided by the theater, I had a hunch, an intuitive hit.

Text messaging had just become a thing in 2000, and I typed in my question to Barney, who was happily ensconced in our Fisher Island apartment in Florida.

I typed, "Do you want a divorce?"

He replied a moment later. Barney sent back, "Where did you get that?"

I responded, "I just did. I picked it up. It's what I do."

I waited for the reply, which came back, "Yes. I am thinking about it. Your radar still scares me."

It wasn't a shock to me. We had been arguing more frequently and making up less and less. Indifference had come to define us. I had always known, deep down, that I made a much better mistress than wife.

During one of our many arguments, right before I left for Chicago, Barney told me of a prediction about the two of us, made by his ex-wife years ago.

"Barbara said you and I would never make it, because we both want to be the star of the show."

I snapped back, "Well, Barbara was wrong! We will never make it because I *am* the star of the show!!"

Barney couldn't help but grin.

"Touché," he said, retreating to his desk.

Barney had been married twice before. His first wife, Joni, was only twenty when they married, twenty-nine when they divorced. His second wife, Barbara, was barely thirty when they married, thirty-nine when they divorced. He had never been married to a woman of my age or my temperament.

He had survived nine years with me being a menopausal mess. And I had lived an equal amount of time with him being a major asshole. What a pair! Now he wanted out.

One day, in the middle of a fight, I yelled at Barney, "Don't you think it's fascinating that every nine years you divorce a wife?"

I swear he paused, looked up at the ceiling, doing the math in his head, and then, his voice filled with wonder, answered, "It *is* fascinating."

What a jerk! I am a saint. He is still alive.

One could no longer contest a divorce by the year 2000, of course, but that didn't stop me from acting like I could.

Completely furious with him, I said, "All right. I'll give you your divorce, but not until I make it to year ten. Because I'm going to beat out the other two! After that, I don't give a fuck what you do!"

"It's a deal," he said.

Months later, I flew in to Los Angeles for the big family dinner to celebrate our tenth wedding anniversary.

Barney has never failed to plan and host perfect parties. He took over the private dining room at Matteo's restaurant on LA's Westside. Everything was impeccable.

He seated himself at one end of the table and me at the other, obviously all the better for us to look adoringly at one another through the tunnel of faces of our family, gathered there to celebrate us. Not one of them—not one—knew we were getting divorced.

Barney rose to his feet to propose a toast.

There I sat, with yet another unfortunate perm topping my almost two-hundred-pound body, thinking, "This ought to be good."

Barney raised his glass to me, smiled, and announced in my direction, "To the winner!"

God. The fucking arrogance.

He still makes me laugh. And he still finds himself fascinating.

Forty-Two

I Love Trouble

Oh, for a dose of trouble! I live for it. Give me a character with some spirit. I'll jump in with both feet.

Among many other roles, I've played a vulnerable receptionist, a virginal daughter, a slutty coed, a spoiled heiress, a square hospital administrator, an observant artist, a variety of doomed stewardesses, a bold cop, a sassy hotel owner, a funny sex-education teacher, a determined journalist, a famous movie star, and a mutilating nurse. But I had never played a powerful queen. And I had never played a character from the twelfth century. Eleanor of Aquitaine was both. I had accepted the female lead in *The Lion in Winter* to be produced at the Cape Playhouse in Massachusetts, one of the oldest theaters in summer stock.

At the time I was offered Eleanor, I was still in Chicago starring in *Cahoots*. I probably should have turned down the role, but I didn't really want to go back to Miami and face the divorce proceedings.

Instead, I sought to engage the finest acting coach in Chicago, and I found him. I knew my life would change with Peter Forster in it. And that's exactly what happened. He is brilliant, very funny, and we "got it" about one another. We became fast friends. Forever.

I still wasn't convinced the part was right for me. I would be playing Eleanor at a time when I felt my personal worst: overweight, prone to mood-swinging depression, soon to be a divorcée, with shriveling self-esteem. Not a good look on me.

Come to think of it, Eleanor's life was not dissimilar, but she handled it better.

One afternoon, before I went to the theater for *Cahoots*, Peter called me from his office. Peter was also an agent for actors. He had a script.

"Have you heard of a TV show called *Queer as Folk*? It's a British show that's been bought by Showtime to make a US version."

I had not heard of it.

"There's a part in it that's perfect for you. I'm going to send a driver to bring you the script. Please read it. Right away."

I did read it. I picked up the phone and I called Showtime.

Carole Smith was now working for Jerry Offsay, the president and programming head of the Showtime network.

I asked her if the role of the mother had been cast.

She said, "You don't want to play the mother."

I said, "Yes, I do."

She said, "It's cable. There's no money."

"I don't care," I answered.

Carole sighed. "It will be filming in Canada. You don't want to live in Canada."

I was unflappable. "Yes, I do."

I wasn't going to give up my shot at playing this part. I had never responded to a role on the page as fully as I responded to Debbie Novotny. Besides which, I had never read a complete TV script like this one before, with its blatant sex scenes.

Carole told me she would run it by Jerry, who happened to be in a casting meeting that very day for *Queer as Folk*.

Jerry got on the phone with me.

"Sharon, I love this idea," he told me. "I think you'll bring a little class to the project."

I said, "Jerry, class is not what I had in mind."

I knew exactly what I wanted to do as Debbie Novotny. She had great honesty, guts, and fierceness, and I loved every word that came out of her mouth.

Jerry said, "Would you mind if we flew you out to Los Angeles to meet with the two producers, Ron Cowen and Dan Lipman? It's their show."

I agreed. On my way to the airport, I spoke to Ron and Dan on the phone. "Before I fly out there, do you both know what I look like now?"

Dan said, "We saw you onstage with Tyne Daly for the recent AIDS benefit. We know exactly what you look like."

Even if they didn't know what I looked like, I wasn't about to let go of an opportunity because of my size. I had done that once before and it remains one of the greatest regrets in my life.

In 1996, Barney, Tyne, and I were getting ready to do a promotional tour for the *Cagney & Lacey* reunion movies on CBS. I was dreadfully unhappy. I had been trying to eat away my menopausal depression and now looked like a plus-size version of Cagney.

Angela Lansbury called. Personally. She said they had written a two-hour episode of *Murder, She Wrote* with me in mind, and she wanted me to play the lead guest star.

I had told Angela for years that I wanted to work with her.

It was a lovely offer. I was an emotional mess.

I stammered out, "Angela, I'm so sorry. I'd give anything to work with you, but I am committed to this press tour with Barney and Tyne for our four TV movies."

What was impossible was for me to honestly tell Angela what I looked like at that time. I was terrified she would see me in person and regret asking me to guest star. I didn't have the nerve to tell her.

It would have been such an honor to work with Angela. My great loss. I know we would have been good together.

This time around, with *Queer as Folk*, I was going to put it all on the table beforehand. Take me or leave me. There was a larger version of Sharon Gless, still an actress, still ready to work, still good at what I do.

So I flew out on my day off from the theater. I wore a T-shirt that said, "Christ is coming. Look busy."

It was the most wonderful interview. We never stopped laughing. I fell in love with Ron and Dan.

"You have Debbie's laugh," Dan told me.

The part was offered to me that day, if I wanted it. I wanted it.

At that time, I was with a new agent, David Shapira.

I told David, "I just went and met the producers of *Queer as Folk*."

Before I could say anything else, he shot back, "I would never let you do that filthy show."

I said, "Well, I already got the filthy part, so negotiate the deal! Please."

He did.

"And get me out of *The Lion in Winter*. Please. Thank you."

He did.

I knew people would remember Debbie Novotny on *Queer as Folk*. She was wonderfully real and hysterically funny. I had no idea how many people would watch it.

"We only have one worry," Ron said. "We know your background. In your past TV shows, you've been the lead. This will be different. This show isn't about Debbie Novotny."

I said, "I understand that."

I smiled, thinking to myself, "Wait till I get on-screen."

Pride cometh before the fall.

I was so enthusiastic about playing Debbie Novotny that I devised a complete look for her. There was a novelty shop in West Hollywood that sold T-shirts with raunchy remarks printed across the chest. I bought out their stock that referred to gay sex. I went to a wig shop in Hollywood and procured seventeen different wigs in a variety of colors from hot pink to emerald green. I had already made up a backstory for Debbie, for my own purpose, about how her goal was to buy her own beauty shop. She worked at the Liberty Diner during high school, got pregnant, and couldn't go on to beauty school because she had a baby son to raise.

The producers loved the T-shirt idea and the wardrobe department made me a rainbow vest. I modeled each of the wigs for the hair and makeup people.

Ron and Dan told me, "We ran the wigs idea by the executives at Showtime. They're against the variety of wigs. They wanted the viewers to know that it was Sharon Gless."

I felt like saying, "Jesus. The second I open my mouth they'll know who it is!"

I was allowed to pick one wig. I chose the red one.

Then the thing that Ron and Dan were concerned might happen did happen. It was my first day of shooting. The show was already in production for about two weeks in August before I came in. I was given a call time of 11 a.m. I arrived on the set and got into costume, wig, and makeup. Every actor on the show had a small dressing room with a makeup mirror over a counter, a bathroom, and a couch. It was fine with me. I knew the deal when I signed on. So, once I was ready, I went to my dressing room, sat on my little couch with my script, and waited to do my scene. I am never late. One hour passed, then three more, then it was midnight. At 5 a.m., I was finally called to the set to shoot my scene. I had been waiting for eighteen hours.

The director did nothing at all to make Debbie Novotny's introduction to the viewers special. The scene takes place in the diner. My son, Michael, comes in with the new kid, Justin. Debbie nicknames him "Sunshine." I had some fun ideas of how to introduce Debbie to the viewers. The director didn't care. He barely made eye contact with me, was uninterested in any suggestion I had, and basically treated me as if I were a person who had never been on a soundstage before.

I tried to keep my cool, but I was infuriated by his arrogance and lack of imagination. Clearly, I had a dose of arrogance myself.

I had been trained early on in my career that at the end of a day of filming, you never leave the set without personally thanking the director. It was a tradition I had always honored—until that morning.

Instead, as soon as we were wrapped, I phoned my agent.

After that, I went to Ron and Dan's office with my complaint. They had one, too. About me. They were unhappy that I had called my agent. They were sympathetic, but it was complicated. A lot was on the line for them with this two-hour launch episode. They pretty much let me know that they had "warned" me. And they had. I was in tears.

The truth was, I didn't understand their key concerns. I had not played a supporting role for decades. I had always been on one of the major networks. I had never done a cable show. I was clueless about the way it might transpire.

I didn't identify it on that day in Ron and Dan's office, but now it's evident to me. This leading lady had to adjust to becoming a supporting player. It was a harsh wake-up call for me, like a cold shower at a campground when you're used to a Jacuzzi tub at the Four Seasons.

I took a deep breath, tamped down my residual anger, and then said, "Here's my request. I will wait for as many hours as the director needs to get his shit together until he gets to my scene. However, once I'm on the soundstage, and it's my time on camera, you have to give me time to work. Don't rush my scene because you got yourselves in a bind. Please."

That was my only ask. They agreed.

I never complained again for the entire five-year run and neither did they.

Showtime did a screening of the pilot for an invited audience in Los Angeles. Barney went with me. He was stunned that I would let myself appear in a TV show looking like that—I was overweight and wearing a cheap red wig and gaudy clothes. He thought it was a career crusher and let me know it.

I didn't have the same worry. I knew I had reinvented my career with the most interesting female television role available that year. The people who attended the screening applauded my scenes and came to talk to me afterward. They fell for Debbie as hard as I had. I knew TV viewers would have the same reaction.

When the lights came up, Barney said, "I was wrong. It works. They love you."

Then he added, "But that director certainly didn't know how to introduce you."

I appreciated his apology.

Often interviewers will ask me why I wanted to be in *Queer as Folk*. I always tell them, "I did it because I thought there would be trouble. And I love trouble."

And I will thank Jerry Offsay, Ron Cowen, and Dan Lipman for the rest of my life for letting me in. They brought me back, and for five years we made wonderful memories.

Forty-Three

I'll Be There

"I had to tell Michael he was gay so he didn't have to tell me first."

Debbie Novotny says these words to Justin's mother after she returns the teenage runaway back to his front door.

Over the years, many people have told me how much they loved that line from *Queer as Folk*.

I didn't write the line. I wrote none of Debbie's dialogue. I didn't alter a word. I was just the lucky one who got to say it. It's why I wanted to play this character. I knew she could cause change.

One morning during the first week of filming, Michelle Clunie, who played Melanie, was in the makeup trailer at the same time I was. When she was finished, she stopped by my chair on her way out.

"None of us would have done this show," Michelle told me, with tears in her eyes. "We were all so afraid that it would end our careers because the content is so shocking. But then we heard you were going to be in it. We all decided that if Sharon Gless thought it was worth the risk, then we could do it, too."

I was both flattered and floored. Ironically, I'd done the show because I thought it would *help* my career!

Filming that first episode, we all knew that we had signed on for a groundbreaker. In those days, truly daring TV shows about gay life didn't exist. TV studios usually want a safe and popular hit. When you sign on for something radical and new, there *is* no safety net.

There was no *Queer Eye for the Straight Guy* or *The L Word* when we debuted. Those shows didn't appear until years later. Somebody had to be brave enough to start it. Jerry Offsay, Showtime president, took the chance.

I think everyone who worked on *Queer as Folk* held their breath the night the show premiered. We expected backlash from the religious right, or strong "warning" reviews, maybe a petition or two against Showtime. We didn't hear a peep. Unbelievably, our premiere happened on the very night that George W. Bush stole the election from Al Gore in Florida. The religious right was focused on their political victory. The rest of America was stunned and sad. The show slid in under the radar and stayed relatively unnoticed by the press until it gained an audience and momentum. The producers had anticipated that gay people would find the show, but their expected audience numbers doubled. It became a pop culture phenomenon.

Showtime discovered that heterosexual women were making *Queer as Folk* appointment TV. They watched by the scores, intrigued by the sexy and beautiful men. Then their boyfriends would watch with them, hoping for payoff with their turned-on girlfriends.

Viewers may have first tuned in out of curiosity about the sex scenes, but they stayed fans for all five years because the show had heart, loyal and tumultuous relationships, and ever-evolving friendships. Okay, it had great sex, too.

Only the actors and the camera operator were allowed on the set during filming of any scene involving sex.

Believe me, I tried to inconspicuously watch, but the director would always laugh and say, "Sharon. Go to your room."

These actors were not exhibitionists. They were real actors, and they courageously gave full life to each character.

Because we were all far away from home, the cast became very close. It was an intimate show. And our friendships reflected that intimacy. We are still close to this day.

One of my all-time favorite scenes was with Gale Harold, who played Brian. Debbie has heard that Brian lost his job, and she goes to his loft to comfort him. She arrives with a tuna casserole in hand to find Brian sitting on the floor, stoned. Despite admitting that she hasn't smoked pot since Woodstock, Debbie joins Brian on the floor to share a joint.

The last time I had smoked pot was in the early 1980s. All I remembered about being stoned was that there were always long gaps in the conversation.

At the table read for this episode, I said to Gale, "Let's make this scene how it really is when you're stoned. Okay?"

Gale nodded. "Following your lead."

We read the scene with a six- to ten-second pause between each line. The actors, producers, and writers at the table broke into laughter and then applauded at the end.

As the relationships developed season to season, it became obvious that Debbie had a potent power over Brian. She could call him on his shit like no one else could. He is vulnerable with her in ways that he never is with other characters. And, God love Gale, he was willing to go there with me every time.

Right before our final season, Rosie O'Donnell was shooting a movie in Toronto and was working with crewmembers from *Queer as Folk*. She told them she loved the show and wanted to be on it. Of course, everyone thought it was a great idea. Rosie had certain caveats, however. She told the producers that she did not want to play herself and that all of her scenes had to be with Sharon Gless.

They honored her wishes.

Rosie played Loretta, a woman who escaped an abusive marriage, came to work in the diner, and fell for Debbie. She brings her roses and homemade candy. Debbie thinks it's a sweet gesture of friendship. Peter Paige's character, Emmett, gives Debbie the wake-up call that Loretta's feelings are romantic.

Then, one evening, after three drinks, Debbie leans in to kiss Loretta. The next day she has no memory of what she did. Loretta hasn't forgotten.

Rosie was in three episodes. She was wonderful. Later, she sent me a dozen red roses, with a card that read, "You're a good kisser."

I was flattered. It was the first time I had heard that from a woman. But then again, it was the first time I had ever kissed a woman.

I've had gay friends my entire adult life, but until I was on *Queer as Folk*, I didn't know a lot about the struggles and concerns of the gay community. Debbie was a true advocate and activist. As a PFLAG (Parents and Friends of Lesbians and Gays) mom, she knew the issues. I learned quickly what they were.

Ever since *Queer as Folk*, gay men will approach me as I am leaving events, movie theaters, restaurants, and even on the street to ask if I will give them a hug. I'm always happy to do that. Many will express how often they had wished to be accepted by their parents. Once, I embraced a young man, and he started weeping in my arms. I stood and held him, thinking, "My God, the damage that has been done to this boy!"

I've never consciously adopted as my own the principles of a character in the way that I adopted Debbie Novotny's. She was a bold advocate for gay and lesbian rights, and I learned a great deal from her. Anytime the gay community needs me, I'll be there.

⇒ • ⇐

One of the first things I did after the show wrapped was to accept Rosie O'Donnell's invitation to be a guest on her second R Family Vacations cruise. She and her then wife, Kelli, wanted to provide an opportunity for the gay community to take a vacation with their kids, friends, and other families like their own. Rosie chartered a complete cruise ship. It was an instant hit. She made a sensational two-hour documentary on the virgin cruise. It was nominated for five Emmys.

For years, Rosie lived part-time on the island next to Fisher Island in Florida. I would ferry to the bridge and walk to her house. We'd talk for hours. She's smart and funny, as well as very politically savvy.

I liked her more and more every time we hung out together.

We were having dinner one night and I said, "Ro, I love you so much. I mean, do you feel . . . do you think . . . ?"

I didn't even know what I was expecting. She was married. I was married. I was obviously confused. She was not.

Rosie smiled and said, "Oh, Glessy, no. Never. You are so straight."

I was disappointed. And very relieved.

So, for all of you who thought since the first episode of *Cagney & Lacey* that I was gay . . . well, I gave it my best fucking shot with the number one lesbian on the planet.

And she turned me down flat.

Forty-Four

Apparently There Were Complaints

In Alcoholics Anonymous, they count the number of years a person has stayed sober in the same way most people count birthdays. I never made it to my Sweet Sixteen. I started drinking again on my actual sixtieth birthday in May 2003. Perhaps, had I attended AA meetings over those fifteen years following my stay at Hazelden, I wouldn't have started again. Who knows? It doesn't matter. It's now many martinis under the bridge.

Barney and I were still considering a divorce, though no one else in our immediate world knew about it. I was still residing in Toronto to film *Queer as Folk*.

With everything in flux, I had not given much thought to my approaching sixtieth birthday. Family members began asking me about how I planned to celebrate. I finally chose a birthday bash weekend in Las Vegas for thirty guests, with rooms at the Four Seasons. We chartered a private bus to drive most of us from Los Angeles to Vegas. On the way, we all viewed my favorite movies and listened to my favorite music. Besides three days of gambling, we arranged tickets for all of us to go to Cirque du Soleil, as well as dinners in the best restaurants.

The night of my birthday dinner, we all gathered at a restaurant where Barney had reserved a private room. As was his custom, he sat me at the head table with my brothers on each side of me.

Before dinner was served, I leaned over to Michael and whispered, "Will you ask the waiter to bring me a martini?"

He never batted an eye.

"With pleasure," Michael responded.

As the evening progressed, I happily sipped on my one martini. I never ordered a second one. Not one person in the room noticed there was a drink in my hand. I hadn't held one for fifteen years.

Since the birthday martini didn't change my personality, I convinced myself that I could have an occasional drink and be perfectly fine. I was sure that all of the cautions I had learned at Hazelden didn't apply to me.

There's a reason it's said that denial is the primary roadblock to recovery. I thought a little cocktail detour would be a harmless way to improve the landscape of my life. And, honestly, it did. I had a lovely time drinking again. No one else in my life seemed to have a complaint about it. My having one cocktail seemed to be acceptable in the "social drinking" realm.

One summer break, between seasons of *Queer as Folk*, I returned to Miami with the intention of figuring out the details of the end of my marriage. It was time to divide the spoils.

Barney said, "Your job is to bring two pads of paper and two pens."

We sat at a table in our Fisher Island apartment, legal pads in hand and a long night ahead.

"Before we start," I offered, "I owe you an apology."

Barney looked up from the notes he was jotting down. "What's that?"

I said, "As you know, I never thought I was pretty. But recently I found photos of myself as Cagney. I looked at one and thought, 'Gosh, I really was pretty, at least in a photo.' I know what I look like now. I want you to know that I'm sorry for what I did."

Barney got tears in his eyes and said, "Sharon, I was a poor Jewish boy from east LA. All I ever dreamed about was a beautiful blonde shiksa. I finally had my dream, and within a year, you were gone."

I said, "I'm sorry, Barney."

He replied, "I'm sorry, too, for being so shallow."

It wasn't as if we allowed the marriage to crumble without trying to fix it. We saw many relationship counselors for couples therapy over our first ten years together.

During regular therapy sessions, we would be horrifically spiteful to one another. It was safe to let it all come out with the therapist in the room, but it was a little scary how mean we could be. Oddly, following each hour-long session, when we were alone, we would be the kindest we had been all week to one another.

Someone highly recommended a specific couples therapist to Barney. I agreed to go, though it was an hour drive from where we lived.

The counselor's office was in a small pool house behind his regular home. The pool was only about ten inches from the side of the garage. There was no other walkway to get to his office. We had to shimmy sideways the length of the pool, our backs hugging the wall, to not fall into the water. Barney was already looking apologetic. I didn't say a word.

The therapy session was equally ridiculous. We had to play word-association games for an hour. I didn't dare look at Barney.

At the end of our session, the therapist got a very serious look on his face, leaned in, and said, "May I ask you both a question?"

We both said, "Sure."

With complete seriousness, he inquired, "Do you know Al Pacino?"

I'm sure the look on my face reflected my thought, "What? What did you just say?"

Finally, I spoke up

"No. I do not. Barney?"

I turned to stare at the side of Barney's face.

He somehow held it together. "No. No, I don't."

We left, silently scooting sideways along the garage wall to get back to our car. Once the car door was shut, I looked over at Barney.

"Al fucking Pacino? Do I happen to know Al fucking Pacino?! Don't ever do this to me again, Barney!"

He didn't.

One of the last couples therapists we saw wisely said, "If I were to give you a relationship diagnosis, I would say that this marriage is over."

Barney and I both stopped talking. This wasn't what we expected.

The therapist explained. "The truth is," he said to me, "you fell in love with Barney because he was powerful. And power is a great aphrodisiac. He made things happen for you. He was the boss. He's not that anymore."

Then he turned to Barney. "And you fell in love with Sharon because she was beautiful. She's not that anymore."

We sat silent. He continued, "The reasons you came together as a couple no longer exist. So what are the two of you going to do?"

We had no answer to his question.

The therapist said, "What I would suggest you do is either call it quits in a kind manner and be done with it all or, when you leave here, go out this door and introduce yourselves again. See if you like one another as you are today. You may. You may not."

It was heartbreaking but true. We walked down the hall and got into the elevator. Someone else got in the elevator with us, but I didn't care. I extended my hand and said, "Hi, I'm Sharon."

Barney took my hand.

He said, "I'm Barney."

We softened after that. We rested from battle. We measured our words more often. We made room for possibility.

We left our "divorce date" off the monthly planner. The weeks passed and the calendar pages turned. A year turned into another year. In the same way I was in no hurry to get married, I was in no hurry to get a divorce. It's one thing to lose a marital status as a matter of record; it's a whole other thing to lose your very best friend. I will continue to love Barney forever. And I know he loves me. To this day, he still refers to me as his "big deal."

= • =

Eventually, my delusional "I can have one drink" detour became two drinks and then three. The booze began to turn on me around age sixty-seven. I would go into blackout, usually after three martinis.

I was still able to function—though not always appropriately—so no one else could tell that I was in blackout, including me. The next day I never remembered what I had done or said the night before.

I would eventually hear from others about the socially inappropriate travesties I had committed, like the evening I joined strangers at their table in a restaurant and ordered food on their bill. I spent the entire evening with them. From what I was told, my chosen tablemates found me to be charming company and apparently had no issue with picking up my tab. I'm sorry I never met them properly. The problem was I had deserted Barney and the couple we had actually invited to dinner at our own table across the restaurant.

I would wake up on some mornings to find Barney staring at the ceiling.

I'd say, "Good morning," with a smile.

He'd reply softly, "Do you have any memory of last night?"

I would admit, "No."

"I didn't think so."

It seemed I was constantly apologizing for things I couldn't remember. My drinking had become unpredictable and, at least for others, embarrassing. I won't bore you with the details of other individual incidents. We've all seen *Absolutely Fabulous*. Although, in alcohol's defense, I've done some pretty stupid stuff while completely sober, too.

I have a video of my incredible and lavish seventieth birthday party, thrown on a high-rise rooftop in downtown Los Angeles.

I cringe at the progression of my drunkenness, shown on the video from the celebration, as the evening goes on. No one appears to be bothered by it, but who knows what was edited out of the reel. Everyone loves the fun party girl until she yells at one of the guests, "I don't give a fuck about your kids!" Oops!

Shortly after that birthday party, I had my first severe pancreatic attack. My body was giving me a red-flag warning. After my second attack, it was obvious that my body would now be directing the show, and my ten-year intermission as a drinker was over.

I quit. Cold turkey.

One day, about a year later, a friend of Barney's asked me why I had decided to get sober again at this point in my life.

I didn't want to go into the medical history of the pancreatic attacks, so I answered, "Apparently, there were complaints."

Barney tipped his head back and roared with laughter.

My book title was born.

Forty-Five

Characters Welcome

"Congratulations. You're going back to work," my manager, Perry Zimel, told me by phone. "*Burn Notice* sold."

"What's *Burn Notice*?" I asked.

I meant it.

Then it all came back to me.

Soon after filming the final episode of *Queer as Folk* in 2005, I shot the pilot for a new TV show by Matt Nix. I thought the writing was clever. Even though it was a drama, I laughed out loud while reading the script. My scenes had been filmed over the course of two days in Miami while I got to stay at a hotel with the other actors and collected per diem. It seems I "forgot" to tell the producers that they didn't need to put me up, since I have an apartment in Miami. It's way too much fun to hang out with the cast and crew when the workday is over.

Seven months had passed since filming that pilot. I'd forgotten all about it. But now Perry was telling me that USA Network had picked up the series. My God, it sold!

I had a new job and a fresh series, and the entire filming would be done in Miami. I guess it was only right to tell the producers that I lived there.

I would be playing the mother of an international spy, sexily played by Jeffrey Donovan, who was fired by the CIA (given his "burn notice"). He had been drugged and dumped in Miami where his mother, Madeline Westen, lives.

It was original. No other TV or film spy had a mother. The closest thing was James Bond's relationship to M, played by Judi Dench. Not so bad!

I wasn't exactly jumping up and down to play a mom again. I thought the mom role of Debbie Novotny on *Queer as Folk* would be hard to beat.

Lucky for me, this *Burn Notice* mom was unique. She was described as a chain-smoking hypochondriac. The slogan of the USA Network at that time was "Characters Welcome." I didn't want to disappoint. I decided to play her full out.

Matt Nix created the character and the story lines. I created her look. I thought she should fit the category of a stereotypical Miami matron, which at that time meant a wardrobe of white capri pants and long, gem-colored blouses. Her earrings had to be big and match the colors of her clothes. I wanted her short hair to be pure platinum, no highlights and no lowlights. Being on a budget, I figured she was a "one dump" color-from-a-box kind of broad.

In the first episode, Madeline, who hadn't seen her son for ten years while he was on a long secretive mission, demands that he drive her to the hospital.

"Just because they can't find anything wrong with me doesn't mean I'm not sick!" she tells him, taking pills by the handful.

When her hypochondria symptoms don't work to control her son, she resorts to other methods, such as telling him there's an emergency at her house. He rushes over to find that the emergency is her malfunctioning blender.

She is horribly and hysterically manipulative. I called her the "mother from hell." As the show progressed, her involvement became richer and sometimes darker.

I enjoyed being able to smoke full-time again, on and off camera, and was soon up to three packs of Marlboro Reds a day. The crew even pumped smoke from a fog machine onto the set that was Madeline's home, reinforcing the joke.

What was originally supposed to be only an occasional appearance by Madeline turned into scenes in almost every episode by the second season. The viewers loved the relationship between Madeline and her son. It was funny and tough and sometimes sad—a dream acting job.

In 2008, during a hiatus of *Burn Notice*, I got a phone call from Ryan Murphy, the creator of *Nip/Tuck*, the hit TV show about the lives of two plastic surgeons. He said he'd seen my guest appearance on the talk show *The View*.

Ryan had come up with an idea for what he described to me as "the sickest character" he had ever dreamed up. He felt I would be perfect for the role. I was flattered.

He first asked if the black suit I was wearing on *The View* was an Armani.

"Yes," I lied.

"Do you actually need the large, round, black-rimmed glasses you were wearing?"

"Only to see with," I answered.

"Good," he said. "I want you to wear that suit and those glasses for this character."

"Have you ever seen *Misery*?" Ryan wanted to know.

I said, "Not only have I seen it, I created the role of Annie Wilkes onstage in the West End of London."

He was happy. "Then you're familiar with insanity."

"Very."

He asked, "Do you know *Nip/Tuck*?"

"Of course I do!" I lied a second time. "My friend Rosie O'Donnell's been on your show. It's great."

"The part is yours if you want it," Ryan assured me. "I'll write it for you."

That weekend I stayed up around the clock and watched twenty-four episodes of *Nip/Tuck* in a row. I got hooked. It was wonderful. I'm not lying.

I went off to film four episodes of *Nip/Tuck* as soon as *Burn Notice* went on its first hiatus.

My portrayal of Colleen Rose, the psycho-villain who weasels her way into the life of one of the plastic surgeons, earned me my ninth Emmy nomination.

I didn't win. I've never said this in my entire career. Ever. But I should have won for that performance.

One morning, during a subsequent *Burn Notice* hiatus, Barney and I had an argument. We always get along better when I'm working. If I'm not busy, I get restless and start buying stuff out of catalogues or eating ice cream out of gallon containers. An addict is an addict.

I was scrolling through emails at my little desk next to the kitchen. Barney appeared at my side, tossed a page from the Sunday *New York Times* on my keyboard, and said, "If you had any balls, you'd go after this."

Since he was already out the door to play tennis, I snapped back to the empty room, "Don't challenge me."

I read the article "Sex and the Single Senior."

Jane Juska, an English professor at Berkeley, had not been touched sexually in thirty years. She decided to take out an ad in the *New York Review of Books* to find a man of her intellectual equal for the purpose of having sex again. It read, "Before I turn 67—next March—I would like to have a lot of sex with a man I like. If you want to talk first, Trollope works for me."

Sixty-three men responded to the ad. She had sex with some of them and had written a best-selling book about her experience, *A Round-Heeled Woman: My Late-Life Adventures in Sex and Romance*. Thirty minutes later I called my attorney on that Sunday afternoon and said, "Option this book for me! Please."

I gave a copy of the book to Jane Prowse, a wonderful British television writer, whom I had met while performing in *Misery*. She fell in love with it and agreed to write the stage adaptation. She took it to Brian Eastman, who bravely came on board as producer. Brian had previously produced *Misery* in the West End. The three of us became inseparable.

When *Burn Notice* would go on break from filming, I would do a production of *A Round-Heeled Woman*, first as a premiere in San Francisco, and then the next year in Miami, at GableStage. The show sold out nightly. The run was extended.

Most of my friends in Miami, including Matt Nix and some of the cast and crew of *Burn Notice*, came to see me in the show. Jeffrey Donovan refused to attend.

"I cannot watch a play where my mother is masturbating onstage. I just can't do it," he explained. I couldn't argue with him, since the play opens with me having phone sex and later multiple orgasms while standing up. That skill is not listed on my acting résumé.

Based on our Miami reviews, we were invited to play London's West End. We started at the Riverside and were then invited to the Aldwych.

The Aldwych is a classic old theater in the best and the worst ways. It had housed the Royal Shakespeare Company for a generation. I had Dame Judi Dench's dressing room, which was on the stage level. It was an elegant space, with an outer sitting room for guests after the show. On the downside, it had no bathroom. The women's restroom was up seven flights of stairs. Seven! Well, that's not going to happen.

There was a large deep sink in the inner dressing room. I realized I had a small footstool and could climb high enough to pee in the sink. One day I confessed to my assistants, Deb Mosk and Daniel Thurman, what I was doing, but I assured them that every night before leaving, I sprayed the sink down with disinfectant.

Daniel laughed and said, "Sharon, do you really suppose that you are the first actress to pee in there?"

If we were ever to meet, I'll bet Dame Judi and I would become friends. After all, we probably pissed in the same sink.

≡ • ≡

Toward the end of our *Burn Notice* run, Tyne Daly came to Miami to shoot an episode as our guest star. The two of us had a ball. She suggested that her character also be a chain smoker. In one scene, Michael enters Madeline's house but can't even find us through the double amount of heavy smoke. It was a funny sight gag.

Tyne and I would start the day in the makeup trailer together, rehearsing our lines and howling with laughter. It's what we always did.

The first time Tyne and I walked onto the *Burn Notice* set together, there was a reverential silence from the crew.

"Jesus! I never get this kind of respect when I walk in by myself!" I complained. A crewman responded, "It's the two of you together."

And still, whenever we are in New York, people on the street will call out to us, "Hey, Cagney! Hey, Lacey!"

The most unexpected reaction was when Tyne and I appeared at the Democratic National Convention for Hillary Clinton in 2016. We all wanted her to go on to the White House. I love Hillary. We were robbed.

Along with Tyne Daly, other top Broadway stars were there: Audra McDonald, Idina Menzel, and Brian Stokes Mitchell, among other notables, to sing "What the World Needs Now Is Love." When the camera panned to Tyne's and my two-line portion of the song, the convention center erupted. We were stunned. Cagney and Lacey, together again! Bigger than Broadway! What an evening!

Tyne will sometimes say to me, "It's an honor to know you."

The honor is truly mine. I'll go anywhere to see her perform or, as is our tradition, have a hot fudge sundae together. I'd do anything for her. We are still very close to this day, and we check in with each other almost every morning by phone. Tyne's mother had an expression that I paraphrase: "Sweat makes a great cement."

For seven years in a row, I loved returning to play Madeline on *Burn Notice*. I received my tenth Emmy nomination for that show. USA Network was eager to give the show season eight, but I think Jeffrey, who never, ever, got a break from shooting, was done. There were no days off for our leading man, as he was in every scene. They kind of killed the golden goose.

I was the last actor on set during the last day of shooting the final episode of the show. Madeline sacrifices her life to save her last living son, Michael, and protect the future of her grandson. The bad guys are closing in. She knows this time they will kill both her and her family unless she takes action.

Even though Jeffrey had completed his time on camera and didn't need to be there, he came in to do our final scene together, a long phone conversation where Madeline and Michael say goodbye. Jeffrey stood offstage to speak his lines, while the close-up shot was on me. He was there so I could hear his voice. We knew it was the last scene we would ever do for the show. His kindness was not wasted on me.

Madeline had rigged her house to explode once all of the "bad guys" enter.

Knowing that her own life will end as the house implodes, she says, "This one is for my boys." She lights her cigarette and flips the switch. It is over.

As the shooting day progressed, I felt an ache in the middle of my chest. It started out gradually and never stopped. I began to worry, but I didn't tell anyone what was going on.

I hugged Matt Nix and the crew goodbye.

Late that night, when I finally got home, I told Barney about the pain in my chest. It wasn't disappearing. He insisted we go to the emergency room.

They ran all the tests. The physician asked me about what was going on in my life. I told him that the show I was working on for seven years had ended that night. The series family I had been a part of and had loved was finished.

I described the intensity of my feelings throughout the day and the continuous pain in my chest. The laughter was over. My *Burn Notice* family was gone.

I was given a diagnosis.

"It's an actual ailment," the cardiologist told me. "It's called Broken Heart Syndrome."

⇒ Forty-Six ⇐

The Wish

A thunderstorm blew across south Miami tonight. The lightning cracked the sky all the way down to the horizon, right before the dark clouds dropped torrents of rain. There's an electrical charge in the air during a storm, which, I believe, holds great power. I always make a wish on that energy, hoping that it might become a reality.

I know my wishes are always heard. Sometimes what I ask for is what I get. Other times, I get something I didn't realize I wanted. Like that bolt of lightning, something I never wished for enters my life.

It was never my wish to write a book. Ever.

In 2013, I was invited to a meeting at CBS where all the brass was present: the heads of comedy, drama, and new series.

"Welcome home, Sharon," said the president of entertainment. Wow! Okay.

For one hour, I told the group of TV decision makers some of the stories from my life. They smiled. They laughed. They listened intently. I had them in the palm of my hand.

I had walked in eager to talk about the possibility of a new TV series. I walked out with a book deal to write my life story. What??

Apparently, they thought the stories that came to me so easily in that CBS office would translate quickly to the page. But, in fact, it has taken me eight years, from book contract to bookshelf.

Here's the deal. I'm an actress. That's what I do. I know how to be "in character." But how to be "in Sharon Gless" and put it in writing on the page? That was a different story. .

Being free of alcohol, drugs, and cigarettes and doing my best to corral my cravings for carbs made it seem even more daunting. Every story I wrote became a mirror . . . with no smoke or inebriated focus to blur the reflection.

Every memory magnified elements of myself I had never taken the time to define: from my determination to succeed to my deep self-doubt, from my shyness in social interactions to my drive to entertain the masses, from my eternal optimism that I will know what to do and how to do it to my ever-present feeling of not being enough. Then there was the overall fear of being boring and yet having the balls to do it anyway.

I realized that I have seldom felt as though I belonged—in adolescence, in adulthood, or in life. Socially, I have always felt like an outsider. The only time I was sure of myself was when I was playing someone else—when I could shape-shift, slip into someone else's skin and hide in plain sight.

It's okay. I'm in therapy. It's probably something most actors share—the sense of belonging only when we are in character.

I found Sharon Gless to be generous and needy, forgiving and flippant, one who persistently preserves the past with diligence and has equally walked away from something she valued to avoid confrontation with others. I am loyal to those I love and as lonely as a foster child left on a doorstep.

I've discovered that the one consistent love of my life has always been my acting career. It is my descendent, my own growing child. I've cherished and nurtured it for five decades.

I've never had a gimmick, or a killer body, or drop-dead looks. I have no university degree in theater or film. I speak only one language—albeit in a husky voice, which I'm told is recognizable. I am genuinely a stranger to the actor's practice of craft and technique. Like all of life, I go with my gut. I'm clueless about the structure of a script. I do, however, know if it doesn't feel true.

My best trait is that I will forever be a willing and enthusiastic student of this "filthy business." Somehow, I learned to put it all together, and it worked for me, despite an occasional complaint. No matter. Even the complaints, more than the compliments, helped form me. Most were accurate. Some are funny . . . now. Some hurt me. And some just made me angry enough to win anyway!

Over the past fifty years, I have been able to turn out a number of memorable performances. As for the many women (and the one man) I've played, it's been an honor.

Tonight's downpour of rain reminded me of the very first time I absolutely knew, to my core, that I belonged in this business.

It wasn't during a thunderstorm. Los Angeles doesn't have many of those.

It happened at Universal Studios in the '70s. Most nights, I'd stay in my dressing room long after the day's filming had ended and the rest of the cast and crew had gone home. I loved being there, savoring the dark silence of 1 a.m. and the smell of the evening rain on the studio asphalt.

I didn't have a driver in those early days, so I would take the long walk to my car in the darkness, guided by the lights on the corners of the now-empty soundstages. I wouldn't see one other person as I made my way across the lot. Not one. Even the Tower, which housed Lew Wasserman and all the other big executives, would be completely dark.

Universal Studios was my private home late at night. I owned it. All by myself.

They paid me, every day, to come to this make-believe world and perform. And every night I'd leave knowing that the next day I'd get to return to this place where everyone shared the same goal: to create magic on film.

In the morning, Scotty, the gate guard, would welcome me back. My very own hair and makeup people would be waiting with all of the pots and paints set up to help turn me into someone else.

I knew everyone, and they knew me. They cared about me. We

laughed all day long. We were good at what we did. We made television.

For ten years, I was an MCA/Universal Studios contract player and, remarkably, I was the very last one to leave the lot when the contract system came to an end. I am the last contract player in the history of Hollywood.

A lucrative career waited for me on the other side of the Universal gates in 1982, thanks to everything I had learned from the studio people who taught me. Those years were my "Rosebud."

Every story in this book is a memory of the people who influenced my life: the guardians of my childhood years, my siblings, my young girlfriends who shaped my humor, the men I've loved—most of whom stay forever young in my memory—the professionals who guided and nurtured me and took a chance on my career, and my fellow performers, most of whom I will always count as my friends.

That's it. I won't take the long walk across my own story again. I'm more intrigued with the possibility of taking on another life, a new character, a new role. I look forward to meeting her—and becoming her.

There's time. I'm going to live forever.

So far, so good.

Acknowledgments

In 2013, the president of entertainment at CBS was the visionary Nina Tassler. She invited me to meet with her in LA. I walked in, thinking it would be about a TV series, and left with an offer to write a book. It all started with you, Nina.

Jonathan Karp, the president and now chief executive officer of Simon & Schuster, invited me to a meeting in New York. I read him one of my stories. The support staff in the next room started laughing. He handed me a book deal. Overwhelmed, I put it in a drawer for a year. Thank you, Jonathan, for your patience and this opportunity.

Thank you to my manager, Perry Zimel, who sealed this deal and pushed me when I needed it most. "So, how's the book coming?"

My deep appreciation goes to my editor, Carina Guiterman, who never questioned if I could do this, cheered me through the challenges, and only killed my "darlings" with the utmost kindness. And, to Lashanda Anakwah, associate editor, it's been said "Love is in the details." Thank you!

Dawn Lafreeda is my very best friend who unfailingly has kept an ongoing list of the many stories from my life that I have told her over the last fifteen years, jotting them down wherever and whenever a memory spilled out of me. From the beginning of our friendship, she insisted that I had a book to write. Her certainty became a reality. But not without her endless willingness to bring order to the memories, digitized photos, schedules, calendars, websites, people, places, and things that comprise my life. Her daily commitment to keeping me on track has been utterly heroic. She has always been a constant source of support and undying enthusiasm for my career and my biggest dreams. She is smart as hell and when other people have to use Google for an answer to a tough question, I text Dawn. She's faster. Also, if she had a dime for every time she has used the Find My

Phone app for me . . . she could buy another Denny's restaurant to add to the eighty-five she already owns. She runs an empire and still finds time for me. I don't know how I got so lucky to have her in my life, but I won't be cashing out anytime soon. There aren't enough ways to adequately thank you, Dawn. You already know how much I love you.

I raise a glass of Sprite in gratitude to my very dear friends Sandi Lifson, Vivienne Radkoff, and the larger-than-life-itself Renée Taylor for reading various versions of this book and always cheering me on. Except when they didn't like something.

To my brother, Michael, the attorney, for telling me *his* version of our childhood. And for keeping me out of prison. And to my brother, Aric, the architect, for faithfully assembling all of our family's history records. The two of you are the surviving witnesses of my childhood and younger years. If any memory in this book doesn't match yours, keep it to yourselves. I love you both with all my heart.

To my cousin, Elizabeth Baur. Your memories were my memories. You were the sister I never had and I'll always be a better person for it. I miss you in so many ways.

To my niece, Bridget Gless Keller. Thank you for keeping a chronicle of my career when you were a teenager, for all of the photographs and the very scary career memorabilia, and for organizing it all for me. I le u, Bug.

To my erstwhile very personal assistant and loving stepdaughter, Allyn Rosenzweig, for never deserting me. You did it all with a smile on your face and a kiss on my cheek. Thank you, my sweet girl.

Carole Smith, you are so much more than our longtime assistant. You are family. You have seen us through it. Thank you.

To my psychotherapist, Dr. Barbara Rose Ponse, who has heard it all for more than thirty years and still takes my calls.

Barney Rosenzweig, my husband, dared me to sit down and write thirty pages. He knows me so well. There would be no jump-start without a challenge. He threw down the gauntlet. I had to pick it up. I always do. Some pages had only nine or ten words on them in twenty-four-point font, but hey, it counted. Barney has rallied the idea of me as a memoir author from the get-go. He stayed the entire course, as my daily motivator, right to the finish line. He has read and reread every line of this book, never mincing his opinion, helping me to put on the page what mattered most. Obviously, a man who can produce a complete story with forty-five minutes of TV time, week after week for hundreds of episodes, knows how to redline a manuscript. I was fortunate to have him clean up my meanderings. For your continuous encouragement and injurious feedback on each draft . . . thank you, Barn. I will love you forever.

And, finally, to Marcia Wilkie. There would be no book without her. If you didn't like it, blame her.

To the rest of my family, many who have both laughed and cried with me . . . or perhaps because of me. I thank you and simultaneously apologize: Kathy Gless, Anita Gless, Bridget Gless Keller, Paul Keller, Kevin Gless, Bryan Gless, Patrick Gless, Gregory Gless, Lesley Worton and Steve Springer. Also Laura Abrahamson, Lisa Hudson, Alexandra Stimson, and Charlotte Stimson. And, to my family on Barney's side: my three wonderful stepdaughters, Erika Handman, Allyn Rosenzweig, and Torrie Rosenzweig, along with my beautiful granddaughters, Hailey Laws and Greer Glassman, and my brave grandson, Alex Rosenzweig. Also David Handman, John Coldiron, Joni Benickes, Miles Benickes, Joel Rosenzweig, Joan Rosenzweig, and Marc Rosenzweig.

I am an actor/actress. I answer to both. It appears I am now also an author. The stories in my book most often include only one other person, two or three at the most. As a result, my stories sadly exclude many that I love. Dearly.

Most of the people in my life, with whom I am close, are not mentioned by name in my book. I'd like to fix that. They are the people with whom I have shared my career, my fellow actors who carried me in each of my television series for the last fifty years.

My love and gratitude for them lives in my heart forever.

FARADAY AND COMPANY:

Dan Dailey, James Naughton, Geraldine Brooks

SWITCH:

Robert Wagner (who saved my considerable ass. I love you, Marv.)

Eddie Albert, Charlie Callas

TURNABOUT:

John Schuck

HOUSE CALLS:

Wayne Rogers (well . . .)

CAGNEY & LACEY:

Thank you for welcoming me in! We never had time to play. The fourteen-hour days and nights never allowed it.

Tyne Daly (as good as it gets! My life went into high definition from working with you and being the recipient of your unfailing friendship. I love you, my partner.)

Stephen Macht (*always* there for me), John Karlen, Al Waxman, Marty Kove, Carl Lumbly, Sidney Clute, Harvey Atkin, Merry Clayton, Robert Hegyes, Dan Shor, and Dick O'Neill (the best dad ever).

THE TRIALS OF ROSIE O'NEILL:

Dorian Harewood, Ron Rifkin, Georgann Johnson, Lisa Banes, Lisa Rieffel, Elaine Kagen, Bridget Gless, Meg Foster, Brenda Vaccaro, and Ed Asner (thank you for it all, dear Ed!)

And, again, Robert Wagner (for the loveliest love scenes. And, for breaking your rule regarding guest spots. You came to save me . . . again. And again. And again. You have my heart forever.)

Carole King wrote my theme song "I Wish I Knew." And Melissa Manchester recorded it for me. How blessed was I? Thank you, brilliant women!

QUEER AS FOLK:

Without question, the bravest actors I know:

Gale Harold, Randy Harrison, Hal Sparks, Peter Paige, Scott Lowell, Robert Gant, Michelle Clunie, Thea Gill, Jack Wetherall, and Peter MacNeill.

Love and thank you to my driver and dearest friend, Al Izumi.

BURN NOTICE:

Jeffrey Donovan (still my boy), Gabrielle Anwar (as beautiful on the inside), Bruce Campbell (funniest man alive), and Coby Bell (a gem).

You've got to have friends. I do. And I am wholeheartedly thankful. I may have met you professionally, but your existence in my world is oh, so personal to me.

Thank you, Jach Pursel and Lazaris, for your decades of love and guidance.

Peter Forster, you were a life-changer for me. I can't begin to show enough gratitude.

Dan Lipman and Ron Cowan, you gave me Debbie and Debbie gave me a whole new career. My deepest appreciation.

Matt Nix, for casting me in my longest-running series.

Brian Eastman and Jane Prowse, your creative vision and dedication are forever part of my favorite memories. I have overflowing gratitude and . . . wait for it . . . respect and love for you both.

For many years, the following magicians personally kept me powdered, puffed, cut, colored, curled, and even sometimes, glowing: Charles Ross, Carolyn Elias, Bob Jermain, Stephen Lynch, James O'Reilly, Tracey Taylor, Luis Gonzales, and Sophia Katzman. Thank you. Sometimes we fooled them!

Marie Osmond and Tracy Baim, thank you for the perfect referral. You got that so right.

To those whose effect on my life has been enormous, my gratitude and love go to: Ann Wilson, Gail Reese, Jackie Danson, Anna Kerslake, Daf Llewelyn, Mary Lea, Helen Cook, Rosemary Bell, Angie Brown, Beverley Faverty, Judy Samelson, Brooke Plantenga, Lee Wallman, Paul Gendreau, Catherine Hamilton, Leena Dunne, Linwood Paul, The Light Group, all my R Family family, Gloria Steinem, Charlie Chaplin, and at last . . . Debra Goodstone.

To those who are my forever friends for many reasons, who are not in the book and should be, but I ran out of room. You exist permanently in the sphere of my smitten heart: Deb Mosk, Dr. Debra Shapiro, Peggy Griffin, Lupita Corbeil, Hannah Shearer, Deeny Kaplan, Marcy Lefton, Ellen Jacoby, Dr. Linda Ford, Stanley Miller and Kristina Park, Sarah Chanin, Daniel Thurman, Adriann Ramirez, Jimmy Hawkins, Frank Gangi, Carole Cook and Tom Troupe, Nancy Heller, Arnie Kane, Dr. Warren and Maxine Finkelstein, Donald Ramsey and Wade Hansen (my Marguerites), Janine Ostow (the Queen of Joe's Stone Crab—Miami Beach), Peter Landroche (Musso and Frank Grill— Hollywood), Craig Susser (Craig's Restaurant—West Hollywood), and . . . Lee Grant, Joe Feury, and Phyllis Fioretti (their kitchen—NYC).

I am blessed.

About the Author

Sharon Gless does not have a hobby. There are no personally handcrafted items in either of her homes, not in Los Angeles or Miami. One time, she roasted some nuts for a Super Bowl party. Other than that, her cookware is virgin. She has no pets. She doesn't even want to foster one, even as a phony service animal. All indoor plants are on their own. She can swim fifty-six lengths in a pool and does so two times a year when a trainer stands poolside shouting "Looking good! Doing great." Twice a year is not a hobby.

Sharon is a multi Emmy Award– and Golden Globe–winning actress, with eighteen total nominations. She has starred in hundreds of TV episodes and played the lead in dozens of TV movies and miniseries, with a long list of character roles and guest-star appearances. She has starred in the West End of London three times. Her list of radio plays is endless. Acting is not a hobby. Acting is her very life force.

Apparently, she is now an author. It's a one-off.

She does have a website: SharonGless.com.